The
Philosopher
as Writer

The Philosopher as Writer

THE EIGHTEENTH CENTURY

Edited by
Robert Ginsberg

Selinsgrove: Susquehanna University Press
London and Toronto: Associated University Presses

Associated University Presses
440 Forsgate Drive
Cranbury, NJ 08512

Associated University Presses
25 Sicilian Avenue
London WC1A 2QH, England

Associated University Presses
2133 Royal Windsor Drive
Unit 1
Mississauga, Ontario
Canada L5J 1K5

The paper used in this publication meets the requirements
of the American National Standard for Permanence of Paper
for Printed Library Materials Z39.48-1984.

Library of Congress Cataloging-in-Publication Data

The Philosopher as writer.

Includes bibliographies and index.
1. Philosophy, Modern—18th century—Methodology.
I. Ginsberg, Robert.
B802.P48   1987   808'.0661   85-63555
ISBN 0-941664-25-2 (alk. paper)

Printed in the United States of America

Contents

Introduction to Eighteenth-Century Philosophic Writing

ROBERT GINSBERG

Philosophy insofar as it is written is a branch of literature. Literary forms and devices, meant for imaginative pleasure, have been adopted easily for the philosophic ends of intellectual exploration, elucidation, and evaluation.

The dialogue, in which discourse is conducted by characters in a setting, has been a perennial attraction for philosophizing since the superb achievements in this form by Plato. In the eighteenth century Berkeley turned to dialogue when he sought a more popular way of assisting his audience to grasp the astonishing philosophical outlook first offered as a treatise concerning the principles of human knowledge (1710). His *Three Dialogues between Hylas and Philonous* (1713) is a radiant composition whose clarity and ease contrast ironically with the paradoxical difficulties and innovations of Berkeley's immaterialism. Hume turned to dialogue for his diplomatic treatment of the existence of God, cushioning the reader from the blows of arguments that severed divinity from human knowledge and concealing the author's position amid the interlocutors. Caution kept the *Dialogues on Natural Religion* unpublished until 1779, after Hume's death. Herder wrote *God* (1787) as a set of conversations that humanize the Spinozist arguments concerning the nature of God; as spiritual refreshment he inserted moving lyric poetry between each day of the argument. Diderot and dialogue are inseparable. The dialogical invitation to explore thought to its very limits was repeatedly accepted by the Encyclopedist. The results show delightful versatility: *The Dream of d'Alembert* (written 1769, published 1830), *Rameau's Nephew* (written 1760s and 1770s, first published in Goethe's translation 1805), *Jacques the Fatalist* (written 1773, published 1796). Of these works one may ask whether philosophy turns into literature, literature turns into philosophy, or both engender a hybrid.

The letter was used by Plato and Cicero as a mode of philosophical discourse, and the epistolary form was widely adopted by Enlightenment thinkers. Locke wrote the landmark *Letter Concerning Toleration* (1689), Diderot wrote the explorative *Letter on the Blind* (1749), Bolingbroke wrote the programmatic *Letters on the Study of History* (1752), Rousseau wrote the polemical *Letters Written from the Mountain* (1764), Schiller wrote the influential *Letters on the Aesthetic Education of Man* (1795).

Philosophical texts in ancient times, such as Parmenides' "On Truth" and Lucretius's *On the Nature of Things*, could be written in verse that organized material, clarified thought, engaged the reader's feelings, and reached memorable heights of expression. Voltaire wrote philosophical poetry, including "Poem on the Disaster of Lisbon" and "Poem on Natural Law" (both 1756), in which biting wit and irony addressed the place of humanity in the scheme of things. Pope's entire career as philosophical poet sparkles with the artful adaptation of verse to that thinker's wit, world view, critique, and reasoning. Pope even wrote his *Essays*—on *Criticism* (1711) and on *Man* (1734)—in verse.

Ancient antecedents of the essay as philosophical form are Plutarch's and Seneca's short moral works. The Renaissance examples of Montaigne (1580) and Bacon (1597) caused the form to be so widely accepted for intellectual discourse that it may no longer be thought of as primarily an instrument of literary pleasure. Hume was tempted to rewrite his *oeuvre* as essays. Dissatisfied with the reception of his *Treatise of Human Nature* (1739–40), as Berkeley had been with *his* treatise, Hume rewrote chunks of it as *Philosophical Essays Concerning Human Understanding* (1748), later renamed *Enquiry*. His *Essays: Moral, Political, and Literary*, covered a wide range of subjects. First published in 1741, they were frequently revised until the posthumous edition of 1777. Hume converted *Four Dissertations* (1757) into *Essays* in 1758. Donald T. Siebert, in a chapter of this book, explores Hume's revised conception of literary "manner," and in the last chapter I offer a paragraph by paragraph reading of one of Hume's essays, "Of the Standard of Taste" (1757).

Kant's mastery of writing is most evident in the late essays he contributed to journals for wide readership. His "What Is Enlightenment?" (1784), one of the many essays proposed by thinkers on that wonderful topic, is a triumph of lucidity and intellectual vigor, analyzed by John A. McCarthy in comparison to the very early philosophical essay by Leibniz, "A Call to the Germans to Make Better Use of Their Reason and Language" (1683). The two works afford McCarthy the history in a nutshell of the German philosophic essay of the Enlightenment.

Shaftesbury worked within the tradition of the philosophic essay of the late seventeenth and early eighteenth centuries, but he also brought to his *Characteristicks of Men, Manners, Opinions, Times* (1711) a concern for stylistic decorum that Robert Markley studies as contributing to Shaftesbury's philosophical thinking. Shaftesbury sought to resolve the crisis in prose style and shape worthy character by his writing.

Other literary forms were put to good use in the eighteenth century: Rousseau wrote confessions, Vico penned an autobiography, Voltaire perfected the philosophical tale, Wollstonecraft produced extended manifestos, Hamann published Socratic memorabilia, and even Montesquieu brought out fictional letters from an exotic locale.

Philosophy is literary not only when it adopts forms of imaginative literature and belles lettres. For whatever the form, the philosophical discourse lives by words. Philosophical writing makes a commitment to style. The professional training of philosophers in the United States in the twentieth century has inculcated systematic neglect of style in both the study of philosophical works and their composition. For style was scorned as mere ornament of texts, inessential to the reasoning, an idiosyncrasy of the author, and at best an emotive appeal to an audience. Literary scholars have known better and have kept alive stylistic interest in the philosophical practice of such giants as Rousseau, Diderot, and Hume. New theories of textuality and criticism are leading philosophers to second thoughts concerning style.[1]

The style of philosophical writing may contribute to the structure of the text, may be concomitant to the activity of philosophizing, and may accomplish the primary aim of such philosophizing in activating an audience. In a word, style may be more than style.

Lester G. Crocker unravels the tangled rhetoric of discourse that is the fabric of Rousseau's discourses *On the Sciences and Arts* (1750) and *On the Origin of Inequality* (1755), for Rousseau is trying to persuade the reader of what he cannot demonstrate. Crocker shows how word choice, sentence structure, appeal to audience, use of the narrator's character, and strategy of composition are taken from the bag of tricks that characterize Rousseau's reasoning and communication. Crocker takes a bold stand against the sophistry in such a philosophical style.

Wollstonecraft faced quite a different rhetorical situation, according to Laurie A. Finke's analysis, for she was addressing men concerning the liberation of women in a language used by men, including Rousseau, to keep women in their place. Wollstonecraft, who has been systematically excluded from the histories of philosophy, heightened awareness of the gender bias of that language as she in turn used it and went beyond it to philosophize about sex, education, and society in her *Vindication of the Rights of Woman* (1792). Finke shows the creative struggle that Wollstonecraft wages as thinker, writer, and woman.

Harry M. Solomon explores the nature and role of a single stylistic device central to Pope's *Essay on Man* (1734)—metaphor—for this helps identify philosophical poetry. Pope's metaphor of Divinity is neither analogical argument nor empirical statement but a regulative hypothesis (similar to Kant's regulative idea), "an *if* instead of a *Since*." Solomon assesses the misinterpretations of critics of the eighteenth and twentieth centuries who treat Pope's metaphor extratextually. In contrast, Wulf Koepke exposes the entirety of Herder's multifaceted career, and the careers of other figures of the German Enlightenment, in terms of the search for the right language in which to advance understanding. Koepke shows Herder as philosopher, preacher, counselor, educator, and poet grappling with the way of expression required by Enlightenment. Style, in this sense, is central to human improvement.

Siebert argues that the meaning of Hume's philosophical efforts is to be found as much in their manner as their matter. In the *Treatise* Hume "is in the process of discovering his philosophy." I argue that Hume engages the reader in that process of discovery not only intellectually but aesthetically. In the essay on taste, Hume's literary strategy is to cause the reader to experience what Hume is talking about.

Even Kant's dry philosophical classic, *The Critique of Pure Reason* (1781), can be better appreciated for its philosophical innovation and internal struggle if we attend to matters of style, demonstrates Stephen F. Barker. The features of Kant's style reveal the status of his thinking. The faculties of mind are like the characters in a soap opera.

The Enlightenment self-consciously explored the literary structures and the literary substance of philosophizing. It was a bold movement in thought that sought appropriate newness of expression. In general, the English-speaking philosophers chose informal structures and selected that style which gave the reader a taste of empirical thinking. John J. Richetti says of the Big Three—Locke, Berkeley, Hume—in his brilliant study, "their thought is a continual return to the act of discovery."[2] French-speaking philosophers chose the path of indirection, writing intellectual pieces protected by literary forms that allowed them currency within a rigid, traditional culture. The ideas of the *philosophes* were susceptible to suppression when expressed straightforwardly. German-speaking philosophers struggled to build a language for their use, freed from academic tradition, as well as to build a suitable readership. They chose forms and styles to create a literate and intelligent audience.

The case studies brought together here are samples of what may be done in analysis and appreciation of the literary dimension to eighteenth-century philosophic texts, and they are invitations to scholars to pursue related studies of other works. The material for seminars and conferences is abundant. The authors have worked independently, with only minor stylistic interference from the editor. They have carved out their subject and designed their method in accordance with their insights.

Yet the studies in this volume share features. All the authors work within Eighteenth-Century Studies. As designation of a field of scholarship that term has had currency for about twenty-five years. As eighteenth-century scholars, the authors have attended to the contexts, language, values, and controversies of that century. They aim to grasp texts from the eighteenth-century viewpoint—not simply from the twentieth-century viewpoint. Usually this means that the text is the locus of consideration, and the context emerges from the text carefully studied. Textual study is enhanced by close attention to language and by broad awareness of contemporary issues and meanings. Thus, the contributors practice explication of texts and make use of the history of ideas. One text leads to another. Thus, to appreciate the strategy, allusions, and choice of terms of one work, we may have to relate it to others, but once a work has been clarified and appreciated, it in turn adds to our understanding of other texts by the same author or by others.

Understanding texts which are literary embodiments of philosophizing is also understanding thinking. Thus, these studies are offered as contributions to philosophy. What they elucidate and assess are often live alternatives for the twentieth-century thinker. We have come to understand philosophy, thanks partly to the eighteenth century, as more than a body of ideas, a set of doctrines, a collection of theories, or an armory of methods, namely, as *philosophizing:* ways of intellectual struggle, confrontation, exploration, puzzlement, protest, experiment, questioning, and questing.

Notes

1. Berel Lang, ed., *Philosophical Style: An Anthology about Writing and Reading of Philosophy* (Chicago: Nelson-Hall, 1980), promises to be a standard volume.

2. John J. Richetti, *Philosophical Writing: Locke, Berkeley, Hume* (Cambridge: Harvard University Press, 1983), p. 21.

The
Philosopher
as Writer

1

Rousseau's Two Discourses:
The Philosopher as Rhetorician

LESTER G. CROCKER

If originality and breadth of influence are hallmarks of a philosopher's importance, then Jean-Jacques Rousseau stands abreast of any other and ahead of many, although in the opinion of some historians of philosophy he may fall below the mark for rigorous abstract reasoning—and even, on a subjective basis, be violently impugned for his ideas. It is not injudicious to assert that Rousseau (like Nietzsche, whom he resembles in many ways)[1] owes a good portion of his influence to the effectiveness of his writing, which in turn is due to the immediate presence and unmistakable commitment of the author as much as to his unique artistry. We cannot say this about most of the great philosophers, for while some (a Plato, a Hume) may engage us by their style, no other combines these two peculiar qualities.

Although we shall be concerned with form and expression, it is not possible to discuss how Rousseau makes his arguments without explaining what they are. I shall be considering three elements in his writing. First, his strategy. Every philosopher has a point, or a number of points, to make and must therefore devise a strategy for developing the argument convincingly. Second, the presentation of that argument, within the overall strategy, involves rhetoric and style. If, like Locke or Kant, the philosopher is not a master of the art of writing, form becomes a negative element, an obstacle to the purpose of attracting and persuading readers, who may find reading the work, however valuable, a tiresome or an arduous task. Third, the acts of writing and reading are ultimately inseparable, inasmuch as a work may be said to exist only in its reading. A number of questions arise from this fact. We must ask whether and to what extent the authorial personality imposes its imprint and its presence. Does the reader sense a voice, a person behind and within the words one is reading, or only—as in the case of Spinoza—a mentality? Viewed from another perspective, is the writer overtly concerned with the reader? Does the writer set forth the arguments or try to make the reader an accomplice? Does the author speak to the reader, endeavoring to establish a one-to-one rapport?

I

In his first philosophical essay, *Discours sur les sciences et les arts* (*Discourse on the Sciences and Arts*, 1750), Rousseau already displays the individual character that gave his writings, with the exception of the *Contrat social*, their vast appeal.

In his effort to win the prize in the Académie de Dijon's contest, Rousseau set himself the difficult task of sustaining a paradox that countered the heart and soul of the faith of the Enlightenment, namely, that progress is beneficial and that the arts and sciences are the working factors in its forward movement. We shall follow his mode of argumentation and refer only incidentally to the quality of his arguments.

What I have called Rousseau's strategy in this Discourse is relatively simple and straightforward. The argument is developed in linear or sequential progression, varied by a few *retournements* (turnings round) that serve to emphasize. The major points are supported by examples, mainly historical. The composition is that of the classical *thème* as taught in the schools. (It was not necessary for him to learn it *in* school.) The structure is readily observable.

Rousseau's strategy is to begin by admitting the glory of humanity's ascent through its own efforts, then, almost immediately, to demolish the admission, denouncing its hollowness. He proceeds from one bad effect to another, in an argument whose thrust is cumulative. Human progress has enslaved us. Transparency in human relationships has been replaced by insincere language, individuality by "une vile et trompeuse uniformité" ("a vile and deceptive uniformity," p. 8).[2] There follows a list of the vices that arose in the wake of this transformation. Then comes the crucial assertion: "nos âmes se sont corrompues à mesure que nos sciences et nos arts se sont avancés à la perfection" ("our hearts have become corrupted steadily, even as our sciences and arts have advanced toward perfection," p. 9). But this bald assertion is what was to be established. Rousseau attempts the proof by referring to corroborative examples: Egypt, Greece, imperial Rome, the Eastern Roman empire, and (again flouting the general opinion of his time) modern China. The examples, all centered on two points, moral corruption and loss of the martial spirit required to resist conquest, are supported by counterexam-

ples, designating peoples where ignorance and rustic hardships produced the contrary virtues: the Persians, Scythians, Germans, early
Romans, and eighteenth-century Swiss. Pursuing his paradox, Rousseau reverses the generally held preference for Athens over Sparta (p.
12). This is one of several notions adumbrated in the Discourse that
Rousseau was to develop in subsequent writings. He then turns, not
disdaining some distortion, to Socrates, "le plus sage des hommes" ("the
wisest of men," p. 13), quoting a passage from the *Apology* as approving
ignorance.

The argument is interrupted by the famous tirade known as the
"Prosopopée de Fabricius," in which that third century B.C. hero is made
to lament the decline of his country, as the consequence of luxury and
the arts. Returning to his argument, Rousseau closes the first part of his
Discourse with two questions. "Quoi! la probité serait fille de l'ignorance? La science et la vertu seraient incompatibles?" ("What then! Can
rectitude be the daughter of ignorance? Can science and virtue be incompatible?" p.16). These two questions set the stage for Part Two.

The refutations that quickly followed publication of the Discourse
point out that examples did not establish a causal relation between the
sciences and the arts and decline and fall. In fact, Rousseau perceived
the causal gap in the development of Part One: asseverations, however
eloquent, and examples resting on weak analogies do not establish the
needed cause-effect relation. His strategy is now to strike in four directions, a strategy he hoped would foreclose refutation. Four words de-
note the directions: origin, sterility, effects, and—a special target—
luxury.

All the sciences, he declares, spring from vices: astronomy from
superstition, geometry from avarice, physics from vain curiosity, ethics
from pride. They are a history of errors and the futile search for truth.
But they are not merely useless; they are positively harmful. The time
wasted could be better spent for the benefit of society. Knowledge does
nothing to increase population and improve government or character.
Quite the contrary. Aiming his guns at what will be a favorite target,
Rousseau asserts that philosophers' "funestes paradoxes" ("fatal paradoxes"—strange charge from a writer of dazzling paradoxes! p. 19)
undermine faith, virtue, and civic commitment.

Worst of all is luxury, companion of the arts and sciences, the greatest
enemy of *bonnes moeurs* (morality, p. 19). Many examples are given to
show how poor and ignorant peoples overcame corrupt and powerful
adversaries. That is what counts. Moreover, luxury leads to frivolity and
so to degenerate taste and to degenerate artists and writers. Then
Rousseau retraces his steps to reemphasize the point about military
virtues, denying (with obvious sophistry) that modern soldiers can be

the equals of those of yore. Next he hammers away at the moral devasta-
tion caused by education, especially the ill-conceived education given in
the schools. Art is prostituted to "les égarements du coeur et de la
raison" ("the aberrations of the heart and reason") instead of being used
for patriotic propaganda (p. 25). At the bottom of all the evil is inequality,
the result of worship of talent instead of virtue: no one asks whether a
book is useful, but only whether it is well written. In such a society, how
can there be citizens?

The conclusion begins with a partial palinode. The situation could be
worse. Fortunately there are enlightened monarchs who found illustrious Academies which give prizes in essay contests designed to
restore virtue! Yet Rousseau is not retreating. The remedy only proves
the evil. Furiously, he decries philosophers and damns the invention of
printing, whose incalculable evils are compounded by writers who
make knowledge available to "une populace indigne d'en approcher" ("a
populace unworthy of coming near it," p. 29). He makes another concession: a few exceptional men should be allowed to practice the arts and
sciences. Even more, such men (Rousseau?) should be the counselors of
kings, for they know how to lead people; they know that it is more
difficult "d'engager les hommes à bien faire de leur bon gré, que de les y
contraindre par la force" ("to induce men to act virtuously of their own
will than to make them do so by force," pp. 29–30). The main drift of
Rousseau's later political writings is contained in these words. In fact,
the germ of his conception of an illiberal, militaristic, rigidly disciplined
society is in evidence throughout the Discourse. But he, Rousseau, an
ordinary man, with no talent, destined to obscurity, will be content with
doing his duty.

The strength of Rousseau's essay clearly does not lie in its argumentation, which falls to pieces even on casual examination. Rhetoric and style
take the place of philosophical rigor and well-founded analysis.

Rousseau was unequaled as a rhetorician in eighteenth-century
France, and on a par, at least, with Burke. Unschooled, he derived his
effects from a natural genius. He would have been unmatched as a
barrister, for he knew how to twist, how to turn weak points to his
advantage and make dubious assertions seem convincing. One of the
outstanding examples of these characteristics is his famous "grande
lettre" to Hume, at the climax of their scandalous quarrel. Let us now
observe some of his rhetorical resources in the Discourse.

Rousseau's foreword is designed to palliate the shocking effect of his
paradox. He presents himself—a man who knows nothing yet who
dares to impugn the sciences before a body of distinguished savants. He
dares, because he is defending truth and virtue. Win or lose, he gets the

greatest prize: "Je le trouverai dans le fond de mon coeur" ("I shall find it at the bottom of my heart").

His judges thus presumably disarmed, Rousseau attacks with a shock effect. Having admitted the "grand et beau spectacle" ("great and beautiful spectacle") of humanity's self-made ascent from rude ignorance, he unexpectedly slips his challenge into the middle of what begins as an innocuous sentence: "les sciences, les lettres et les arts, moins despotiques et plus puissants peut-être, étendent des guirlandes de fleurs sur les chaînes dont ils [les hommes] sont chargés, étouffent en eux le sentiment de cette liberté originelle pour laquelle ils semblent être nés, leur font aimer leur esclavage et en forment ce qu'on appelle des peuples policés" ("sciences, letters, and arts, less despotic and more powerful, perhaps, cover with garlands of flowers the chains with which they [men] are weighed down, stifle in them the feeling for that original freedom for which they seem to have been born, make them love their enslavement, and make of them what are called civilized peoples," p. 7).

As Rousseau develops, step by step, the chain of arguments we have followed, he uses a wealth of rhetorical devices. Sometimes he postulates as certain what is in question. After a first, brief statement of our moral corruption, he declares: "Où il n'y a nul effet, il n'y a point de cause à chercher: mais ici l'effet est certain, la dépravation réelle, et nos âmes se sont corrompues à mesure que nos sciences et nos arts se sont avancés à la perfection" ("Where there is no effect, there is no cause to look for; but here the effect is certain, depravity real, and our hearts have become corrupted step by step as our sciences and arts have advanced toward perfection," p. 9). Assuming that what does not foster the patriotic and martial spirit is useless, he concludes, "c'est un grand mal que de ne point faire de bien; et tout citoyen inutile peut être regardé comme un homme pernicieux" ("it is a great evil not to do good; and every useless citizen may be considered a pernicious man," p. 18).

Rousseau is a master of the art of building to a climax and of skillfully varying his tone. After developing his initial presentation over several pages, he bursts into a paean to Sparta, "cette république de demi-Dieux plutôt que d'hommes. . . . O Sparte! opprobre éternel d'une vaine doctrine!" ("that republic of demigods rather than of men. . . . Oh Sparta! eternal shame of a vain doctrine!" p. 12), and so on. Then he lapses into a calm, persuasive mode which ends with a leading question: "De tels monuments vaudraient-ils moins pour nous que les marbres curieux qu'Athènes nous a laissés?" ("Would such monuments be worth less to us than the curious marbles that Athens has left us?").

Sophistry was an accusation leveled against the whole of the Discourse, an accusation Rousseau (with some additional sophistries) combated in his rejoinders. The modern reader may agree or not. However, little tricks of the barrister are evident. (Rousseau was to urge the use of trickery in later writings, a fact that those who insist that to criticize him is to be his "enemy"—reflecting his own paranoia—tend to evade.) Thus, he distorts Socrates' point (p. 13) and falsifies Plato's meaning (pp. 17, 1247 n.2). Penning an egregious paradox himself, he several times accuses his targets of practicing noxious paradoxes and "maximes singulières" ("peculiar maxims," p. 19). He fashions an argument, then turns into "facts" what are only opinions. Thus *littérateurs* and *philosophes* (literary persons and philosophers) are the worst poisoners, since they are the most effective practitioners of the arts, all of which are poisonous. They praise luxury for promoting the splendor of a state, but forget that a state needs good morals, and that the two cannot coexist (p. 19). The valor of modern soldiers is meaningless, because (unlike Spartans) they are not inured to the rigors of hardship and deprivation. (The Spartans were not always victorious.) Schools teach everything but what is useful, and the schoolboy would be as well off playing games (p. 24). Rousseau invents a speech by Fabricius—an excellent *tour de force*, superbly carried out, in which he conveys Fabricius's dismay with an eloquence and a "sincerity" so effective that the "jury" cannot help being moved.

Rousseau assumes, and tries to make us assume, that the *origin* of arts and sciences being vices (another opinion stated as incontrovertible fact), their *effects* or results are also vices, worse vices; and beyond this, that without their cultivation, those vices could be avoided. He picks his examples to suit his plea, and assumes that there were such ancient realms (and Switzerland as well) unstained by vice, and that modern nations are by contrast corrupt through and through. This use of exaggeration or extravagant asseveration is effective in Rousseau's hands because his emotional commitment gives it a patina of truth and avoids the taint of caricature. The same remark applies to the insistent offensive, which informs the Discourse, against the arts and sciences, directed at demolishing the unquestioned assumption that they are useful. Having done this to his satisfaction, he attempts to evade the onus of obscurantism by explaining that they could be useful if the state allowed a few persons to practice them, provided they were used to further its civic purposes.

I have mentioned adroit changes of tone. The resounding crescendo of the last paragraph of the first part subsides into a calm statement of what is to follow. The second part resumes on the same tone for the first paragraph. Then the crescendo starts again: one paragraph of excited questions, and the harsh accusations: "Nées dans l'oisiveté, elles la nourrissent à leur tour; et la perte irréparable du temps est le premier préjudice qu'elles causent nécessairement à la société" ("Born in idleness, they nourish it in turn; and irreparable waste of time is the first harm they necessarily cause to society"). More questions and more accusations accentuate the pounding effect. "Répondez-moi donc, Philosophes illustres; vous qui savez . . ." ("Answer me, then, illustrious philosophers; you who know . . ."). And Rousseau lists what useless knowledge they pretend (how falsely!) to possess, only to repeat his peremptory summons, loaded with irony: "Répondez-moi, dis-je, vous de qui nous avons reçu tant de sublimes connaissances . . ." ("Answer me, I say, you from whom we have received so much sublime knowledge . . ."). Would we be worse off without your knowledge? "Revenez donc sur l'importance de vos productions. . . . Dites-nous ce que nous devons penser de . . ." ("Look anew at the importance of your productions. . . . Tell us what we should think of . . . ," pp. 18–19). The artful combination of inferentially accusatory questions, arrogant imperatives, and effective repetition in this development is one example, among many in the work, of Rousseau's mastery of the art of pleading.

The line between rhetoric and style is a fine one, since the former depends on the latter. Take, for instance, one of Rousseau's favorite devices, the use of questions. A question may be used for emphasis. "Que-dis-je, oisifs?" "O fureur de se distinguer, que ne pouvez-vous point?" ("What am I saying, you idlers?" "Oh fury for distinction, of what are you not capable?" p. 19). This combined exclamation and rhetorical question caps the peroration and clinches an effect. Other questions are transitional. "Que dirai-je de cette métropole de l'Empire de l'Orient?" "Mais pourquoi chercher dans ces temps reculés. . . ?" "De quoi s'agit-il dans cette question du luxe?" ("What shall I say of that metropolis of the Eastern Empire?" p. 10; "But why seek in those distant times. . . ?" p.11; "What is at stake in this question of luxury?" p. 20.)

They are usually leading questions. Sometimes the answer follows quickly and explicitly: "Dira-t-on que c'est un malheur particulier à notre âge? Non, Messieurs. . . ." "D'où naissent ces abus, si ce n'est de l'inégalité funeste. . . ?" ("Will you say that it is a misfortune peculiar to our times? No, gentlemen. . . ," p. 9; "Whence spring these abuses, if not from fatal inequality. . . ?" p. 25). Elsewhere a question may have an implied answer. "Que faudra-t-il conclure de ce paradoxe si digne d'être né de nos jours; et que deviendra la vertu, quand il faudra s'enrichir à quelque prix que ce soit?" ("What must we conclude from this paradox, so worthy of being born in our age, and what will become of virtue, when it is necessary to get rich at any cost?" p. 19).

The questions become more frequent as he continues and whenever he wishes to strike a higher emotional pitch. The "Prosopopée de Fabricius" (pp. 14–15) is a model of Rousseau's technique of building on a succession of questions, framed by exclamation. "Dieux! eussiez-vous dit, que sont devenus. . . . Quelle splendeur funeste a succédé. . . . Quel est ce langage étranger? Quelles sont ces moeurs efféminées? Que signifient. . . ? Insensés, qu'avez-vous fait?" (" 'Oh gods!' you would have said, 'what has become of. . . ? What fatal splendor has followed. . . ? What is this foreign language? What are these effeminate manners? What means. . . ? Madmen, what have you done?' "), and on and on, until he drives home with exclamatory imperatives: "Romains, hâtez-vous de renverser ces amphithéâtres; brisez ces marbres; brûlez ces tableaux; chassez ces esclaves . . ." ("Romans! Hurry and throw down those amphitheaters; break those marbles; burn those paintings; drive out those slaves . . ."). And the alternation continues.[3]

More and more, the questions imply unquestioning assent to a self-evident truth. "De quel oeil, en effet, pense-t-on que puissent envisager la faim . . . des hommes que le moindre besoin accable. . . ?" "Que contiennent les écrits des philosophes les plus connus?" "Ne suffit-il pas pour apprendre tes loix de rentrer en soi-même et d'écouter la voix de sa conscience dans le silence des passions?" ("In what way, indeed, do you think that men whom the least need crushes can contemplate hunger. . . ?" p. 23; "What do the writings of the best known philosophers contain?" p. 27; "Is it not enough, to learn your laws, to withdraw into yourself, and listen to the voice of conscience in the silence of the passions?" p.30).

Exclamations, like questions, adroitly punctuate the rhythms. Thus, beginning with a rhetorical question, the abrupt insertion of "O Sparte! opprobre éternel d'une vaine doctrine!" ("Oh Sparta! eternal shame of a vain doctrine!" p. 12) has the desired shock effect.

Rousseau has many other strings to his stylistic bow. He knows how to employ contrast and antithesis. "Nous avons des physiciens, des géomètres, des chimistes, des astronomes, des poètes, des musiciens, des peintres; nous n'avons plus de citoyens" ("We have physicists, geometers, chemists, astronomers, poets, musicians, painters; we no longer have citizens," p. 26). In this sentence we also see his effective use of rhythms, here as part of contrast. Antithesis can be concealed in a tendentious oxymoron, "cette heureuse ignorance" ("this happy ignorance," pp. 12, 15), "heureux esclaves" ("happy slaves," p. 7), or brought out in a longer development: the Spartans, called "barbarians," are dubbed by him "demi-Dieux" ("demigods," p. 12).

The first quotation in the preceding paragraph also displays Rousseau's use of accumulation for emphasis. One could cite several instances. "Plus d'amitiés sincères; plus d'estime réelle; plus de confiance fondée. Les soupçons, les ombrages, les craintes, la froideur, la réserve, la haine, la trahison se cachent . . ." ("No more sincere friendships; no more genuine esteem; no more assured confidence. Suspicions, umbrage, fears, coldness, reserve, hatred, betrayal are hidden. . . ," p. 8). This rhetorical device may be used differently, to pound hard in the initial words of sequential sentences. "On ne profanera plus. . . . On ne vantera pas. . . . On n'outragera point . . ." ("We shall no longer profane. . . . We shall no longer boast. . . . We shall no longer insult . . . ," p. 9). A series of unfavorable examples is followed by a series of counterexamples, much more vigorously hammered out, of admirable nations: "Tels furent les premiers Perses. . . . Tels furent les Scythes. . . . Tels les Germains. . . . Telle avait été Rome. . . . Telle enfin s'est montrée jusqu'à nos jours cette nation rustique [les Suisses] . . ." ("Such were the first Persians. . . . Such were the Scythians. . . . Such the Germans. . . . Such Rome had been. . . . Such, finally, has that rustic nation [the Swiss] shown itself. . . ," pp. 10–11).

Rousseau's mastery of tonal variations is evident throughout. He is fond of irony, of a scathing kind. Blasphemies, he writes, are heard "sans que nos oreilles scrupuleuses en soient offensées" ("without our scrupulous ears being thereby offended," p. 9). "Telle est la pureté que nos moeurs ont acquise. C'est ainsi que nous sommes devenus gens de bien" ("Such is the purity that our moral laws have acquired. That is the way we have become honorable people"), and in this way literature, art, and science have performed "un si salutaire ouvrage" ("such a salutary task," p. 9), and we have acquired "tant de sublimes connaissances" ("so much sublime knowledge," p. 19), thanks to these "hommes merveilleux" ("marvelous men," p. 27).

Where irony, an intellectual weapon, falls short of the emotional driving force and desired effect, another weapon, invective, lies at hand. We read of "jargon scientifique" (p. 6), "une vile et trompeuse uniformité" (p. 8), "ce troupeau qu'on appelle société" (p. 8), of "auteurs obscènes," "orgueilleux raisonneurs" (p. 12), "vains et futiles déclamateurs . . . armés de leurs funestes paradoxes" (p. 19), "une troupe de charlatans" (p. 27), etc. ("scientific jargon," "a vile and deceptive uniformity," "this herd that we call society," "obscene authors," "haughty reasoners," "vain and futile reciters . . . armed with their fatal paradoxes," "a band of quacks").

In contrast to these harsh, at times frenetic outbursts, calm reasoning can reassure and poetic effect enchant.

L'élévation et l'abaissement journalier des eaux de l'océan n'ont pas été plus régulièrement assujettis au cours de l'astre qui nous éclaire durant la nuit, que le sort de [nos] moeurs et de la probité au progrès des sciences et des arts. On a vu la vertu s'enfuir à mesure que leur lumière s'élevait sur notre horizon, et le même phénomène s'est observé dans tous les temps et tous les lieux. (The daily rise and fall of the ocean's waters have not been more regularly subjected to the course of the star that illuminates us during the night than the fate of [our] morals and probity to the progress of the sciences and arts. We have seen virtue flee in proportion as their light rose on our horizon, and the same phenomenon has been observed in all times and all places. P. 10)

Or again, ecstatic over the simplicity of primitive times: "C'est un beau rivage, paré des seules mains de la nature, vers lequel on tourne incessamment les yeux, et dont on se sent éloigner à regret" ("It is a beautiful shore, adorned only by nature's hands, toward which we constantly turn our eyes, and from which we see ourselves with regret moving away," p. 22).

Cadence, accumulation, antitheses, irony, epithets, examples, questions, exclamations, artfully varied and interwoven, add up to eloquence. The opening pages, cadenced and solemn, with strong emphases, build to the outburst beginning "Qu'il serait doux de vivre parmi nous . . ." ("How sweet it would be to live among us. . .," p. 7), then subside only to rise again. Calm reasoning rests the reader and prepares for the moments of exaltation that is born of anger interfused with feigned sorrow or regret—the outstanding moment being the "Prosopopée de Fabricius"—an anger that pervades the fiery Discourse,

Que contiennent les écrits des philosophes les plus connus? Quelles sont les leçons de ces amis de la sagesse? A les entendre, ne les prendrait-on pas pour une troupe de charlatans criant, chacun de son côté sur une place publique: Venez à moi, c'est moi seul qui ne trompe point? (What do the writings of the best known philosophers contain? What are the lessons of these friends of wisdom? To hear them, wouldn't we take them for a band of quacks shouting, each in his spot in a public square: Come to me, it is I alone who does not deceive? P. 27)[4]

Even more intriguing, and more subtle to delineate, is the role of the author and his relation to the readers—both the judges of the contest to whom he overtly speaks and the ideal reader he ultimately desires to persuade.

Throughout, Rousseau intrudes himself as the writer *who is speaking*. The foreword is unabashedly personal and boastful behind the transparent mask of modesty. Rousseau had a gift for posturing; the most remarkable example is the celebrated opening page of the *Confessions*. From time to time in the Discourse, he indicates his presence. "J'ajouterai seulement une réflexion" (p. 9). "Que dirai-je de. . . ?" (p.

10). "Oublierai-je de. . . ?" (p. 12). "Ce n'est point en vain que j'évoquais les mânes de Fabricius; et qu'ai-je fait dire à ce grand homme que je n'eusse pu mettre . . ." (p. 15). "Qu'on me dise . . ." (p. 25). "Qu'on ne m'oppose point . . ." (p. 27). "Je demanderai seulement . . ." (p. 27) ("I shall add only one reflection." "What shall I say about. . . ?" "Shall I forget to. . . ?" "It is not in vain that I invoked the shade of Fabricius; and what have I made that great man say that I could not have put. . . ." "Let me be told. . . ." "Let me not be opposed. . . ." "I shall only ask. . . .") In a word, Rousseau hides behind no curtain. He uses the first person pronoun, when "on" or other impersonal expressions would be available. He makes it clear that he is speaking for himself and is proud of what he says—proudly defiant. Openly, he challenges his judges, his readers, the world.

Never forgetful that he is in a prize contest, he speaks directly to the judges, the readers of first instance, intermittently. In the foreword, he flatters them, but in a way warns them that they will overlook him at their peril: "A ce motif qui m'encourage, il s'en joint un autre qui me détermine: c'est qu'après avoir soutenu, selon ma lumière naturelle, le parti de la vérité; quel que soit mon succès, il est un prix qui ne peut me manquer: je le trouverai dans le fond de mon coeur" ("To this motive which encourages me is joined another that determines me: it is that after having upheld, according to my natural lights, the side of truth, whatever be my success, there is a prize that cannot fail me: I will find it at the bottom of my heart," p. 5). Later we encounter phrases in which the barrister addresses the judge: "Dira-t-on. . . ? Non, Messieurs" (p. 9); "Voyez l'Egypte. . . . Voyez la Grèce . . ." (p. 10); "Ce qu'il fera, Messieurs" (p. 21) ("Would we say. . . ? No, gentlemen." "Look at Egypt. . . . Look at Greece. . . ." "What he will do, gentlemen")—or again flatters them (p. 25).

Rousseau aims beyond the judges to the ideal reader. He admonishes or lectures that reader. "Peuples, sachez donc une fois que la nature a voulu vous préserver de la science . . . que tous les secrets qu'elle vous cache sont autant de maux dont elle vous garantit, et que la peine que vous trouvez à vous instruire n'est pas le moindre de ses bienfaits" ("Peoples, know then for once that nature has tried to protect you from knowledge . . . that all the secrets she hides from you are so many evils from which she shields you, and that the labor learning costs you is not the least of her boons," p. 15). The ultimate rhetorical purpose of Rousseau's persistent use of questions is not rhythmic but persuasive. The questions either are followed by the answer, or else imply the desired answer, which supposedly must be that of any reasonable reader. A few citations will suffice to illustrate this constant rhetoric. Unanswered: "Mais est-il quelqu'une de ses leçons dont nous ayons su profiter, ou que nous ayons négligée impunément?" (p. 15). "Que ferions-nous des arts, sans le luxe qui les nourrit?" (p. 17). "Qui est-ce d'ailleurs, qui la [vérité] cherche bien sincèrement?" (p. 18). "Avec quel courage les soldats supporteront-ils des travaux excessifs dont ils n'ont aucune habitude?" (p. 23) ("But is there one of her lessons that we have known how to profit from, or that we have neglected with impunity?" "What would we do with the arts, without the luxury that nourishes them?" "Besides, who looks for [truth] sincerely?" "With what courage will soldiers bear excessive labor to which they are not accustomed?"). Answered: "Croit-on que s'il [Socrate] ressuscitait parmi nous, nos savants et nos artistes lui feraient changer d'avis? Non, Messieurs, cet homme juste continuerait de mépriser nos vaines sciences" (pp. 13–14). "De quoi s'agit-il donc précisément dans cette question du luxe? De savoir lequel importe le plus aux empires . . ." (p. 20) ("Do you think that if he [Socrates] was brought back amongst us, our savants and artists would make him change his mind? No, gentlemen, that just man would continue to despise our vain sciences." "What exactly is at stake in this question of luxury? To know which matters most to empires . . .").

Rousseau associates the reader with himself and tries to make the reader his accomplice. He takes the reader into his confidence: "Qu'il serait doux de vivre parmi nous . . . si nos maximes nous servaient de règles. . . !" (p. 7). "Mais pourquoi chercher dans des temps reculés des preuves d'une vérité dont nous avons sous les yeux des témoignages subsistants?" (p. 11). "Mais franchissons la distance des lieux et des temps, et voyons ce qui s'est passé dans nos contrées et sous nos yeux. . . . Ce n'est point en vain que j'évoquais les mânes de Fabricius; et qu'ai-je fait dire à ce grand homme, que je n'eusse pu mettre dans la bouche de Louis XII ou de Henri IV? Parmi nous, il est vrai . . ." (p. 15) ("How sweet it would be to live among us . . . if our maxims were our rules. . . !" "But why seek in distant times proofs of a truth for which we have constant testimony beneath our eyes?" "But let us leap over the distances of places and times, and let us see what has happened in our countries and under our eyes. . . . It is not in vain that I summoned up the shade of Fabricius; and what have I made that great man say, that I would not have put into the mouths of Louis XII or Henry IV? Amongst us, it is true . . ."). He may speak to the reader indirectly, by association: "Dites-nous, célèbre Arouet . . ." ("Tell us, celebrated Arouet. . . ," p. 21). Again: "Répondez-moi [philosophes], dis-je, vous de qui nous avons reçu tant de sublimes connaissances; quand vous ne nous auriez jamais rien appris de ces choses, en serions-nous moins nombreux, moins bien gouvernés. . . ? Dites-nous ce que nous devons penser de cette foule d'écrivains obscurs et de lettrés oisifs . . ." ("Answer me [this to philosophers], I say, you from whom we have received such sublime knowledge; if you had taught us nothing about these things, would we be less populous, less well governed. . . ? Tell us what we ought to think of that swarm of obscure writers and idle men of letters. . . ?" p. 19). He may address the reader directly: "Que penseriez-vous que représentent ces chefs-d'oeuvre de l'art exposés à l'admiration publique. . . . Ce sont des images de tous les égarements du coeur et de la raison . . . présentées de bonne heure à la curiosité de nos enfants" ("What do you think these masterpieces of art exposed to the public admiration represent. . . ? They are images of all the aberrations of the heart and of reason . . . displayed to our children's early curiosity," p. 25).

My opening contention about Rousseau's uniqueness is now (if I may use his own rhetorical technique) unmistakably evident. Not cool reasoning, spirited dialectic, or arid logic but the impassioned notes of the author's voice build and irresistibly carry forward the rhetorical dynamics of his Discourse. We hear that voice throughout speaking to us, and as it does, we hear the author speaking for himself, expressing personal, even extravagant feelings. In his irony, his invective, and above all his anger, we never lose sight of his presence or fail to hear the sound of a man's voice behind the printed lines. We know his conviction, which he is striving to make our own. "Oublierai-je que ce fut dans le sein même de la Grèce qu'on vit s'élever cette Cité aussi célèbre par son heureuse ignorance que par la sagesse de ses lois, cette république de demi-Dieux plutôt que d'hommes? . . . O Sparte! opprobre éternel d'une vaine doctrine!" ("Shall I forget that it was in the very heart of Greece that arose that city as celebrated for its happy ignorance as for the wisdom of its laws, that republic of demigods rather than of men? . . . Oh Sparta! eternal reproach to a vain doctrine!" p. 12). We feel the lash of his anger, as in the heated paragraph of which I shall quote only the climactic lines:

Allez, écrits célèbres dont l'ignorance et la rusticité de nos pères n'auraient point été capables; accompagnez chez nos descendants ces ouvrages plus dangereux encore d'où s'exhale le corruption des moeurs de notre siècle, et portez ensemble aux siècles à venir une histoire fidèle du progrès et des avantages de nos sciences et de nos arts. S'ils vous lisent, vous ne leur laisserez aucune perplexité sur la question que nous agitons aujourd'hui: et à moins qu'ils ne soient plus insensés que nous, ils lèveront leurs mains au ciel, et diront dans l'amertume de leur coeur: "Dieu tout puissant, toi qui tiens dans tes mains les Esprits, délivre-nous des Lumières et des funestes arts de nos pères, et rends-nous l'ignorance, l'innocence et la pauvreté, les seuls biens qui puissent faire notre bonheur et qui soient précieux devant toi." (Go forth, famous writings, of which our ancestors' ignorance would have been incapable; accompany amongst our descendants those works, more dangerous still, which exhale the corruption of the morality of our century, and together bring to the centuries to come a faithful history of the progress and the benefits of our sciences and arts. If they read you, you will not leave them in any perplexity about the question we are debating today; and, unless they are madder than we, they will raise their hands to heaven, and say with bitter hearts: "All-powerful God, thou who holdest the spirits in thy hands, deliver us from enlightenment and the fatal arts of our forebears, and give us back ignorance, innocence, and poverty, the only possessions that can make our happiness and that are precious before thee." P. 28)

Do we know this man who is haranguing us? If we do not really know him (did he know himself?), we are keenly aware of the persona he displays *as* his self. From the foreword to the closing lines, he displays that persona.[5] He is proud of it, to the point of arrogance. He defies the world and its great, even his judges. He—and he alone—knows what is wrong. He will tell it to the jury, really to the world at large, even as the prophets of yore.

The *Discours sur les sciences et les arts* is less a philosophical discourse than a sermon, less a sermon than a barrister's plea. It persuades less by sound argumentation than by the brilliance of paradox, the cleverness of the *rhéteur*, and the fire of the Old Testament prophets. It won the coveted prize. It convinced no one, doubtless not his judges. But it was the best of the submissions. And Rousseau won not only the prize, but also the fame or notoriety he had craved.

II

Just as Rousseau had not respected to the letter the question posed by the Académie de Dijon in 1749,[6] in the *Discours sur l'origine de l'inégalité parmi les hommes (Discourse on the Origin of Inequality among Men,* 1755) he again alters, but more significantly, the subject for the 1753 prize, which was "Quelle est l'origine de l'inégalité parmi les hommes, et si elle est autorisée par la Loi naturelle" ("What is the origin of inequality among men, and whether it is authorized by natural law"). In analyzing the writing of this second Discourse, I shall concentrate on his strategy of exposition, with occasional references to rhetoric; to go over again the detail of his stylistic repertoire would be tedious. Moreover, because the subject requires more complex reasoning, the structure is more interesting, while the rhetoric is thinner. Perhaps that was one reason—I shall suggest others—why Rousseau, on his second try, did not win the prize.

The Discourse is preceded by a very long Dedication "A la République de Genève." It has nothing to do with the subject, and its eloquent tone, which resembles that of the first Discourse, differs from the prevailing

tone of the second.[7] Yet it is of interest because of its personal, autobiographical, and apologetic character. In the combination of flattery,
self-abasement, and pride, the man reveals himself, indeed more than
he intends. The picture of an idealized Geneva, which Rousseau per-
fectly well knew did not exist, might be considered by his aspersers as
another instance of sophistry. It would be described more accurately as a
projection of his political ideals and his love for the homeland he had
lost, deliberately and with unending regret and self-reproach. I shall not
examine here the autobiographical elements of the Dedication. However,
the ideas expressed in it will become so central to his later political
theory that they are worthy of mention. The ideal state, as he pictures it,
is small enough so that all the citizens know each other and can exercise
surveillance over each other in the civic interest. There is no conflict of
interests; a single interest moves all parts of the machine toward the
general welfare. This requires that the people be sovereign. The people
are both free and docile. No one is above the law. Military ardor and
puritanical severity distinguish their way of life. The citizens enact the
laws, but only the "magistrates" may draw them up and propose them;
then the citizens vote on them, "sur le rapport des chefs" ("on the
recommendation of the leaders"), the latter being elected (or reelected?)
annually.

This outline—whether intended as a eulogistic, ideal description of
Geneva's government or as a covert monitory criticism of its degeneration, I cannot say—proves that, as Rousseau himself maintained, all his
writings on society are of a piece. However sketchily, he already knew
what was wrong about existing societies and where to head to discover
the right way. Students of the *Social Contract* have too often ignored this
Dedication. Ultimately, it is connected with the body of the Discourse,
because one must know what went wrong in order to project what is
required to make things right. The Discourse will tell us what went
wrong.

The Dedication was added later, for publication. The Discourse itself
begins with a skillfully planned and reasoned Preface. Its tone is ponderous, and it is punctuated by classical allusions. Knowing in what
direction he is heading, Rousseau resets the question on his own terms.
The Preface is designed to establish two points that are essential to his
project.

The first point is that the question of inequality cannot be addressed
head-on. He establishes it in a development that starts with a rhetorical
question: "Car comment connaître la source de l'inégalité parmi les
hommes, si l'on ne commence par les connaître eux-mêmes?" ("For how
can we know the source of inequality among men, if we do not begin by
knowing men themselves?" p. 122). This apparently innocuous, self-

answering question prepares the reader for the vital kernel of the Discourse, which Rousseau immediately announces. It is an upsetting proposition. We cannot know Man through an empirical study of men. Men—the simile is revealing—are like the statue of Glaucus (Plato, *Republic,* 10.611); they have been transformed and disfigured by the work of time. Thus Rousseau is attempting, poetically and not by abstract argument, to posit an axiomatic notion: we must look for Man outside of or prior to men. We must reconstruct the original Man.

Rousseau at once tells us what Man was. Any analysis would show the picture that follows to be sheer speculation ("méditant sur les premières et plus simples opérations de l'âme humaine," "meditating on the first and simplest operations of the human soul," p. 125), as indeed it had to be, given the search for a Man who existed before and outside of social or even elementary human relationships. Nevertheless, it is rhetorically effective, because of Rousseau's earnestness and his commitment through direct authorial presence. "Ce qu'il y a de plus cruel encore. . . . Il est aisé de voir que . . ." ("What is even more cruel. . . . It is easy to see that . . ."). He disarms potential critics: "Que mes lecteurs ne s'imaginent donc pas que j'ose me flatter d'avoir vu ce qui me paraît si difficile à voir" ("Let my readers not imagine, then, that I dare to flatter myself that I have seen what seems to me so difficult to see," p. 123). He concedes that he is advancing conjectures about something that may never have existed. But those conjectures, he argues, are necessary. He does not tell us why they are necessary, *unless* we are captivated, as he intends, by his assertion that there was such a Man and that we must reconstruct him in order to understand men (hence, inequality). Moreover, he will henceforth disregard his own caveat and write *as if* the developments pictured in the Discourse were historical realities. This, then, is his initial rhetorical strategy.

This assumption made, the question automatically follows: what are—rather, were—the characteristics of Man? Rousseau tells us that Man acted upon certain and invariable principles—animal instincts, apparently—undistorted by passion or reason. There can be only two such prerational principles. The first is personal well-being and self-preservation. The other is a natural repugnance at seeing a fellow man suffer. From the second principle it follows that he will never hurt another man or a sensitive animal except when the first principle requires it. This statement is basic to the ensuing argument.

The second objective of the Preface is to eliminate from Rousseau's presentation the question posed in the adjunct to the Academy's subject—"et si elle est autorisée par la Loi naturelle" ("and whether it is authorized by natural law")—and to justify its exclusion. Rousseau adroitly inserts this point in the midst of his first argument. Because we

are ignorant about Man, natural law theorists have fallen into confusions. Rousseau's reasoning is important in the context of eighteenth-
century thought. He agrees with Pufendorf and Burlamaqui that we
must distinguish, contrary to the Roman jurisconsults, between nature's
law and "natural law." The former pertains to the "rapports généraux
établis par la nature entre tous les êtres animés, pour leur commune
conservation" ("general relationships established by nature among all
living beings, for their common self-preservation," p. 124). The latter is a
law prescribed by nature to a free and rational being, thus a moral being,
meaning man alone. However, the notions of earlier theorists not only
are contradictory, but are so "metaphysical" as to be useless—inevitably,
Rousseau declares. Not knowing Man, they have retrojected into the
original "natural" nature of Man (necessarily, since they were searching
for "natural" law) knowledge, conditions, ideas, and rules that came into
being in the course of historical and cultural development. Therefore,
theories of natural law are useless in the pursuit of original Man, whom
we must discover if we are to know what natural law, which really
speaks "immédiatement par la voix de la nature" ("immediately by the
voice of nature," p. 125) might really be, and if we are to discover the
origin of inequality, which is, then, the meaningful part of the Academy's question, the part Rousseau proposes to address.[8]

As if Rousseau were throwing off the constraints of rational argumentation, to which he has disciplined himself in this course of reasoning, he
abruptly concludes the Preface with a poetic flourish, doubtless designed to express his own feelings or to capture those of his readers.

A short but dense opening to the body of the Discourse delimits his
subject, as he conceives it, with clarity and eloquence. The exposition
displays both rational acumen and his very personal conception of the
set question. After a brief, obsequious bow to his judges, he distinguishes between natural and conventional inequality. Swiftly he eliminates the first as supererogatory and denies any connection between it
and the second form. The denial is rhetorically loaded: it contains the
assumption that if the two inequalities corresponded, then the second
might be justifiable, and the further implication that in our unjust societies, they do not correspond.

Having thus gotten rid of another possible obstruction to his scheme,
Rousseau can define his subject. The rhetoric is skillful:

De quoi s'agit-il donc précisément dans ce Discours? De marquer dans
le progrès des choses, le moment où le droit succédant à la violence, la
nature fut soumise à la loi; d'expliquer par quel enchaînement de
prodiges le fort a pu se résoudre à servir le faible, et le peuple à
acheter un repos en idée, au prix d'une félicité réelle. (What, precisely,

is the question in this Discourse? To discern, in the progress of things, the moment when law [*le droit*] replaced violence and nature was submitted to law; to explain by what chain of prodigies the stronger could resolve to serve the weak, and the people to buy a fictitious security at the price of real happiness. P. 132)

This is obviously a loaded definition. It implies the answers which will produce the body of the Discourse and justify their truth.

Abruptly, with no transition, Rousseau comes to grips with the question that will underlie the whole development, the state of nature. He *must* establish the falsity of accepted conceptions. This he does by expounding the idea expressed in the Preface: the theories of Grotius, Pufendorf, and Hobbes must be discarded. Justice, property, and authority are all conventional notions. In a word, all earlier writers "ont transporté à l'état de nature des idées qu'ils avaient prises dans la société" ("have transported into the state of nature ideas they found in society," p. 132). Another exclusion, then. Rousseau makes a hasty bow to Christian dogma, and repeats that he is presenting hypotheses.

He eliminates another issue that might hinder him or provoke criticism. Biological transformism was already a nascent idea among advanced speculators.[9] By excluding any consideration of human evolution, Rousseau *ipso facto* obviates the possibility of an evolution of human nature, that is, the gradual emergence and development of essential generic characteristics, or their association with interpersonal, group, and social relationships that might depend on or accompany such biological transformations. On the contrary, the abstract Man is assumed to be what he is, or what Rousseau tells us he is, as pure intrinsicality. In this way, abstraction and separation are completed: there was the natural man, there is the artificial man. A decisive break occurred. On this "fact" will rest Rousseau's whole notion of inequality.

Even at this early point, we can see that the strategy of argumentation in the second Discourse is far more complex than the straightforward progression of the first. Before developing his theses Rousseau has done two things. (1) He has set forth in summary fashion some primary hypotheses, posited as self-evident facts. (2) He has gotten rid of questions, conceivably aspects of the general problem, that might impede or contravene his theses. The first of these accomplishments will inevitably beget repetition and expansion of the three basic points he has fleetingly made: (a) abstract, natural Man; (b) criticism of retrojection of traits belonging to men as we know them now into the primitive, essential Man; (c) the two inequalities, natural and artificial. Repetitiousness, in fact, is the major rhetorical defect of the second Discourse. It may have been a second reason for Rousseau's failure to win the prize, although his submission was superior in originality and animating power to those of his competitors.

Having thus seen the groundwork, we must ask where he is heading and then see how he gets there. The road he takes, and so the one we shall take, corresponds to the following analytical table.

I. His ultimate objective, the *terminus ad quem*, was not the one contemplated by the proposers of the subject. It is not really the *origin* of inequality (the second part having been dismissed, as we have seen). It goes altogether beyond that. It is essentially homiletic and admonitory, grandiose in its sweep; a radical critique and condemnation of society, together with a hint that something better is possible.

II. To reach this objective, he must establish (1) that inequality had an origin, and what it was, and (2) that the origin (now newly discovered and revealed) was the fountainhead of what he condemns in I.

III. If there was an origin to inequality, there must have been a prior state of equality. He must demonstrate not only its existence, which is a logical *sequitur*, but (1) that it was a better state, and (2) that it was better because of the absence of social relationships.

IV. To justify the third set of hypotheses, he must account for the passage from the initial state to its subsequent one.

Analysis of the argumentation of the Discourse shows this table of reverse or deductive progression to be its real ratiocinative skeleton. However, it is not the essay as we read it. By examining the way Rousseau actually proceeds, and how he makes his points, we shall see how he gives the skeleton its flesh, its rhetorical appeal. The underlying logical order might have been carried out by a descent down the ladder of steps marked out by the ultimate objective. Rousseau prefers not to pursue this deductive chain of reasoning, or more exactly, to mask it for the purpose of persuasion. His order of exposition is the reverse, but only roughly so, for it several times folds over on itself. Rousseau's choice was probably made to give a specious impression of an inductive chain. In following the course of his presentation, I shall refer to the numbers in the table set forth above.

Rousseau, then, chooses to begin his demonstration with III. This starting point was dictated by the groundwork he had laid out. The process of elimination we have examined left him with an abstract Man, whom he reifies as "natural man." Since no such creature now exists, the prior state required by III is imposed on the reader as a veracious corollary, despite the fleeting defensive disclaimer of its being no more than a justified hypothesis.

By telling us next who or what this natural man *was* or *might have been*, Rousseau *pari passu* takes a first step toward establishing the superiority of the original state, or state of nature (III, 1). I shall not recapitulate the well-known details of the description (pp. 135ff.), but the presentation calls for some comments.

"Je le vois . . ." ("I see him"), Rousseau begins, thus inviting the reader to "see" along with him. The reader is further involved by the rhetorical device of speaking in a series of questions. "S'il avait eu une hache, son poignet romprait-il de si fortes branches?" ("If he had had a hatchet, could his wrist have broken such strong branches?" p. 135), etc. And by a tendentious imperative: "Mettez un ours ou un loup aux prises avec un sauvage robuste, agile, courageux, comme ils sont tous, armés de pierres, et d'un bon bâton, et vous verrez que le péril sera tout au moins réciproque" ("Put a bear or a wolf in combat with a robust, agile, courageous savage, as they all are, armed with stones and a good club, and you will see that the peril will at least be equal," p. 136). Taking fantasy for fact, Rousseau describes his natural man as not subject to disease, devoid of aggressive impulses, and erotic only in volatile, animal encounters. Another disease man does not have is thinking. The conclusion is then set forth directly, as established fact deduced from the preceding description: "Gardons-nous donc de confondre l'homme sauvage avec les hommes que nous avons sous les yeux. . . . En devenant sociable et esclave, il devient faible, craintif, rampant, et sa manière de vivre molle et efféminée achève d'énerver à la fois sa force et son courage" ("Let us then be careful not to confuse savage man with the men we see. . . . By becoming sociable and a slave, he becomes feeble, fearful, cringing, and his soft and effeminate way of life completes the enervation of both his strength and his courage" p. 139). The conclusion is confirmed by a great "truth": all domesticated animals are degenerate. In an abrupt change of mode, Rousseau speculates ("doit aimer à dormir," "doivent être," "il aura" ["must love to sleep," "must be," "he would have"]) about his model's way of life.

What he has said thus far deals mainly with "l'homme physique" ("the physical man"). What was this naked man's metaphysical and moral life? Mentally, he was little different from animals. There is, however, one distinguishing difference. Man is free from the mechanical fixity of instinctual behavior. Aware of his freedom, he can change his ways of life. This distinction, Rousseau tells us, only reinforces the same conclusion (III, 1): it is "la source de tous les malheurs de l'homme" ("the source of all of man's misfortunes"), for it will eventually draw him out of his innocent, tranquil state and give birth to his knowledge, virtues and vices, and enslavement (p. 142). Foreshadowing IV, Rousseau indicates a chain: new circumstances, new needs, passions, mental development. The first, and the worst new feeling will be awareness and fear of death, unknown to natural man. Rhetorical devices clinch the point: "Il me serait aisé, si cela m'était nécessaire, d'appuyer ce sentiment par les faits" ("It would be easy for me, if that were necessary, to support this opinion by facts"); but the "facts" that he alleges he might use, if they were any longer necessary, are evasively alluded to (pp. 143–44). Instead, he drives home his contention by repeating himself in another way, still appealing directly to the reader in a manner that takes the reader's assent for granted. Instead of calling on "unreliable" facts, he asks: "qui ne voit que tout semble éloigner de l'homme sauvage la tentation et les moyens de cesser de l'être?" ("who does not see that everything seems to remove from savage man the temptation and the means to cease being savage?" p. 144)—sans imagination, sans needs, sans curiosity or foresight, sans everything.

Point IV is thus broached again. Arguing once more by a long series of self-answering questions (pp. 144–45), Rousseau tries to convince the reader that change through progress was so nearly impossible that the original state seemed destined to go on forever—this despite "perfectibility." And here III, 2 is introduced, but brushed over: even if discoveries had been made, they would have been useless and lost among men living in isolation, who did not need each other, and did not want or have each other's company. From the "fact" of isolation also follows that they had no language, hence no communication.

This new "fact" leads Rousseau into a long excursus on theories of the origin of language. Interesting as this subject is, we shall pass it by, because it interrupts the flow of his argument. Yet the idea that natural man had no language (to which this disquisition is directed) is important for the chain of reasoning. As the editor, Jean Starobinski, remarks in a note, "Démontrer la contingence du langage, c'est du même coup démontrer le caractère relatif et dérivé de tout ce qui résulte de l'emploi du langage. Contre les philosophes qui, avec Aristote (*Polit.*, I) définissent l'homme par la sociabilité et le langage, Rousseau entreprend de prouver que sociabilité et langage ne sont pas des attributs liés à l'essence de l'homme" ("To demonstrate the contingency of language is at the same time to demonstrate the relative and derivative character of everything that results from language. Against the philosophers who, with Aristotle [*Politics* 1] define man by sociability and language, Rousseau undertakes to prove that sociability and language are not attributes linked to the essence of man," pp. 1322–23 n.2). As our logical table indicates, Rousseau must define the presocial state as one of solitary men (III, 2), or else his major thesis (I), that society has led them into a corrupted state, falls. Therefore he at once brings to bear an argument to which he had already assigned great weight in discussing natural law: to suppose that men lived in families (which would ensure communication) is only another false retrojection from the present social state (p. 146). Thus he assumes—and tries to make the reader assume—as self-evident, that

there really was an original state such as he depicts. Accusing others of a
fault in reasoning, he masks the poor grounding of his own assumption.
In this, as in his assumption that natural man could not think, having no
language, he retrojects the reverse: natural man—in order to make him
unsocial—had to be deprived of what social men possess. We see how
his argumentation hangs on III, 2.

What follows makes this assertion even more evident. Natural man—
it is to be remembered that Rousseau is speaking not of savages but of
"Man" in his original, unaltered, quintessential being—had no moral
notion or sense of obligation. He cannot then be called good or evil—and
here Rousseau adroitly slips in a hint of what he is ultimately aiming at
(I): we must suspend judgment about this state until we have examined
"s'il y a plus de vertus que de vices parmi les hommes civilisés . . . si le
progrès de leurs connaissances est un dédommagement suffisant des
maux qu'ils se font mutuellement" ("whether there are more virtues
than vices among civilized men . . . whether the progress of their
knowledge is a sufficient compensation for the evils they mutually inflict
on each other"), and whether they would not be happier in a state of
independence (pp. 152–53).

Parenthetic diatribes against Hobbes and Mandeville follow. They
allow Rousseau to attribute to natural man something better, or purer,
than virtues: compassion for his fellow men, a feeling Rousseau "justifies" by attributing it to some animals as well. "Tel est le pur mouvement
de la nature, antérieur à la réflexion" ("Such is the pure impulse of
nature, prior to reflection," p. 155).

After recapitulating the last phase of his demonstration (p. 157), Rousseau, apparently feeling that he has not adequately forestalled a predic-
table objection, turns back to argue at greater length that the powerful
sexual urge, which creates disorder and wreaks havoc among socialized
men, was harmless in the state of nature, because it was purely physical
and free of "le moral de l'amour," "un sentiment factice" ("the moral
aspect of love," "a factitious sentiment," p. 158). This repetition serves
also to reconfirm the point of III, 1.

The first part of the Discourse concludes with a long summation (pp.
159–63). Rousseau has shown that a state existed in which there was only
natural inequality, and that it was innocent and innocuous. In this
summation the style becomes eloquent and metaphorical. For eloquence
he again relies on a series of purportedly apodictic questions, for example, "Que sera l'esprit à des gens qui ne parlent point, et la ruse à ceux
qui n'ont point d'affaires?" ("What could wit matter to people who don't
speak to each other, and ruse to those who have no dealings?"). Metaphor is emphatic. About education: "car qu'un géant et un nain
marchent sur la même route, chaque pas qu'ils feront l'un et l'autre

donnera un nouvel avantage au géant" ("for let a giant and a dwarf walk the same line, every step that each of them takes will give a fresh advantage to the giant," p. 160). Or again: "Si l'on me chasse d'un arbre, j'en suis quitte pour aller à un autre" ("If I am chased from one tree, all I have to do is go to another," p. 161).

Before opening the second part of the Discourse, Rousseau does two other things: (1) He defends his method. If he has indulged in conjectures, they become "reasons" when they are the most probable conjectures, because they are based on the nature of things and are the most heuristically productive. (2) Moreover, the consequences he is about to deduce cannot be called conjectural "puisque, sur les principes que je viens d'établir, on ne saurait former aucun autre système qui ne me fournisse les mêmes résultats, et dont je ne puisse tirer les mêmes conclusions" ("since on the principles I have just established, it would be impossible to form any other system that would not produce the same results, and from which I could not draw the same conclusions," p. 162). This is a remarkable example of circular reasoning, or of *petitio principii,* one that merits the epithet *sophistry.*

At the same time, Rousseau hints at what those results and conclusions will be. Two parts of the exposition, II and IV of our table, have yet to be put in place to produce the conclusion of I. In perfect control of his general rhetorical design, he writes: "Il me reste à montrer son origine [celle de l'inégalité] et ses progrès dans les développements successifs de l'esprit humain" ("I still have to show its origin [that is, of inequality] and its progress in the successive developments of the human mind"). He will show (II, 1) that to leave the original state, a "concours fortuit de plusieurs causes étrangères qui pouvaient ne jamais naître" ("a fortuitous coincidence of several extraneous causes which might never have come into being") was requisite. He will consider (II, 2) these "hasards qui ont pu perfectionner la raison humaine, en détériorant l'espèce, rendre un être méchant en le rendant sociable, et d'un terme si éloigné amener enfin l'homme et le monde au point où nous les voyons" ("chance events that may have perfected human reason, while debasing the species, made a being wicked by making him sociable, and from so remote a time brought man and the world at last to the point at which we see them now," p. 162). Rousseau is clearly heading toward point I. All of the first part has been a "demonstration" of point III of the logical table. The others will follow.

The second part begins with a resounding sentence, that has continued to echo down the years. "Le premier qui ayant enclos un terrain, s'avisa de dire, *ceci est à moi,* et trouva des gens assez simples pour le croire, fut le vrai fondateur de la société civile" ("The first man who, after enclosing a piece of ground, took it into his head to say, *this is mine,* and found people simple enough to believe him, was the real founder of civil society," p. 164). The writer's emotions surge unchecked:

> Que de crimes, de guerres, de meurtres, que de misères et d'horreurs n'eût point épargnés au genre humain celui qui arrachant les pieux ou comblant le fossé, eût crié à ses semblables. Gardez-vous d'écouter cet imposteur. Vous êtes perdus, si vous oubliez que les fruits sont à tous, et que la terre n'est à personne. (From how many crimes, how many wars, how many murders, how many misfortunes and horrors, would that man have saved mankind, who, pulling up the stakes or filling in the ditches, would have cried to his fellow men: Beware of listening to this impostor. You are lost, if you forget that the fruits [of the earth] belong equally to us all, and the earth itself to nobody. P. 164)

These lines purport to state a historical fact, not a proof or argument. That fact would establish a one-to-one causal relation between property and society. However, Rousseau has again chosen, for rhetorical impact, not to follow a linear logical order. This time he takes the reader into his confidence and makes the reader aware of it. That fatal act depended, he writes, on many prior developments. He has thus exploited the "fatal act" to achieve a rhetorical shock effect. What follows, then, is a flashback. He will tell us what actually happened. He will set forth a series of developments, as if they had really occurred, and accompany each with a vivid description, written as if he had witnessed them and is telling the reader what he saw. Some of these developments did occur, but not in the way he describes and not necessarily with the effects he ascribes to them.

His Man lived an animal life of pure sensation. He learned to use weapons, but not to make them. For several reasons that are suggested, food gathering eventually became more difficult. The Man learned to fish, make weapons and clothing, use fire, and cook. Since these changes involved perception of relationships, Man learned to think. Now he feels superior to other animals—a pride of species that foreshadows individual pride. Then, on islands, he became aware of other creatures like himself. Sometimes they cooperated, transiently, in hordes ("troupeaux"). In so doing they acquired a rude idea of reciprocal commitments ("engagements") and experienced fleeting rivalries and hostilities. Such contacts gave rise to articulate cries and gestures. Tools are made. Huts are built.

Many centuries have passed. Families form. Conjugal and paternal love are born. The sexes acquire distinct roles for the first time. People become more attached to conveniences: "ce fut là le premier joug qu'ils s'imposèrent sans y songer, et la première source des maux qu'ils préparaient à leurs descendants" ("that was the first yoke they put upon themselves without realizing it, and the first source of all the ills they were preparing for their descendants," p. 168).

With this first revolution, deterioration begins its long course. Everything changes. Floods, volcanic eruptions, geological alterations force men to live together. They learn to speak, on islands, first. More lasting social groups (tribes?) are formed, but there are still no rules or laws. Comparison brings about rivalry, especially for the best sexual partners. Finally, love is discovered, and with love, jealousy and discord. Rousseau tells us how *he* feels about this: "et la plus douce des passions reçoit des sacrifices de sang humain" ("and the sweetest of passions receives the sacrifice of human blood," p. 169).

Assemblies for singing and dancing intensify comparison and sharpen the desire for esteem and preeminence. This, then, "fut le premier pas vers l'inégalité, et vers le vice" ("was the first step toward inequality and toward vice," p. 169). Entirely new feelings spring forth: vanity, shame, envy, scorn. This is the end of innocence.

Referring to our table, we now have an explanation of II, 1 and a preliminary notion of its causative relation to I. But this is only the beginning.

Inevitably, some men become predominant, some have to obey. Now they know "les premiers devoirs de la civilité" ("the first duties of civility," p. 170). Moral ideas, newly born, produce the idea of offenses, which provoke vengeance. This, Rousseau claims (incorrectly), is the state in which present-day savages live; it explains the "false idea" that men are naturally cruel and need to be governed. According to Rousseau's "history," men have traveled a long way to the savage state. But there is still a long road ahead. The savage state, thus described, is the golden age, "l'époque la plus heureuse, la plus durable" ("the happiest, the most durable epoch," p. 171). Only a "funeste hasard" ("fatal chance")—we are now linked to the opening trumpet blast—could have put an end to it and consummated "la décrépitude de l'espèce" ("the degeneration of the species").

What was that cause? Division of labor, work requiring more than one, the end of self-sufficiency. Such a change puts an end to equality (which, however, seems already to have ended), establishes property, allows accumulation. But the cause had to have a cause. How did it come about? Metallurgy and agriculture were the culprits. They spawned "cette grande révolution" ("that great revolution") and ruined humanity. But this cause, too, had to have a cause. Rousseau explains the obstacles that long postponed these two arts (pp. 172–73). In the end, it comes down to metallurgy, which made the tools that made systematic agriculture possible. Rousseau attributes little agriculture to the stone age.

With agriculture comes property. The fence so eloquently put up in the opening paragraph is now historically in place. Rousseau does not condemn property now; it comes with agriculture. So do rules of justice. Inequality continues its unstoppable growth.

Point IV of our table has been established. It, too, requires further elaboration and a clearer connection with I. Rousseau sets about this by interrupting momentarily his pseudo-historical narrative and re-introducing the narrator. "Je ne m'arrêterai pas à décrire l'invention successive des autres arts . . . que chacun peut aisément suppléer" ("I shall not pause to describe the successive inventions of the other arts . . . which each one can easily supply," p. 174). Instead, he gives us his impression of the effects of "ce nouvel ordre de choses" ("this new order of things"). His technique is descriptive here, not developmental. Eloquence soars, as he tells us how transparency gave way to the fatal dichotomy of *être* and *paraître* (*being* and *appearance*), and how freedom gave way to enslavement. Even the powerful are enslaved now: "riche, il a besoin de leurs services; pauvre, il a besoin de leurs secours" ("if rich, he needs their services; if poor, he needs their succor," p. 175). All are dependent, all are rivals, all are impelled to surpass others. This is our state I. It inspires in all men "un noir penchant à se nuire mutuellement . . . et toujours le désir caché de faire son profit aux dépens d'autrui" ("a sinister penchant for hurting each other . . . and always the hidden desire to profit at the expense of others," p. 175). Hypocrisy, then, and the mask of good intention. "Tous ces maux sont le premier effet de la propriété et le cortège inséparable de l'inégalité naissante" ("All these evils are the first effect of property and the inseparable accompaniment of nascent inequality"). It is a state of domination, violence, and rapine. Like an Old Testament prophet, Rousseau swells with anger as he denounces our societies: "semblables à ces loups affamés qui ayant une fois goûté de la chair humaine rebutent toute autre nourriture, et ne veulent plus que dévorer des hommes" ("like famished wolves who having once tasted human flesh disdain all other food and want to devour only men," pp. 175–76).

With this tirade Rousseau has tied together the logical chain of our table. It is not quite complete. He has taken us only to the point at which civil societies, in his scheme, come into being. He must go further in his demonstration of our miserable state, because our societies are societies of governments. He seethes as he describes how this came about, the result of the most infamous conspiracy "qui soit jamais entré dans l'esprit humain" ("that ever entered the human intellect," p. 177). He is again present at the scene. He puts the rich man on the stage and puts into his mouth a speech rich in deceit and demagogy, as he addresses the oppressed:

"Unissons-nous, leur dit-il, pour garantir de l'oppression les faibles, contenir les ambitieux, et assurer à chacun la possession de ce qui lui appartient: Instituons des réglements de justice et de paix auxquels tous soient obligés de se conformer, qui ne fassent acception de personne, et qui réparent en quelque sorte les caprices de la fortune en soumettant également le puissant et le faible à des devoirs mutuels. En un mot, au lieu de tourner nos forces contre nous-mêmes, rassemblons-les en un pouvoir suprême qui nous . . . maintienne dans une concorde éternelle . . ." ("Let us unite," said he, "to secure the weak from oppression, restrain the ambitious, and secure to every man the possession of what belongs to him. Let us form rules of justice and peace, to which all may be obliged to conform, which shall give no preference to anyone, but may in some sort make amends for the caprice of fortune by submitting the strong and the weak alike to the observance of mutual duties. In a word, instead of turning our forces against ourselves, let us collect them into a sovereign power, which may . . . maintain a perpetual concord and harmony among us." P. 177)

The spectator draws us with him as he sees the deluded masses seduced, running to embrace "leurs fers croyant assurer leur liberté" ("their chains, thinking to assure their freedom," p. 177). He makes us see it, too, makes us feel his towering wrath.

The explanation is now complete.

Telle fut, ou dut être l'origine de la société et des lois, qui donnèrent de nouvelles entraves au faible et de nouvelles forces au riche, détruisirent sans retour la liberté naturelle, fixèrent pour jamais la loi de la propriété et de l'inégalité, d'une adroite usurpation firent un droit irrévocable, et pour le profit de quelques ambitieux assujettirent désormais tout le genre humain au travail, à la servitude et à la misère. (Such was, or must have been the origin of society and of law, which gave new fetters to the weak and new power to the rich; irretrievably destroyed natural liberty, fixed forever the laws of property and inequality; changed an artful usurpation into an irrevocable right; and for the benefit of a few ambitious individuals subjected the rest of mankind to perpetual labor, servitude, and misery. P. 178)

We need not follow Rousseau as he goes into further effects (massacres, wars), or indulges in conjectures, given out as reasonable suppositions, about early forms of government, and again trains his guns on Hobbes. Then, suddenly, as if this effort of calm reasoning has spent his patience, emotional lyricism, unwilling to be so long dammed, bursts out in a famous passage that conclusively brings together III, 1 and I of our table.

Comme un coursier indompté hérisse ses crins, frappe la terre du pied et se débat impétueusement à la seule approche du mors, tandis qu'un cheval dressé souffre patiemment la verge et l'éperon, l'homme barbare ne plie point sa tête au joug que l'homme civilisé porte sans murmure. . . . Quand je vois des animaux nés libres et abhorrant la captivité se briser la tête contre les barreaux de leur prison; quand je vois des multitudes de sauvages tout nus mépriser les voluptés européennes et braver la faim, le feu, le fer et la mort pour ne conserver que leur indépendance, je sens que ce n'est pas à des esclaves qu'il appartient de raisonner de liberté. (As an unbroken steed erects his mane, paws the ground, and rages at the bare sight of the bit, while a trained horse patiently suffers both whip and spur, just so the barbarian will never reach his neck to the yoke which civilized man carries without murmuring. . . . When I see freeborn animals through a natural abhorrence of captivity dash their brains out against the bars of their prison; when I see multitudes of naked savages despise European pleasures, and brave hunger, fire and sword, and death itself, to preserve their independence, I feel that it is not for slaves to argue about liberty. Pp. 181–82)

Now emotion is spent. The Discourse is complete. If Rousseau had called a halt with this lyrical outburst, he might have won the prize, despite his outrageous theses and conjectures. He does not. He is obsessed by man's fate. His mind's eye is fixed on the great work on which he will engage later. Making a weak attempt (p. 184) to attach the discussion of the social contract which follows to his subject, he speculates on its nature, and on the origin of diverse forms of government. His speculations are imaginatively conceived, and again his imaginings are set down as facts.

Perhaps realizing that this long discursus has broken the thread and diluted the force of his composition, Rousseau tries weakly to connect it to his subject by an arbitrary schematization of the progress of inequality into three stages: (1) the establishment of law and property, (2) the institution of the "magistrature," (3) the assumption of arbitrary power by rulers. In reality, this schema, which has little to do with the body of the essay, is an effort to rescue the lost unity of composition. His sights are still set beyond the confines of the Discourse, as we see immediately after. The vices that made social institutions necessary, he goes on, also made their abuse inevitable. History testifies to only one exception— Sparta. Lycurgus, Rousseau's supreme hero, instilled mores that made laws practically superfluous. Even at this early stage, Rousseau is dreaming his seminal dream of behavioral control. Where behavior is regulated by a quasi-mechanical habituation, government is unnecessary: "il serait aisé de prouver . . . qu'un pays où personne n'éluderait les lois et n'abuserait de la magistrature n'aurait besoin ni de magistrats ni de lois" ("it would be easy to prove . . . that a country where no one evaded the laws or made an ill use of the magistracy would require neither magistrates nor laws," p. 188). He does not prove it, since it is too easy!

Rousseau seems to have difficulty in ending his essay. He almost apologizes for going back to his subject: "Si c'était ici le lieu d'entrer en des détails, j'expliquerais facilement . . ." ("If this were the place to go into details, I could easily explain . . ."). Nevertheless, he does repeat himself (p. 189), denouncing again the jungle "society" of competition and thirst for destruction, crystallized in wealth gained at the expense of others. He is holding his indignation in check—we feel it as his—with difficulty.

> Je prouverais enfin que si l'on voit une poignée de puissants et de riches au faîte des grandeurs et de la fortune, tandis que la foule rampe dans l'obscurité et dans la misère, c'est que les premiers n'estiment les choses dont ils jouissent qu'autant que les autres en sont privés, et que, sans changer d'état, ils cesseraient d'être heureux, si le peuple cessait d'être misérable. (I could prove, in short, that if we behold a handful of rich and powerful men seated on the pinnacle of fortune and greatness, while the masses grovel in obscurity and want, it is merely because the former prize what they enjoy only in the degree that others are deprived of it, and that, without changing their condition, they would cease to be happy the minute the people ceased to be wretched. P. 189)

But not for long. The barrister senses the moment of his summation and raises the pitch of eloquence. If he showed all the things he sees, then others would see. "On verrait la multitude opprimée. . . . On verrait l'oppression s'accroître. . . . On verrait les droits des citoyens. . . . On verrait. . . . On verrait. . . . On verrait. . . . On verrait. . . . On verrait . . ." ("We should see the masses oppressed. . . . We should see the oppression increase. . . . We should see the rights of citizens. . . . We should see. . . . We should see. . . . We should see. . . . We should see. . . . We should see. . . ," p. 190). All is lost. Men are back to where they started—all *equal*—with the equality of servitude in a state of moral corruption. The lash continues to fall (p. 192). Isn't this where he intended to go all along—to the I of our table?

And still he feels the need for one last rhetorical flourish. It is the well-known paean to the noble savage (Rousseau never used that phrase). This passage (pp. 192–93), too long to quote here, with its exclamations, interrogatives, antitheses, and harsh language, is a model of the *plaidoyer* (address to the court) and the summation of his moralizing purpose. The tone abruptly descends to a placid final paragraph, a simple résumé for the jury, ending with only a moderately intensified but firm concluding clause, whose revolutionary import is no less resounding: ". . . puisqu'il est manifestement contre le loi de nature, de quelque manière qu'on la définisse, qu'un enfant commande à un vieillard, qu'un imbécile conduise un homme sage, et qu'une poignée de gens regorge de superfluités, tandis que la multitude affamée manque de nécessaire" (". . . since it is evidently against the law of nature, however defined, that children should command old men and fools lead the wise, and that a handful should gorge themselves with superfluities, while the starving masses lack the barest necessities of life," p. 194).

The logical and rhetorical order of the *Discours sur l'origine de l'inégalité* is clearly more complex than the tightly knit argument of the *Discourse sur les sciences et les arts*. It is by far the richer work, but the less perfect composition. Not only does it lack the neat and simple order of the first Discourse, but it is marred by a diffuseness that doubtless put off the Academy's judges. The ideas overflow the composition. The nineteen long notes, some of them essays in themselves, add to the prolixity. They treat a wide variety of subjects about which Rousseau wished to express his opinions. They are unequal in interest and in their connection with the theme of the Discourse. Note IX (pp. 202–8), which contrasts the savage and the civilized life and ends with a homily, is most pertinent, but belongs with the praise of savages at the end of the Discourse, not where it is. Note XV (pp. 219–20) contains a distinction between *amour de soi* (love of self) and *amour-propre* (self-esteem), the first natural and innocuous, the second artificial and competitive, of such importance to Rousseau's thought that it merits a place in the body of the essay, at one of the places where he sets forth the leap between "natural" and social living.

In arguing his paradoxical conception of human history, Rousseau has few facts to go on. His essay is conjectural, poetic, passionate, personal. Nevertheless, the flights of eloquence are fewer and more interspersed than in the first Discourse. Not having facts, he presents a quasi-factual experiential history, designed to be accepted as quintessentially true, hence supportive of his main contention, I in our table. His concept of "Man in himself," for instance, is meaningless, for man is a social animal or he is not of the species *homo*. Rousseau uses every resource of reasoning, pleading, and rhetoric to make his idea persuasive. Taken as fiction, it hangs together consistently; but it is presented—indeed, imposed—as hypothesized fact, not as fiction. Rousseau's wild man is not man, in any sense. His fantasized picture was dictated by the *conclusion* he also wishes to impose, the political and moralizing lesson (I). It did not convince his judges nor, probably, anyone else.

Rousseau's style is that of a great literary artist. He is the master of rhetorical resources—simile, metaphor, oxymoron, antithesis, sequential repetition, interrogation, exclamation, and pure lyricism. Rousseau's most significant oxymoron is "the harsh yoke of liberty." However, it is not felt by him to be such; it is not a mere rhetorical device like "heureux esclaves" ("happy slaves"). The two nouns are intended as equivalents. A yoke is a restraint, compulsion to follow a path traced by a guide, controlled behavior. Liberty lies in voluntary acceptance of the yoke, in willingness to follow what is determined to be the one right way. Thus he says that for a law to be valid, "il faut que la volonté de celui qu'elle oblige puisse s'y soumettre avec connaissance" ("it requires that the will of the one it obliges can submit to it knowingly," p. 125). *Yoke* is one of Rousseau's word fixations. It occurs six times in the Discourse. Another will be *docile, docilité, docilement*, although there is only one use of the adverb in this work (p. 112).

Rousseau's omnipresent technique is to use assertions or assurances to effectuate certainties. His argumentation is mostly persuasion. Thus he assures us that man was rarely frightened in the state of nature, "où toutes choses marchent d'une manière si uniforme, et où la face de la terre n'est point sujette à ces changements brusques et continuels, qu'y causent les passions, et l'inconstance des peuples réunis" ("where everything proceeds in so uniform a manner, and where the face of the earth is not subject to those sudden and unending changes which are caused by the passions and the inconstancy of socialized people," p. 136). Sickness "appartient principalement à l'homme vivant en société" ("belongs mainly to men living in a society," p. 137). "Les mâles et les femelles s'unissaient fortuitement selon la rencontre. . . . Ils se quittaient avec la même facilité" ("Males and females coupled haphazardly as they chanced to meet. . . . They left each other as easily," p. 147). "On voit du moins, au peu de soin qu'a pris la nature de rapprocher les hommes par des besoins mutuels, et de leur faciliter l'usage de la parole, combien elle a peu préparé leur sociabilité" ("At least we can see, by the little care nature has taken to draw men together by mutual needs, and to facilitate their use of speech, how little it has prepared them for sociability," p. 151). About all these things Rousseau knew absolutely nothing; but in positive statements he pretends to the reader that he does. He knows that in the state of nature there was no unhappiness: "or je voudrais bien qu'on m'expliquât quel peut être le genre de misère d'un être libre, dont le coeur est en paix, et le corps en santé" ("now, I'd like someone to explain to me what is the nature of the unhappiness that can afflict a free being, whose heart is at ease and whose body is healthy," p. 152). He *knows* how differently original men felt toward each other: "Or il est évident que cette identification a dû être infiniment plus étroite dans l'état de nature que dans l'état de raisonnement. C'est la raison qui engendre l'amour-propre" ("Now it is evident that this identification must have been infinitely narrower in the state of nature than in the reasoning state. It is reason that engenders *amour-propre*," pp. 155–56). In this assertion we see how Rousseau makes instinct and reflection say what he wants them to say; the proposition could be reversed.

At crucial moments Rousseau tries to establish an emotional relationship with the reader by injecting his emotion and making his presence felt, even as he obviously wants the reader to know that he is aware of the reader's presence. The reader rarely loses this consciousness of authorial presence. Rousseau projects himself into his *narrative*, as well as into his argument. He sees what he is relating ("Je le vois se rassasiant sous un chêne" ["I see him eating his fill under an oak tree"]), reacts to it, involves the reader in his anger or nostalgic fantasy, makes the reader his accomplice. When he is, occasionally, rhapsodic or ecstatic, the reader is swept along by the power of his feeling and the force of its expression. Conviction can be convincing. Thus, when Rousseau denounces the disparity between the power and worth of those who command, asking whether they are better than those who must obey, he ends with an exclamation that envelops the reader: "Question bonne peut-être à agiter entre des esclaves entendus de leurs maîtres, mais qui ne convient pas à des hommes raisonnables et libres, qui cherchent la vérité" ("A good question, perhaps, to raise among slaves overheard by their masters, but one that is unsuitable for reasonable and free men who are searching for the truth," p. 132). No reader wants to be a slave.

Rousseau is an eminent philosopher, because he shook and still shakes many minds. The power of his work derives, in significant measure, from the qualities of a great writer. He knew how to do what he will tell his leaders of people to do: capture minds and hearts. By his artful and impassioned rhetoric, his vivid imagination, his luminous personal presence, he largely succeeds in overcoming the deficiencies of substance in these two Discourses. We must remember, however, that his fame did not rest on them, notorious and exciting as they were.

Notes

1. See L. G. Crocker, "Hidden Affinities: Nietzsche," in *Studies on Voltaire and the Eighteenth Century*, vol. 190 (Oxford, 1980), pp. 119–41.

2. *Discours sur les sciences et les arts*, in *Oeuvres complètes*, éd. Pléiade (Paris, 1964), 3:8. Page references will be given in parentheses to this edition. Spelling has been modernized. Translations are my own.

3. For another typical example, see the first paragraph on p. 18.

4. Among the many other passages one could quote, the one beginning "Allez, écrits célèbres" ("Go, celebrated writings," p. 28) is noteworthy.

5. See the revealing paragraph beginning: "Pour nous, hommes vulgaires, à qui le ciel n'a point départi de si grands talents et qu'il ne destine pas à tant de gloire, restons dans

notre obscurité" ("As for ordinary men like us, to whom heaven has not dealt out such great talents, and whom it does not destine for so much glory, let us remain in our obscurity," p. 30).

6. "Si le rétablissement des Sciences et des Arts a contribué à épurer les moeurs" ("Whether the restoration of the sciences and arts has contributed to refining morals").

7. See for instance the dithyramb, pp. 115–16.

8. Rousseau explains that natural man cannot know natural law as *law*, but nonetheless obeys it (pp. 125–26).

9. See my "Diderot and Eighteenth-Century French Transformism," in *Forerunners of Darwin*, ed. Bentley Glass (Baltimore: Johns Hopkins University Press, 1959), pp. 114–43.

2

The Philosopher as Essayist:
Leibniz and Kant

JOHN A. McCARTHY

I

The importance of Gottfried Wilhelm Leibniz (1646–1716) and Immanuel Kant (1724–1804) for the German Enlightenment is well known. They were instrumental in promulgating that age's optimistic belief in the teleology of the universe and in the perfectibility of humanity. Leibniz's contribution to the *Aufklärung* lies in his advance beyond Cartesian logic. Substituting a pluralistic universe for Descartes's dualism, he introduced the concept of becoming. Cassirer calls this change an extension of Cartesian logic: "the logic of 'origin' and . . . the logic of individuality" which "leads from mere geometry to a dynamic philosophy of nature, from mechanism to organism."[1] Kant's singular achievement is a monumental synthesis of the two main currents of philosophy—rationalism and empiricism—into an integrated whole. Both thinkers were also catalysts for intense activity in the realm of aesthetic theory. Leibniz's influence was primarily indirect, via Christian Wolff on Johann Christoph Gottsched and Alexander Baumgarten, to name but three famous theoreticians. Kant's impact was more direct, eliciting responses to his *Kritik der Urteilskraft* (*Critique of Judgment*, 1790) from thinkers as diverse as Schiller and Hegel.[2]

Despite the critical appreciation of Leibniz and Kant as central figures in the development of aesthetic (as well as philosophic) thought since the eighteenth century, scarcely any attention has been accorded their stature as writers. I know of only one substantial study of Leibniz as a writer and none of Kant. Even the consideration of Leibniz does not examine him as a prose writer but rather as a Baroque poet of German verse.[3] In his study of Leibniz, Olan Brent Hankins is guided by the philosopher's considerable reputation during his lifetime as a composer of occasional poems in Latin, French, and German. However, Kant enjoyed no such fame. Yet Kant, like Leibniz, frequently published his work in journalistic form designed for the layperson. Although these shorter pieces have not escaped the attention of critics, their style has been ignored in preference to their content. Even Eric A. Blackall, who accords a special place to Leibniz in the evolution of German as a literary language, is more concerned with the philosopher's views on language than with the literary use of German in his writing. Blackall's lack of attention to Leibniz's style is perplexing, given the fact that he does note the philosopher's ideal for the language of philosophy as popular, accessible to all.[4]

This general neglect is surprising, since both Leibniz and Kant envisioned a central role for the written word in fulfilling the ultimate purpose of human nature. That goal was "to achieve a moral community founded upon the advancement of science . . . and the fine arts."[5] While the sciences were perceived to regulate human thinking, the fine arts, above all literature, disciplined one's feelings and sensibilities. Culture for the eighteenth century was a hybrid, the result of science as well as the arts. Art and science were the two great humanizing forces for the entire age of Enlightenment. Thus, it would be surprising if Leibniz and Kant had failed to imbue their popular writing with more than cold reason. Leibniz was widely acclaimed for his poetic talent while Kant spent so much time ruminating on the role of art in life that "we cannot isolate [his] aesthetics from his theoretical or practical philosophy nor . . . isolate the theoretical or practical from the aesthetic."[6] Was there no transfer from theory, from verse, to prose practice? In the following pages we will not be concerned so much with the thought of these philosophers as with their manner of presentation manifested in representative examples of their popularistic writing. In other words, we will examine the philosopher as writer.

I have chosen to analyze Leibniz and Kant as essayists because of the intimate—and causal—relationship between the incidence of the Enlightenment and the rapid rise of the profession of letters which accompanied the movement. This is characteristic not only of Germany but also of England (Pope) and France (Voltaire, Diderot). Enlightenment occurred to a great extent by the written word and the process of reading. Thus, the "age of criticism" also became known as "le siècle des journaux," and the "Age of Reason" was also the "Age of Sentiment." My purpose is to portray the place of Leibniz and Kant in the history of the German essay. The essay was a major vehicle of enlightenment and a nascent literary genre which reached first full bloom in Germany at the end of the eighteenth century. The history of the German essay in the

eighteenth century has yet to be written, and the ensuing comments are
offered as a contribution to that undertaking.[7]

Although the essay is a protean literary form which seems to defy
final definition, Richard Exner provides a useful approximation, which
will help to focus our discussion:

> The essay is a sample of artistic prose, which has evolved in an organic
> manner both stylistically and thematically. Its essence must be es-
> sayistic [i.e., tentative, truth seeking]; it must stimulate thought and
> the desire to think an idea through to its conclusion; finally, the essay
> portrays the problem in question in its entire complexity. The tend-
> ency of the essay is to weigh and to consider. An essay is either
> linguistically exceptional or it is not a genuine essay. It may, however,
> assume the form of a speech, a learned treatise, or a narrative. Never-
> theless, important is its structural proximity to lyric writing.[8]

In addition to the points raised by Exner—artistic, thought-provoking
prose in compact form which develops an idea in a multifaceted yet
organically unified manner—we can cite other traits necessary for full
understanding of the literary form. Thus, Klaus Günther Just emphasizes the progressive, avant-garde quality of all genuine essays.[9] The
essay thrives in the atmosphere of conflict which normally accompanies
the transition from one historical-cultural age to another. The relationship between these phases is ambiguous. On the one hand, the new
cultural era arises as a reaction to the foregoing one; on the other hand, it
evolves as a continuation of it. The ambiguity attached to that forward-
looking quality of an age marks many essays. Note Annamarie Auer's
conclusion: "essayism evolves at any given time from the historical
writing or philosophy of a culture because humankind's existence in any
given epoch is its very topic."[10]

Essayism, furthermore, is consistently regarded as a hybrid genre,
part poetry, part science. It is concerned with enhancing knowledge but
also with evoking an aesthetic response. Its origins and intent give the
essay an ambivalent quality.[11] For these reasons, the examination of
philosophers as potential or actual essayists is most appropriate. Finally,
we must remember that the philosophical bent of mind which gives rise
to essayism is skeptical. Consequently, the attempts to get at the truth of
the matter are tentative; using the technique of comparison and contrast
they move in close to the core only to back off to try another tack. This
method is referred to variously as a "process of encirclement"
(Einkreisungsprozess),[12] "weighing the possibilities," or "processuality"
(Möglichkeitserwägung, Prozessualität).[13] These are all attempts to approxi-
mate Montaigne's comparison of essayistic writing to a leisurely walk or
to a cautious testing of the subject matter: "Of the hundred parts and

aspects that each thing has, I take one, sometimes merely licking it, sometimes scraping its surface, and sometimes punching it to the bone. I stab it as deeply, but not as widely as I can; and I generally like to seize it from some unaccustomed viewpoint."[14] The dynamic process of approximation is a chief characteristic of the essay. We should not expect an essay to provide definite syllogisms. In a true essay we will encounter the dynamism of the thought process itself, not as a neatly packaged, inalterable conclusion.

The qualities of the essay outlined here are reminiscent of the principle of continuity which forms the basis of the Leibnizian system. Cassirer defines the importance of the principle as follows: "Continuity means unity in multiplicity, being in becoming, constancy in change."[15] We also hear a faint echo of Kant's concept of the "aesthetic idea" which broadens our understanding while enriching our sensibility. Kant wrote: "In a word, the aesthetic idea is a representation of imagination, annexed to a given concept, with which, in the free employment of the imagination, such a multiplicity of partial representations are bound up, that no expression indicating a definite concept can be found for it."[16] Although not identical to the qualities of the literary essay, the principles of continuity and aesthetic idea have application to essayistic style.

The literary essay is marked by two basic authorial attitudes: one intentional, the other relational. The first has to do with the author's purpose in composing the piece and is more a matter of authorial relationship to the subject matter at hand. The second is marked by a definite concern for the reader's response to the written word. This latter stance involves the author's attitude toward the potential reader, which helps give shape to the style and form of the particular essay. These two stances are traceable to Sir Francis Bacon (1561–1626) and Michel de Montaigne (1533–92), the inaugurators of the essay genre. Of the two basic attitudes, the awareness of the reading public is more critical in the writing of essays because it lends not only a personal note to the style but also determines the impression of dynamic thinking.[17] With these characteristics in hand let us turn to the two philosophers selected for analysis.

II

Of Leibniz's numerous shorter writings, I have selected his epistle of 1683 entitled "Ermahnung an die Teutsche, ihren Verstand und Sprache besser zu üben, samt beigefügten Vorschlag einer teutschgesinnten Gesellschaft" ("A Call to the Germans to Make Better Use of Their Reason and Language, Together with a Proposal for a Pro-German

Society").[18] Its date of origin readily marks it as a product of the early German Enlightenment and is included here for that very reason. The "Ermahnung" and its companion piece "Unvorgreifliche Gedanken" ("Tentative Comments," ca. 1709) have been identified as representing a clear break with the stylistic concepts of the seventeenth century. I have elected to analyze the "Ermahnung" which was not published until 1846, rather than the "Unvorgreifliche Gedanken" (published in 1717) because it is the earlier form of the essay and treats the topic in greater depth.[19] Moreover, my selection is guided by its topic of cultural development. Cultural and literary questions proved to be a favorite topic of later essayists.[20] If we assume that literary genres undergo a developmental process, then we should not expect a contribution to an emerging form to possess the traits of the perfect model. Furthermore, critics of the German essay date the beginning of the genre in the German-speaking territories from around 1750. Thus Leibniz's "Call to the Germans" predates the commonly accepted date of inception of the genre by a good fifty years.

Content and form of a successful essay are inseparable. In twenty-one pages Leibniz presents an appeal to his compatriots to upgrade their language (and thus their culture) which was then far inferior to that of the English, French, and Italians (p. 69). This argument is presented in two principal parts with a demarcation between the two stages of reasoning and the clearly formulated, concluding summation of the proposal's intent. Generally speaking, the first part of the argument presents a positive view of the German situation, while the second takes a critically negative look at the same conditions. The first part culminates in a utopian vision of a highly civilized Germany, the second with the proposal to found a "Teutschgesinnte Gesellschaft" ("Pro-German Society") to further the ideal of an enlightened Germany (p. 80). Despite the clear organization, the argument is not presented in a straightforward, strictly syllogistic manner. The markers for the division of the line of reasoning are all internal; there are no external signs to guide the reader through the train of thought. As we shall see, length, topic, manner of presentation, and use of rhetorical techniques expose "Ermahnung an die Teutsche" as an excellent example of the German essay. On the basis of its exhortation for cultural reform, we readily identify it as a "kulturkritischer Essay" ("culturally critical essay"), one of the six categories recommended by Just.[21]

Leibniz begins by conjuring up a thoroughly positive picture of the Holy Roman Empire of the German Nation with the images of its wealth and superfluity. The country is blessed with natural resources and political strength which make it the envy of Europe. Nowhere are natural resources more abundant, the aristocracy more competent, the numerous free city-states more prosperous, or freedom more prevalent. Even the peasantry is better off than expected with excellent prospects for future improvement (pp. 61–64). These images of prosperity and growth-potential are designed to arouse the reader's sense of patriotism to which Leibniz had appealed in his opening paragraph ("exordium"). The Germans' national and cultural identity is derived above all from their common customs and language (p. 60). Leibniz concludes from his detailing of Germany's blessings that the Germans' happiness and contentment is dependent solely on the individual's will to be happy and content. All the prerequisites are there (p. 64). The true patriot will endeavor to increase the welfare of the nation by taking carefully considered action which will lead to concrete results (p. 65).

Leibniz emphasizes the practicality of the suggestion for betterment which he makes because no real benefit can be derived from empty dreams or from projects unrealizable by private individuals due to the complexity of the problems. Consequently, he rules out actions involving high-level political activity such as a fixed constitution, improved communications within the empire, common coinage, the establishment of manufacturing and commercial enterprises, introduction of religious tolerance and universal justice, the reinstitution of military discipline (p. 65). Having done so he asks rhetorically: What's left? What else could be done? And he immediately answers in an ironic vein: nothing, if all of the above political problems had already been solved. Once an edifice has been erected, there is no need for the daylaborer *(Handlanger)*, that is, the "Privatmann." But the natural course of events precludes such perfect coincidence. A few "minor" tasks do remain to be accomplished, bagatelles really, but nonetheless beneficial (pp. 65f.). Instead of introducing his proposal at this point, Leibniz keeps his reader in suspense by drawing back from his main purpose. He employs the typically essayistic technique of weighing the different possibilities: "One might think that a reform of the schools and universities was being considered, an important undertaking to be sure. But no, that is not the purpose" (p. 66). No, educational reform is not his objective. Nevertheless, Leibniz cannot refrain from saying a few words about that of which he does not wish to speak. He suggests that the problem lies not so much with the educators as with the lack of support for educator and institution. This digression further arouses the reader's curiosity and impatience to know what the actual proposal is.

Finally the reader thinks that the author is about to come out with his proposal, for we read that the recommendation is not concerned solely with the savant's profession but with all persons, "who are willing to nurture their minds with good books and good company" (p. 66). But the reader is held off once again. Leibniz does not formulate his main idea here. Instead, he establishes the nature of the audience at which it is aimed. The group is comprised not only of scholars and students, but also administrators, men of the world, and especially women. In short, those classes of people are included who are not numbered among the common folk (der gemeine Mann). In German they are designated as "die Gebildeten" (pp. 66f.).

Even now the concrete proposal is not forthcoming. Leibniz interjects yet another moment of retardation. Before specifying his purpose, Leibniz takes time out to clarify the "Stand der Gebildeten" ("the station of the educated classes") by contrasting that group to the "gemeiner Mann." The difference is not based on wealth, power, or birth but only on one's level of sophistication, that is, on the level of education. The comparison and contrast is accomplished in vivid terms using easily intelligible diction and similes with a delightful touch of irony. All of these elements are essayistic traits. For instance, the common people are characterized as "dummes Volk ohne Erregung und Feuer" ("a dumb people without spirit or fire"). They delight in slandering their neighbors and amuse themselves with "viehisches Saufen oder spitzbübisches Kartenspiel" ("bestial drunkenness or mischievous card playing"). They think only of eating, live only for each day, and are as nimble as cattle. Historical accounts are the same to them as fairy tales; descriptions of other countries and customs mean nothing. Furthermore, they are so ignorant of religious matters that they are as capable of appreciating a magnificent concert as is a person born deaf (Taubgebohrener, p. 67). By contrast, the educated classes are freer in their movements and outlook, an attitude reflected by their choice of reading matter. They are inquisitive of mind, sociable in manner, and noble in spirit. Because they are far-sighted they have a greater understanding of the difficulties encountered by the government and are therefore more useful to the state. In everything they do, the "Gebildeten" reveal "more sensibility and good sense" ("mehr Herz und Verstand," p. 67). The final sentence of this first part of Leibniz's overall argument summarizes the foregoing: "The more people of this type that we have in a country, the more that nation is polished or civilized; and consequently all citizens will be happier and more resolute" (pp. 67f.). This is not the concrete proposal the reader has been led to expect. Instead, in a strange, ironic way we are presented with an assessment of the consequences of the unstated proposal. The reader's level of curiosity and expectation is raised one notch higher by this exercise in contrast and comparison enlivened with vivid images and similes. What comes next is the axis of the two-part discourse.

The crucial thought is formulated in two brief paragraphs. The first paragraph is phrased in the conditional mode: the greatest service that the private citizen could render one's country would be to join the number of educated, sensitive people. This select group is marked by a love of wisdom and virtue and represents both sexes as well as all social classes. Only at this point does the reader recognize the purpose of the foregoing, apparently digressive discussion of the necessity for defining realizable goals and for characterizing the group of scholars and "Gebildete." Now we see how apparent asides are integral to the whole. In the second paragraph of the axis we find the explicit formulation of Leibniz's purpose: "This is our purpose . . . this is the suggestion, which we not only propose, but can also . . . achieve. These are the goals which we advocate. To achieve them, the German Patriots Society is to be founded" (p. 68). To understand the "this" the reader must bear the first paragraph in mind with its concept of enlarging the class of educated, refined persons.

Language with its full range of connotations is the focus of the second part of Leibniz's argument (pp. 68–80), for it is through the written and oral use of language that we learn more refined thinking (p. 68). This line of reasoning culminates in the assessment that language mirrors one's level of understanding, erudition, and eloquence. In short, language is viewed as "an interpreter of the human spirit and as a guardian of science" ("eine Dolmetscherin des Gemüts und eine Behälterin der Wissenschaft," p. 80). However, the path to that direct assertion is a meandering one. For example, after having stated what his focus will be, Leibniz commences his argument with a discussion of the possible reasons for the Germans' backwardness in comparison to their neighbors. That backwardness is most apparent in the quality of German writing, which is an embarrassment to Leibniz personally and should be one for all patriotic citizens (cf. pp. 71–73). German books are either a tedious compendium of excerpts from foreign works or, when they do offer original thoughts, are so obtuse and confusing that they prove unreadable and incomprehensible.

In the second part of his presentation Leibniz has greater recourse to rhetorical devices. We find the full range of such tactics from simple examples and popular phrases to paradox and prolepsis. Their purpose is to present the argument in more graphic and forcible terms. The reader is supposed to react to the proposition in the author's predetermined manner. In the words of a contemporary eighteenth-century writer, that purpose is expressed as follows:

Rhetoric is the ability . . . to express oneself well; that is, to convince the listening audience by logical reasoning, to win them over through emotional appeal, and to manipulate them toward a predetermined goal. Then, oratorical ability is granted us by nature for no other purpose than to communicate our thoughts to one another, to influence each other, and to advance our own personal ends. Or, to put it differently: by means of rhetoric we impact upon the minds and wills of others. Thus it follows that the mark of the accomplished orator is the ability to persuade others by the power of the word to accept an idea or to take action.[22]

Thus Leibniz speaks of the German books as uninspired and lifeless ("ohne Kraft noch Leben . . . ohne Schmack oder Saft," p. 68). Moreover they are referred to metaphorically as worthless chaff ("Eicheln, Spreu und Kleye") which has been substituted for finely winnowed wheat ("wohl gesichteten Weizen," p. 69). These designations even the most common reader could understand and remember.

Having made this association between disagreeable German books and plant life, Leibniz continues the metaphor in his ensuing discussion of the apparent reasons for the German atrophy. The plant and garden metaphors stand out because they are imbedded in a three-page explanation of what he does not wish to talk about. This device of stating what the discourse is not concerned with is a favorite one of classical essayists. For instance, Leibniz is not going to address himself to the hindrances to cultural evolution posed by past wars, nor to the lack of a capital city, nor to the failure to elevate culturally aware officials to high posts, nor to the division of Germany along confessional lines, nor to the role of enlightened patrons. The popular explanation that Germany has suffered from the lack of a cultural focal point, such as London or Paris, is not taken very seriously. A capital city does function as a fruitful source of inspiration and as a sounding board without which new ideas wither and die like so many plucked blossoms ("ein Brunnquell der Mode und Richtschnur der Nation . . . aus welchem Mangel erfolget, . . . daß manche gute Gedanken sozusagen wie zerstreute und abgebrochene Blumen verwelken müssen," p. 69). But Italy provides an example of a nation which lacked a focal point and which nevertheless experienced the flourishing of its language and culture. More important than a geographical locus is the patronage by such persons as Leo X (Giovanni de Medici, 1475–1521), François I of Angoulême (1494–1547), or Cardinal Richelieu (Armand Jean du Plessis, 1585–1642). Germany itself had patrons whose efforts had not been entirely fruitless (p. 70); however, German scholars did not respond to the initiative as did their counterparts elsewhere. The opposition of German scholars to the use of the vernacular in their writing proved to be the decisive hindrance to the development of a common, eloquent language in Germany. While culture and knowledge of the sciences spread to all classes by clear, unaffected prose in England, France, and Italy, the appreciation of the arts and sciences remained largely the property of the learned in Germany. The German writers (that is, scholars), whom Leibniz brands as overblown pedants ("aufgeblasene Pedanten") persisted in their time-honored tradition of publishing unoriginal ideas in turgid Latin prose ("Wortgezänke"). Because the vast majority of readers at the beginning of the century did not read Latin fluently they were virtually barred from participating in the activities of the intellectually elite. Consequently, the filtering down process which transformed the languages of neighboring countries into polished crystal ("ein rein poliertes Glas") while promoting keen and clear thinking ("die Scharfsinnigkeit des Gemüts," p. 70) did not occur in Germany.

The advantages of a refined mother tongue—insightful thinking, mature judgment, fine sensitivity—were not available because German scholars nurtured a slavish attachment to a foreign language and a non-German way of thinking ("Sind wir also in den Dingen so den Verstand betreffen, bereits in eine Sklaverei geraten und werden durch unsere Blindheit gezwungen, unsere Art zu leben, zu reden, zu schreiben, ja sogar zu gedenken, nach fremden Willen einzurichten," p. 71). The German spirit needed to be liberated. But how go about it? What action had to be taken?

Leibniz notes that writing in the German vernacular was then limited to the realm of belles lettres. Consequently, authors had experience in writing poetic German but none in a more popular vein. The tide of incompetent writing had risen so high that the beneficial influence of belles lettres was no longer sufficient to stem it. Much more vigorous writing was called for ("ander Zeug von mehr Gewicht und Nachdruck"). To underscore his point, Leibniz utilizes striking similes. Just as a strong arm cannot toss a feather as far as a stone, neither can the sharpest intellect achieve much with literature which is designed only to amuse (p. 71). A new kind of writing is required which combines intellectual profit with aesthetic pleasure. The nucleus of such writing is composed of weightier matter, something for the intellect as well as for the senses. This hybrid style is more effective than either erudite or literary writing alone. Profound substance must be paired with poetic lightness. Leibniz writes: "Utility must be paired, therefore, with pleasantness just as an arrow must be equipped with feathers and crowned with a metal tip if it is to be shot from a crossbow over a great distance through the air" ("Muß also der Nutzen mit der Annehmlichkeit vereinigt werden, gleichwie ein Bolzen, so von einem stählinen Armbrust in die ferne Luft getrieben werden soll, sowohl mit Federn versehen, als mit Metall gekrönet zu sein pfleget," p. 71). The feathers at the end of the arrow stand metaphorically for the light touch of poetry, while the heavy metal tip represents the weightier substance of scientific studies. The allusion to weapons suggests the need for forceful liberation from the bonds of linguistic and cultural slavery perpetuated by stuffy academicians. Only by cultivating German as the language of science and scholarship can the German people hope to close the cultural gap between themselves and their neighbors.

By this point the reader has forgotten the plant motif. But Leibniz has not. To profile more distinctly the need for introducing eloquent German in all areas of writing, the philosopher returns to the garden metaphor. The world of German writing is depicted as a garden bed in which all kinds of plants—flowers, fruit, herbs—must grow side by side so that the overall prosperity can be sustained: "Our German garden dare not contain only exquisite lilies and roses; it must also include sweet apples and healthful herbs. The former quickly lose their beauty and pleasant scent, the latter prove much more useful" ("Dann unser teutsche Garten muß nicht nur anlachende Lilien und Rosen, sondern auch süße Äpfel und gesunde Kräuter haben. Jene verlieren bald ihre Schönheit und Geruch, diese lassen sich zum Gebrauch behalten," p. 72). An allusion to the "Fruchtbringende Gesellschaft" (1617–80), a society founded for the promotion of the German language and its literature, serves to equate poetry to flowers and scholarly writing to fruitbearing plants. The name of the society, Leibniz contends, was a misnomer, for it did not produce fruit, only tender blossoms which die quickly if not nourished with the powerful nutrients of immortal art and science ("einen nährenden Saft der unvergänglichen Wissenschaften," p. 72).

Leibniz is quick to grant that his proposed language reform might appear a futile effort to some people. Why should his chances of success be any better than those of illustrious reformers who had preceded him? Would it not be better to let oneself go, to swim with the current (p. 72)? This occurrence of prolepsis, of anticipating an opponent's counterargument, is followed rapidly by a second one protracted over the next few pages which anticipates yet another possible objection to Leibniz's proposal; namely, that French evolved from a mixture of Old French and Latin. Why could not German evolve in similar fashion? Examples exist of German writers who quite effectively ("das ist vornehmlich und kräftig," p. 74) employ foreign citations and expressions in their works. Is it necessary to ban all foreign phrases? Would not elegance suffer? Leibniz answers the first objection by inserting the metaphor of a dam erected to stem the tide of ponderous and barbarous writing. The problem lies not in the reform effort but in the quality of stone, sand, and earth used to construct the dike (p. 72). His proposed reform would be made of firmer stuff. Leibniz's response to the second objection is that negligence and laziness are no excuse for not practicing a polished German style purified of extraneous elements. With a little effort appropriate German terms could be found, while preserving a sense of refinement.

Interspersed in these two prolepses are personal appeals to the reader to reject obtusely macaronic style and barbaric customs ("Ich rufe zu Zeugen an . . . ich [laβ] einen jeden bei sich selbst prüfen, ob er teutsch Blut in seinen Adern habe," "I call to witness . . . I leave it to each person to verify if he has German blood in his veins," p. 73). Leibniz's case is strengthened by personal anecdotes (pp. 73, 75) as well as by contrasting the apparent decline of German culture into chaos with the dawning of a new age of enlightened harmony everywhere else (p. 73). Examples of excellent writing composed by nonscholars in a universally intelligible and appealing style are cited from history (pp. 76f.) to show that the reform effort would not be in vain. History moves in cycles; the signs of enlightenment elsewhere indicate that the twisted state of German customs can also be reversed. The style *(Sprachrichtigkeit)* of those historical documents of the past are held up as example of what the Germans could easily do again, if they really wanted to. That laudable command of language is marked by a number of features: (1) the elegance of its diction, (2) the quality of its syllogisms, (3) the inventiveness of its conceits, (4) the particular preciseness of its formulation, (5) the organic nature of its embellishments, and finally, (6) the overall unity of its composition ("Reinigkeit der Worte . . . den Arten der Vernunftschlüße, den Erfindungen, der Wahl, der eigentlichen Deutlichkeit, der selbstwachsenden Zierde und Summe der ganzen Einrichtung").

These traits evolve in a natural manner as a kind of dialogue between author and reader and are free of patent artifice. They are revealing of the literary essay in general which Ludwig Rohner summarized as "tranquil, graceful, conciliatory, and familiar" in tone.[23] In a sense, Leibniz enumerated those qualities which set his dialogic discourse apart from the usual sedate fare. A careful reading of Leibniz's essay reveals that the philosopher is not interested in presenting us with the results of his cogitation. He is more concerned with leading us through the thought processes themselves so that we might become fully convinced of his conclusions, yes, so that his conclusions might become our conclusions. If we were seeking a description of the early German essay, we could stop right here, for the enumeration Leibniz offers is astonishingly accurate for 1683! We could consider Leibniz's entire "Ermahnung an die Teutsche" not only as an early example of the essay form but also as embodying an early theory of the nature and quality of essayistic writing predating Friedrich Schlegel's famous theoretical remarks by a hundred years: "We should write an essay as if we were just thinking a thought through for the first time, writing just for ourselves, speaking freely on a topic, or composing a letter—in each case focusing on a moral topic out of pure interest without philosophic or poetic intent."[24] To be sure, there are differences. Leibniz does not use the term essay as does Schlegel, nor does he stipulate the most desirable length. But the philosopher does specify key traits of essayistic writing, he does envisage the critical role that the author's awareness of the audience must play in achieving that special dialectic quality, and he does recognize the need for an author to wax enthusiastic about the topic (for example, Leibniz writes that he has argued his point "nicht ohne Gemütsbewegung," "not without agitation," p. 79). At a decisive point in his argument Leibniz contends that German scholars were largely unsuccessful in their writing because they wrote only for one another. If they were to take aim at the generally educated reader, at the courtier, and at women, as their counterparts in France and Italy had done, they would also learn to adjust their tone to the less esoteric needs of that anonymous group (cf. p. 70). The repeated designation of language as "a true mirror of the mind" ("ein rechter Spiegel des Verstandes") is an implicit reference to the interrelationship of audience and style (cf. pp. 76, 73). The new audience and innovative language are both marked by reasonableness as well as by elegance.

The means to cultivate the new receptive audience and to acquire the necessary rhetorical skills prove to be one and the same. One attains both objectives gradually by reading stimulating books *(nachdenkliche Bücher)* and conversing on pleasant topics *(annehmliche Gedanken)* (p. 77). Education is depicted as capable of overcoming all obstacles (p. 79). All the reformer need do is provide the proper example, and, as the young gradually become accustomed to the new ideas and manner, they will be inspired with hope, pride in their country, and love of virtue. Ultimately, they will become confident in their nation's ability to prosper; that is, to bring about universal enlightenment and felicity. Leibniz formulated this utopian vision, which parallels the concluding imagery of the first part of his discourse as follows: "In the case of those nations which enjoy prosperity and excellent prospects for the future we can detect important qualities even among the non–university-trained, such as: a love for and respect of one's country, a high estimation of virtuous behavior, keen understanding, and—as a result of the former—fluent and correct use of the vernacular" ("Dahingegen bei den Völkern, deren Glück und Hoffnung blühet, die Liebe des Vaterlandes, die Ehre der Nation, die Belohnung der Tugend, ein gleichsam erleuchteter Verstand und daher fließende Sprachrichtigkeit sogar bis auf den gemeinen Mann herabgestiegen und fast durchgehends sich spüren lassen," p. 79). This visionary projection of the effects of education, democratic ideals, and common refulgence accompanied Enlightenment thought throughout the eighteenth century. Equally valid for the later Enlightenment is the prerequisite of correct grammar for clear, "correct" reasoning.[25]

Imitation is the path to that goal—but not the indiscriminate "Nachäffung" then fashionable in Germany. Thus, before invoking his concluding utopian vision, Leibniz interpolates yet another prolepsis. These prolepses have the effect of reining in the reader's and Leibniz's own forward drive, for each time the reader is reminded of something already known. Thus, the occurrence is a moment of intellectual relaxation, an exhaling. In concert with the energized movement of the rest of the argument, the prolepses function as the systole to their diastole.[26] While objecting strongly to the indiscriminate imitation of things French which he brands as "eine ansteckende Landseuche" ("a contagious epidemic," p. 77) and for which he provides specific examples (mania for chocolate, tea, silver, porcelain, tapestry, peasant dolls from Paris, fashionable clothes, p. 78), Leibniz does grant the validity of the objection that this mania for French luxuries is an improvement over the coarse intemperance of the preceding age. Nevertheless, the fact remains that "whatever is forced and slavishly copied, is in bad taste" ("was gezwungen und nachgetan, abgeschmackt ist," p. 78). An original is always better than a copy. Thus, Leibniz would almost argue that "a drunken old German displays more sense in his speech and writing than a modern, sober frenchified monkey" ("ein trunkener alter Teutscher in Reden und Schreiben mehr Verstand spüren lassen, als anjetzo ein nüchterner französischer Affe tun wird," p. 78). Moreover, these frenchified monkeys are likened to foolish, small-town school children who neglect everything else in order to imitate foppish, itinerant actors. Itinerant acting troops were generally in ill repute at the time. If such imitational buffoonery is not halted, the German people will eventually impair irrevocably their capability for common sense. Use of poignant similes, metaphors, and images combined with the salient choice of diction and measured set of rhetorical questions, give this prolepsis and its resolution graphic force. These diverse elements also lend the argument a hint of entertaining levity.

The conclusion of Leibniz's "Ermahnung an die Teutsche" is a masterpiece in the best rhetorical tradition. As Friedrich Schlegel was to note: "The wittier and more rhetorical an essay is, the more effective it will be."[27] An effective conclusion does not merely repeat the body of the argument. While summarizing essential points, it must intensify them in singular fashion. The central idea must be presented for the last time in a concentrated, highly intelligible form. In this regard Heinz Lemmermann averred in his *Lehrbuch der Rhetorik: Die Kunst der Rede und der Diskussion*: "A summative repetition is important: however, the conclusion must not be a mere repetition of the argument. Instead, the main points of the talk must be presented in a more salient manner. Formulate the conclusion so that it can be remembered. Paint a poignant picture, use an easily comprehensible phrase, a striking sentence. Above all, the central ideas must be crystal clear."[28] Leibniz succeeded in utilizing the various rhetorical devices in this cogent combination.

Having spent so much time elaborating upon the ills of German society, Leibniz felt constrained in his conclusion to counteract any impression that the nation is beyond recovery. He accomplishes this task with a few brisk strokes of the quill. His concluding paragraph reiterates earlier points. If there were not a glimmer of hope ("keine glimmende Funke") under the ashes of devastated German traditions, for him to expose the failings ("unsre Wunde aufdecke[n]") would be cruel. As long as the patient (der Kranke) still feels pain, then he is not hopelessly benumbed. A switch in imagery to divine, paternal chastisement strengthens the impression of stern yet caring concern for the ailing nation's welfare ("und wer weiß, warum uns Gott gezüchtiget, dessen väterliche Rute wohl gemeinet," p. 79). The intervention of doctor or Divine Being can have little effect if the citizenry does not have the will to rebound. Thus, the general will for improvement must be the focus of any recovery efforts. At this juncture Leibniz reformulates his recommendation for the founding of a "Teutschgesinnte Gesellschaft."

With such an organization a few patriotic persons can instigate a general cultural reform. The goal of the society would be the advancement of "common sense, erudition, and eloquence." Since these qualities are mirrored in the language itself, the select group of reformers would write and publish key works in German which would be provocative, useful, and pleasurable all at the same time ("allerhand nachdenkliche, nützliche, auch annehmliche Kernschriften in teutscher Sprache," p. 80). These works would "stem the tide of barbarism," teach other authors how to write well, and train ever greater numbers of readers to discern the difference between well-written and shoddily composed books ("zu unterscheiden als das Huhn die Perl vor einem Gerstenkorn zu schätzen weiß," "to differentiate like the chicken does between the pearl and a barley kernel"). Because of the enjoyment attendant upon it, the new mode of writing would spread rapidly from the courts right into the living rooms of private homes; that is, the official as well as personal attitudes and judgment would be affected ("gar bald die Hof- und Weltleute, auch das Frauenzimmer selbst"). Leibniz's concluding sentence offers a series of advantages in a crescendo. The philosopher succinctly enumerates all the spheres of public and private life to be invigorated by the new, popular style of writing. People would become better mannered and more intellectually aware. Patriotic fervor would increase, indiscriminate imitation of foreign customs would cease. The final thought is that the dissemination and accumulation of knowledge would redound to the credit of the entire nation ("mit einem Wort zum Ruhm und Wohlfahrt teutscher Nation gereichen," p. 80). Leibniz's summary is thus both precise and concise. His intricate, lively argument finds a fittingly spirited resolution, which echoes the theme of patriotism sounded in the opening lines of his article.

The proximity of Leibniz's "Ermahnung an die Teutsche" to essayistic writing is evident. It partakes of the provocative, avant-garde tendencies of the essay and is, like that genre, a dialectic hybrid of scientific tract and artistic *tour de force*. Cognizant of his audience, Leibniz the essayist approached his task in a nonphilosophic manner; that is, non-syllogistically. His writing is gauged to lead the reader on a dynamic journey of "encirclements" which, while revealing the ambiguity of the situation at hand, suggests possible solutions. Neither aphoristic nor effusive, neither pedantic nor flowery, Leibniz's engaging prose composition foreshadows Friedrich Schlegel's ideal essay: "The essay is a mutual galvanism of author and reader; it is, moreover, an inner charging of each one alone; that is, a systematic alternation between paralysis and palpitation. The essay should bring about movement, it should combat intellectual arthritis and promote nimbleness."[29]

III

Writing almost ninety years later in the *Berlinische Monatsschrift* (1784), Kant had the advantages offered by stylistic advances and linguistic refinement achieved in German since the turn of the century by such writers as Gellert, Lessing, and Wieland.[30] Moreover, Kant had greater experience in writing for journals; his collected works contain several volumes of shorter essayistic compositions on numerous topics.[31] We expect, therefore, that Kant's writings will reveal even greater affinity to the essay genre. The new genre, moreover, was fairly well established by the 1780s.

Because of its seminal role in discussions of eighteenth-century Enlightenment, Kant's "Beantwortung der Frage: Was ist Aufklärung?" ("An Answer to the Question: What Is Enlightenment?") first published in the December 1784, issue of the *Berlinische Monatsschrift*, has been selected for analysis here as a literary work. Tone and style are different from those in Leibniz's "Ermahnung." Despite this divergence Kant's piece can be considered an essay, since the exact form of the genre is hard to pin down. The decisive criterion is always the impression a discourse imparts as a "Denkerzählung" ("narrative thought"), "intellecktuelles Gedicht" ("intellectual poem"), or a "lyrisches Philosophem" ("lyrical philosophical statement").[32] Strikingly, recent studies of the piece tend to focus precisely on this aspect of Kant's argument; that is, its call for the critical exercise of "Selbstdenken" ("autonomous thinking").[33] Kant's "Was ist Aufklärung?" with its mere ten paragraphs covering but seven pages, more closely approaches the "ideal" length of the essay.[34] Perhaps because of its more compact form, Kant's composition comes across in a more focused and forceful manner. For the same reason we notice a lack of personal tone. Kant presents us with a sparkling, translucent house of crystal, whereas Leibniz offered us the view of a vital, verdant garden on the verge of bursting into first full bloom. These differences are due to the period of gestation each piece experienced and to the difference in philosophical mind. Whereas Leibniz approached philosophical questions in an unsystematic fashion, Kant was a careful dialectician who placed importance on systematic analysis. The latter qualities mark much of Kant's "Was ist Aufklärung?"

Like Leibniz's "Ermahnung" Kant's composition was intended for a broader audience. Its publication in the popular *Berlinische Monatsschrift* bears witness to that intention. Although Kant might not have had the professional scholar in mind in this particular instance, he did apparently expect his reader to be interested in the topic from the outset. This expectation was fully justified by the circumstances surrounding the posing of the question, "Was ist Aufklärung?," in the pages of the *Berlinische Monatsschrift*. It was a widely discussed subject.[35] Even though he could presume interest, Kant made extensive use of the rhetorical devices of personal appeal, graphic images, striking metaphors, repetition, and rhetorical questions to involve his reader more deeply in his line of reasoning. In contrast to Leibniz, Kant made sparing use of imagery and he included no overt emotional appeal to his audience as Leibniz had done, for example, in regard to love for one's country. The lack of such personal appeal is due to the philosophical nature of Kant's topic.

The tone is set by the opening paragraph, the exordium, which is direct and sober because it is a definition of terms:

> *Enlightenment is humankind's release from self-incurred tutelage. Tutelage* is the inability to make use of one's understanding without direction from another. *Self-incurred* is this tutelage when its cause lies not in the lack of reason but in the lack of resolution and courage to use it without direction from another. Dare to know! Have the courage to *think independently!*—that is the motto of the Enlightenment.[36]

How very different from Leibniz's emotionally charged exordium! Nevertheless, how effective as a definition. It is a typical instance of the literal or determinate concept.[37] As the essay progresses, however, the dichotomy of art and science becomes evident with the introduction of the metaphorical and indeterminate. The reader's attention is immediately caught by the opening sentence. Because it is italicized the sense of electricity underlying it is enhanced. The statement is electrifying precisely because of its clarity and directness. The reader is induced to read on in order to learn how human beings are themselves responsible for their intellectual dependency. The immediate repetition of the italicized word *"Unmündigkeit"* ("tutelage") at the beginning of the second sentence draws one on. The third sentence uses the same technique with "selbstverschuldet" ("self-incurred"). In each instance the key term is concisely defined. The concluding sentence makes unmistakably clear the intent of the preceding definitions: humanity must dare to use reason freely. The repetition of the Latin *sapere aude* ("dare to know") in German paraphrase lends greater weight to the exhortation. Finally, that exhortation is identified as the motto of the *Aufklärung*. Instead of deadening the reader's curiosity, the matter-of-factness of these opening lines unexpectedly kindles intense interest. The economy of words is classic in its impact.

Kant does not let up. In the second paragraph he immediately moves to the causes of intellectual dwarfishness: laziness and cowardice (*Faulheit und Feigheit*, p. 55), for which he provides a series of examples: "If I have a book which understands for me, a pastor who has a conscience for me, a physician who decides my diet, and so on, I need not trouble myself" ("Habe ich ein Buch, das für mich Verstand hat, einen Seelsorger, der für mich Gewissen hat, einen Arzt, der für mich die Diät beurteilt u.s.w., so brauche ich mich ja nicht selbst zu bemühen," p. 55). And he concludes using again the inclusive first person pronoun, *ich*, to invite reader identification: "I need not think for myself, if I can only pay: others will readily undertake the irksome work for me" ("Ich habe nicht nötig zu denken, wenn ich nur bezahlen kann; andere werden das verdrießliche Geschäft schon für mich übernehmen," p. 55). The pointed reference to money characterizes the reluctance to think for oneself as a luxury which, in the long run, one can ill afford. Kant follows up the money motif and its implications of privilege with the metaphor of the unthinking majority of citizens as domestic cattle (*Hausvieh*) tethered by their guardians (*Vormünder*) to a cart with harness (*Gängelwagen*) who have become too timid to attempt independent action. In his first two paragraphs Kant succeeds in totally captivating his reader. The writer is firmly in control; the reader plunges on.

The third paragraph is closely integrated into the line of movement established by the preceding two. This continuity is achieved on two levels: by means of the literal concepts (argument) and by means of the metaphorical language (imagery). The argument is clear: because individuals are unpracticed in the free use of reason, they find it difficult to think for themselves. Besides, the force of habit has something comforting about it. Only in isolated instances has an occasional person succeeded in breaking free of the set patterns, thereby liberating the powers of reason. The immense difficulty of achieving this freedom is underscored by images of shackles *(Fußschellen)* and an uncertain gait *(Gang)*. Kant argues that most of those few individuals who succeed in ridding themselves of the "shackles of continuing dependence" are scarcely able to leap over the smallest ditch ("würde dennoch auch über den schmalesten Graben einen nur unsicheren Sprung tun," p. 56). Only the rare individual is able to walk with sure step ("einen sicheren Gang zu tun"). These allusions to walking and jumping echo similar motifs of the second paragraph where Kant speaks of "den Schritt zur Mündigkeit" ("the move toward intellectual maturity") and of an individual's inability to venture a "Schritt außer dem Gängelwagen" ("step from the harness cart") in which one is held captive (p. 55). In view of the frequent use of metaphors *(Gängelwagen, Hausvieh)* and images *(Fußschellen, unsicherer Gang)* we recall that aesthetic ideas included for Kant such rhetorical devices as similes, tropes, metaphors, and poetic analogies. The metaphor for Kant was not just ornamental but also of cognitive value. Indeed, "the metaphor raises important questions concerning the origins and limits of knowledge," while also serving as "the hallmark of artistic genius."[38]

The same rhetorical techniques are repeated in paragraph four, which begins to focus more clearly on the essential element of freedom in this process of liberation. Given the opportunity to develop their critical faculties, the people would naturally strive for self-realization. The sine qua non, however, is that the "yoke of tutelage" ("des Joch der Unmündigkeit") must first be thrown off. Kant introduces at this important juncture the idea that enlightenment evolves gradually, whether for the fortunate individual or for the commonweal. Revolution might free the individual from political or economic oppression, but it would never lead to a genuine reform of one's mode of thinking (p. 56). True and permanent change only comes with the eradication of prejudice.

In four brief paragraphs, Kant leads his reader deep into the labyrinth of his thinking without the reader having suspected how demanding the philosopher's line of reasoning really is. The impression of ease in moving from one idea to the next is conveyed largely by Kant's judicious and appropriate use of images, all related to the need to walk and move about freely. But we are not dealing here with the topos of the leisurely walk which may occasion all sorts of thoughts and has become the hallmark of the literary essay.[39] The reader is completely persuaded to follow Kant's lead on a journey of explanation. Thus, the reader hardly realizes that the next two paragraphs (#5 and #6) run on for four pages (each paragraph covers two pages of print) and form the crux of the philosopher's argument. The main idea of paragraph five is the concept of "Freiheit" in Kant's specific context, while paragraph six explores the idea of moral responsibility for bringing about enlightenment. The ideas of freedom and obligation were first sounded in paragraph four. The middle part of the essay is thus devoted to an elaboration of views introduced in the first page and a half.

The protracted discussion of freedom avoids tediousness by employing devices such as definition, prolepsis, repetition, rhetorical questions, direct quotation, and examples drawn from everyday experience. As he had done before, Kant begins paragraph five with a definition, this time of freedom: "to make public use of one's reason without restraint" ("von seiner Vernunft in allen Stücken *öffentlichen Gebrauch* zu machen," p. 56). This definition is immediately followed up by a series of terse sentences which anticipate objections and thus form a prolepsis. They also have a dialogic quality designed to engage the reader more intensely. The prefatory comment, "But I hear on all sides: *Do not think!*" ("Nun höre ich von allen Seiten rufen: *räsonniert nicht!*"), introduces variations of the main dictum. Exhortations not to think are heard from such pillars of society as a military officer, a finance minister, and a cleric. Each has his own reason to urge the citizenry not to think (for example, "obey, pay, believe"). The sole exception to this litany of "do-nots" is Friedrich II's exclamation: "*Think* as much as you will and about whatever you will, *but obey!*" ("*räsonniert, so viel ihr wollt, und worüber ihr wollt; aber gehorcht!*") which is cited parenthetically here (p. 56). Kant's use of the statement lent it great notoriety. Its function is to underscore how diametrically opposed to freedom are all the usual "räsonniert nicht!" commands. To his rhetorical question about what is beneficial or detrimental to enlightenment, Kant replies that we must distinguish between public and private use of critical thinking. Public use of one's reasoning powers is equated to views published in print for a general audience, whereas private use designates the application of reason by persons in public service who are required by their positions to execute the will of others. While the "öffentlicher Gebrauch" of reason can tolerate no restrictions, the "privater Gebrauch" is frequently subject to curtailment. Restrictions in the latter area are not detrimental to the ultimate evolution of critical, enlightened thinking. In speaking of the need for compliance to a general will in the government sector, Kant refers to the administrative apparatus of society as a machine which necessarily must operate in a mechanical way ("ein gewisser Mechanismus notwendig, Maschine," p. 57). The use of the machine image to designate the nature of government is noteworthy apart from all the associations it can evoke because Kant reintroduces the concept at the conclusion of his essay to imply the opposite of its designation in its current context.

In an effort to explain fully the differentiation between public and private use of reason, Kant cites several examples of "public" persons— an officer, a taxpayer, a cleric, a teacher—acting in both a public and private capacity. In the moment of battle, for instance, the officer may not question decisions; however, after the battle he may—and should— analyze in public view mistakes in deployment, timing, tactics, and so forth. Only by means of such public analysis can military strategy be improved. Analogous cases are made for the benefit to other areas of government and church administration. Whenever an expert (Kant wrote "Geistlicher" ["cleric"] but by implication he meant all leaders of society) addresses himself "durch Schriften zum eigentlichen Publikum, nämlich der Welt" ("through print to the actual public, namely the world") on matters within his jurisdiction, he enjoys unrestricted free-dom in the use of reason and in the expression of personal views (p. 58). It would be nonsensical, the philosopher concludes, to claim that the cleric (or officer, or teacher, etc.) has knowledge of his profession only when speaking as a functionary of church or state but not as an individ-ual human being. In Kant's words: "That the guardians of the people . . . should themselves be incompetent is an absurdity which amounts to the eternalization of absurdities" (p. 58).

Paragraph six begins with a classic example of a prolepsis. Kant anticipates the counterargument that the clergy could agree to propound officially and individually always and everywhere the same views; that is, to create an "unceasing guardianship" over each of its members. The prolepsis is effective because the reader is now taking every step with the writer. The added effort is deliberately to narrow the focus to freedom of thought in religious matters. Kant's response to the objection is clear and curt: "I answer that this is altogether impossible" ("Ich sage: das ist ganz unmöglich," p. 58). The ensuing demonstration of his contention is apodictic, much more syllogistic than metaphorical. The only rhetorical attempt to persuade the reader to accept his view is the allusion to the "Obervormundschaft" ("guardianship") as a "criminal act against human nature itself the foremost destiny of which lies precisely in the advancement of enlightenment," adding that "future generations would be fully justified in rejecting those decrees as having been made in an unwarranted and malicious manner" (p. 59). Enlightenment is a moral obligation which no individual may deny others or even oneself. Enlightenment and human nature are identified so intimately that they prove inseparable. You cannot have the one without the other.

Kant reverses the argument. Not only do those in authority *not* have the right to prescribe beliefs for others, they carry the primary responsibility for ensuring the progress of enlightenment from generation to generation. Thus, the monarch must safeguard the right to freedom of speech. Unnecessary and excessive censorship would prove injurious to the king's majesty, for such censorship is tantamount to supporting the spiritual tyranny of the few over the many. To underscore his point, Kant takes recourse to the tried rhetorical technique of citing authority. He interjects the apparent quotation in Latin: "Caesar non est supra grammaticos" ("Caesar is not above the rules of language," that is, above the law, p. 60). After the long, intellectual argument of paragraph six, these words are the last impression. They also succinctly summarize Kant's overall argument. No monarch, no bishop can deprive the individual of the innate right to freedom of thought.[40]

As if sensing that he might have overtaxed the reader's willingness to think the philosopher's thoughts by the unusual length and cerebral quality of the last two paragraphs, Kant returns to the technique of segmenting his ideas into more manageable size. The final four paragraphs frame the central argument regarding freedom and moral obligation by mirroring the structure of the opening four paragraphs. The first and final sections of the essay, therefore, provide an attractive symmetry. Moreover, the tripartite structure is a feature of many essays.[41]

Paragraph seven shifts the reader's attention to the question of whether the current age is an enlightened one. The response takes the form of a word play: no, author and reader were not then living "in an *enlightened* age . . . but rather in an *age of Enlightenment*" ("in einem *aufgeklärten* Zeitalter. . . , aber wohl in einem Zeitalter der *Aufklärung,*" p. 60). The substitution of "Aufklärung" for "aufgeklärt"—another rhetorical device (polyptoton)—stresses the *process* rather than the completion of the development. The paragraph concludes with the suggestion that the age could also be labeled "das Jahrhundert Friedrichs," an allusion to the dominant role played by Friedrich II in the political world. With that the topic of the ensuing paragraph is sounded.

Friedrich is honored in this manner because he granted his subjects freedom of thought in matters of conscience. The free use of reason in religious questions was an important first step. The reader's half-conscious inquiry as to whether this freedom is restricted to the realm of religion is answered almost in the same breath: we read that the spirit of open inquiry had already begun to spread to political concerns (p. 60).

In the penultimate paragraph Kant explains why he has addressed himself first and foremost to enlightenment in religious matters. The answer, Kant implies, is self-evident "because our rulers have no interest in playing the guardian to the arts and sciences" (p. 61). Besides, tutelage in questions of dogma is the most serious kind of prescriptive guidance. To indicate that the free use of reason is equally applicable to the political situation, Kant employs synecdoche as a means to invite the reader to complete his line of reasoning: "But the way a monarch thinks, who favors religious enlightenment, goes even further, recognizing that there is no danger even to his lawgiving in allowing his subjects to make public use of their reason and to publish their thoughts as a better formulation of that legislation . . ." (p. 61). Without naming him, the reference to the chief of state is sufficient to prompt the reader to conclude: Kant means Friedrich II.

Even as the repetition of the term *"öffentlicher Gebrauch"* (*"public* use") recalls its previous use, so does the concluding paragraph act as a summation of the entire article. It achieves its impact by repeating key terms and ideas. Friedrich's remark ("räsonniert, so viel ihr wollt") is repeated in its entirety. The benefit of greater political freedom for an enhanced atmosphere of intellectual freedom of inquiry is acknowledged, but the preeminence of "Freiheit des *Geistes"* ("intellectual freedom") is emphasized as the critical factor. Thereupon Kant reminds his reader that humanity is destined to think freely and critically ("Hang und Beruf zum *freien Denken"*) and that it is only a matter of time before human potential (and rights) evolve fully. Freedom of thought will naturally and logically lead to freedom of action, action based on reasoned choice. For Kant a natural affinity exists between rationality and moral freedom. "Mündigkeit" ("majority") proves, therefore, to be a rational category.[42]

The final sentence of the essay offers another striking synecdoche, achieved by an allusion to Julien Offray de Lamettrie's celebrated work, *L'homme-machine (Man as Machine,* 1748). The reintroduction of the motif of mechanicalness in this new context highlights an important parallel between the bureaucratic machinery mentioned earlier and the genesis of the human spirit as envisaged in the final paragraphs. Both administrative bodies and the human personality operate according to a set of internal laws. However, the *punctum saliens* in their difference lies in the preeminence of the individual human being whose destiny is to evolve in a morally and intellectually unrestricted manner. This penchant of humanity for freedom is seen as the nucleus *(Keim)* of civil life. By contrast, governmental bureaucracy is bound by nonvital laws which allow no deviation from a self-prescribed path. These external structures of society are referred to as a hard shell *(diese harte Hülle).* Placed in this light, the concluding allusion to the mechanism of the human individual is reversed, for the government must eventually recognize this difference, acknowledging that the human being "[ist] nun mehr *als Maschine"* ("is now more than a *machine,"* p. 61). Forced to cede the point, the guardians of state would then be moved to treat the individual as the free agent that every person is and not as an automaton programmed to execute the official will. Consequently, the bodies of state and church would be restructured according to the human propensity and vocation to free thinking ("Hang und Beruf zum *freien Denken*"). Kant expresses these complicated ideas in the final sentence with an admixture of scientific rigor and poetic imagination: "When nature, therefore, has uncovered from under this hard shell the nucleus which she most carefully nurtures—namely, the propensity and vocation to *free thinking*—then this nucleus gradually affects the people's way of thinking (by means of which they gradually become ever more capable of *free action*). Ultimately, the premises of governance are affected as well so that the *governing body* will find it to its own advantage to treat all men—who are now recognized as more than mere *machines*—according to their inherent dignity" ("Wenn denn die Natur unter dieser harten Hülle den Keim, für den sie am zärtlichsten sorgt, nämlich den Hang und Beruf zum *freien Denken*, ausgewickelt hat: so wirkt dieser allmählich zurück auf die Sinnesart des Volks [wodurch dieses der *Freiheit zu handeln* nach und nach fähiger wird], und endlich auch sogar auf die Grundsätze der *Regierung*, die es ihr selbst zuträglich findet, den Menschen, der nun mehr *als Maschine* ist, seiner Würde gemäß zu behandeln," p. 61). The concluding words poignantly express the underlying conviction of this brief discourse: mankind must be treated with dignity according to its basic nature. The external shell of restrictive convention must be pierced and peeled away so that the inner being might evolve freely, thereby providing the basis for social and political reform.

IV

Critics of the essay form have frequently noted that the genre shares qualities with other prose forms ranging from the novella to the feuilleton, dialogue, aphorism, and poem. The foregoing literary appreciation of Leibniz and Kant is designed to place these two figures of Enlightenment thought within the tradition of the German (and ultimately European) essay. Their affective use of language gives evidence of their ability to enlist the power of the poetic image and turn of phrase to more expressively formulate philosophic ideas. In their practice of popular prose as evinced in the two discourses examined here, Leibniz and Kant apparently distinguished between mere rhetoric and genuine poetry. They valued the latter as an ally in scientific argumentation. Kant's comment in his *Kritik der Urteilskraft* on these functions can be applied with as much validity to his own "Was ist Aufklärung?" and to

Leibniz's "Ermahnung an die Teutsche." Kant argued that rhetoric promises something serious while giving only an "entertaining play of the imagination." Poetry, on the other hand, promises only amusement while accomplishing "something worthy of being made a serious business, namely, the use of play to provide food for the understanding, and the infusion of life in its concepts."[43] Both Leibniz and Kant made significant strides in achieving the proper admixture of poetry and scholarship in their journalistic writing, which can now be seen as contributions to the eighteenth-century German essay. On the basis of internal evidence, Leibniz's "Ermahnung" can be identified as a "kulturkritischer Essay" ("culturally critical essay"), whereas Kant's "Was ist Aufklärung?" falls under the rubric of "begrifflicher Essay" ("conceptual essay").[44] Both compositions are noteworthy products of two remarkable philosopher-essayists.

Notes

1. Ernst Cassirer, *The Philosophy of the Enlightenment*, trans. Fritz C. A. Koelln and James P. Pettegrove (Boston: Beacon Press, 1966), pp. 35–36.

2. Francis X. J. Coleman, *The Harmony of Reason: A Study of Kant's Aesthetics* (London: University of Pittsburgh Press, 1974), p. 180, and Theodore E. Uehling, Jr., *The Notion of Form in Kant's "Critique of Aesthetic Judgment"* (Paris: Mouton, 1971), p. 13.

3. Olan Brent Hankins, *Leibniz as Baroque Poet: An Interpretation of His German Epicedium on the Death of Queen Sophie Charlotte* (Bern: H. Lang, 1973). An earlier essay on Leibniz as author of prose works is Johann Vahlen's "Leibniz als Schriftsteller. Festrede gehalten zum Leibniztag am 1. Juli 1897," *Sitzungsberichte der Königlichen Preußischen Akademie der Wissenschaften zu Berlin* 2 (1897): 687–701.

4. Eric A. Blackall, *The Emergence of German as a Literary Language, 1700–1775* (Cambridge: Cambridge University Press, 1959), pp. 2–9.

5. Coleman, *Harmony of Reason*, p. 179. See also Hans Heinz Holz, "Einleitung," Gottfried Wilhelm Leibniz, *Politische Schriften* (Frankfurt am Main: Europäische Verlagsanstalt, 1967), 2:12–20. Holz speaks (p. 14) of Leibniz's "Kulturpolitik als Angelpunkt der Gesellschaftspolitik, allgemeine Bildung als Bedingung der Möglichkeiten eines vollkommenen Staatswesens . . ." ("cultural policy as the pivot of his social policy, universal education as the prerequisite for the possibility of a perfect government").

6. Uehling, *Notion of Form*, p. 15.

7. The most important studies of the essay genre in eighteenth-century Germany are: Vincent J. Dell'Orto, "Audience and the Tradition of the German Essay in the 18th Century," *Germanic Review* 50 (1975): 111–23: Heinrich Küntzel, *Essay und Aufklärung: Zum Ursprung einer originellen deutschen Prosa im 18. Jahrhundert* (Munich: Fink, 1969); Helmut Rehder, "Die Anfänge des deutschen Essays," *Deutsche Vierteljahrsschrift* 40 (1966): 24–42.

8. Richard Exner, "Zum Problem einer Definition und einer Methodik des Essays als dichterische Kunstform," *Neophilologus* 46 (1962): 171.

9. Klaus Günther Just, "Der Essay," *Deutsche Philologie im Aufriß*, unter Mitarbeit zahlreicher Fachgelehrter hrsg. von Wolfgang Stammler (Berlin, 1954, 1960), vol. 2, cf. col. 1897.

10. Annamarie Auer, *Die kritischen Wälder: Ein Essay über den Essay* (Halle [Saale]: Mitteldeutscher Verlag, 1974), p. 133.

11. Just, "Der Essay," col. 1897.

12. Eva Acquistapace, *Person und Weltdeutung: Zur Form des Essayistischen im Blick auf das literarische Selbstverständnis Rudolf Kassners* (Bern: H. Lang, 1971), p. 10.

13. Gerhard Haas, *Essay*, Sammlung Metzler M83 (Stuttgart: Metzler, 1969), pp. 33, 50.

14. Michel de Montaigne, *Essays*, trans. J. M. Cohen (Middlesex, England: Penguin, 1981), pp. 130–31 (1:50). See also 3:3.
15. Cassirer, *Philosophy of the Enlightenment*, p. 30.
16. Coleman, *Harmony of Reason*, p. 164. The original German reads: "Mit einem Worte, die ästhetische Idee ist eine einem gegebenen Begriffe beigestellte Vorstellung der Einbildungskraft, welche mit einer solchen Mannigfaltigkeit der Theilvorstellungen in dem freien Gebrauche derselben verbunden ist, daß für sie kein Ausdruck, der einen bestimmten Begriff bezeichnet, gefunden werden kann. . . ." I. Kant, *Gesammelte Schriften*, hg. von der Königlich Preußischen Akademie der Wissenschaften. Erste Abteilung: *Werke* (Berlin: G. Reimer, 1908), 5:316.
17. Cf. part I of Dell'Orto, "Audience and the Tradition," pp. 111–19.
18. Because it is convenient as well as reliable, H. H. Holz's edition of Leibniz's "Ermahnung an die Teutsche" is used: G. W. Leibniz, *Politische Schriften*, vol. 2 (Frankfurt am Main: Europäische Verlagsanstalt, 1967), 60–80. Future references to this edition will be cited in the text by page number. The translations are my own.
19. Blackall, *Emergence of German* (pp. 3–9), and Paul Böckmann, *Formgeschichte der deutschen Dichtung*, 3d ed. (Hamburg: Hoffman und Campe, 1967, pp. 477–83) discuss the content of both essays. The "Unvorgreifliche Gedanken" appeared in 1717 and was reprinted in full in 1732 by Gottsched. Thus, the "Unvorgreifliche Gedanken" was more broadly known. Nevertheless, both versions had the same goal. Böckmann's purpose is to argue that Leibniz's concept of language represents a break with the superficial, merely decorative rhetoric of the seventeenth century. For Leibniz language is no mere "Zierde" ("ornament") but rather "ein Spiegel des Verstandes" ("a reflection of the mind"), that is, language acquires the quality of logical semiotics and it becomes more akin to mathematics (pp. 482–83). Because of his efforts to show how innovative Leibniz was, Böckmann discounts the role of rhetoric in Leibniz's own writing and summarizes the philosopher's significance for the eighteenth century as follows: "Man will mit Begriffen ebenso wie mit Zahlen rechnen lernen und logisiert dadurch die ganze Sprachwelt" ("Just as one learns to count with numbers so will one learn to reckon and logicize in the entire speech-world by means of ideas," p. 483). My analysis of Leibniz's early essay will show that Böckmann's categorical statement regarding Leibniz's view of language as "durchaus unrhetorisch" ("thoroughly unrhetorical," p. 482) is extreme. Blackall (p. 5n.) has already noted Böckmann's unwarranted stress on the rationalism of Leibniz's language.
20. See Just's classifications, "Der Essay," cols. 1902–6.
21. Ibid., col. 1903.
22. Christoph Martin Wieland, *Theorie und Geschichte der Red-Kunst und Dicht-Kunst. Anno 1757*, *Wielands Gesammelte Schriften* (Berlin: Akademie der Wissenschaften, 1909), Ser. 1, vol. 4, p. 303: "Wir verstehen unter der Red-Kunst eine auf die Kenntniß der Regeln gegründete Fertigkeit, wohl zu reden, d.i. durch seine Reden die Zuhörer zu überzeugen, sich ihrer Affekten zu bemeistern und sie zu dem Zweck zu lenken, den man sich vorgesetzt hat; denn das Vermögen, zu reden, ist uns von der Natur zu keinem andern Zweck gegeben, als damit wir dadurch einander unsere Gedanken beybringen und einander determinieren können, uns in unsern Absichten beförderlich zu seyn; oder, mit andern Worten, vermittelst der Rede würken wir auf den Verstand und auf den Willen der andern menschen. Es folget also von selbst, daß nur derjenige wohl reden kann, der andere durch seine Vorstellungen würklich bewegen kann, etwas zu glauben oder zu thun." For an overview of rhetorical techniques see Heinz Lemmermann, *Lehrbuch der Rhetorik* (Munich: Goldmann, 1964).
23. Ludwig Rohner, *Der deutsche Essay* (Neuwied: Luchterhand, 1966), p. 307: "die klassische Methode des Essays sei ruhiger, anmutiger, konzilianter als die [moderne] Proklamation. . . . [Der moderne Essay] hat weitgehend den familiären Ton verloren. . . ."
24. Friedrich Schlegel, *Sämtliche Werke*, Kritische Ausgabe, hg. Ernst Behler (Munich, 1963), Bd. 18, 2. Abt., 206: "Der Essay ist so zu schreiben, wie wir denken, sprechen, für uns schreiben oder im Zusammenhang frei reden, Briefe schreiben—über einen sittlichen Gegenstand, aus reinem Interesse daran, nicht philosophisch und nicht poetisch."
25. Cf. John A. McCarthy, "The Art of Reading and the Goals of the German Enlightenment," *Lessing Yearbook*, 16 (1984): 79–94.
26. Cf. Rohner, *Der deutsche Essay*, p. 307.

27. Fr. Schlegel, *Sämtliche Werke*, p. 203.
28. Lemmermann, *Lehrbuch der Rhetorik*, p. 101.
29. Fr. Schlegel, *Sämtliche Werke*, p. 221.
30. Blackall gives a fine analysis of the stylistic advances made during the period under consideration.
31. Aside from the "Vorlesungen" and shorter "nachgelassene Schriften," vols. 1, 2, and 8 of the Akademie Ausgabe contain journalistic pieces.
32. Rohner, *Der deutsche Essay*, p. 305.
33. See, for example, Jochen Schulte-Sasse, "Einleitung," *Aufklärung und literarische Öffentlichkeit*, ed. Christa and Peter Bürger and Jochen Schulte-Sasse (Frankfurt am Main: Suhrkamp, 1980), pp. 12–16; Werner Schneiders, *Die wahre Aufklärung. Zum Selbstverständnis der deutschen Aufklärung* (Munich: Karl Alber, 1974), passim; Frederick M. Barnard, "*Aufklärung* and *Mündigkeit*: Thomasius, Kant, and Herder," *Deutsche Vierteljahrsschrift* 57:2 (1983): 278–97. Gerhard Sauder, "Aufklärung des Vorurteils—Vorurteile der Aufklärung," *Deutsche Vierteljahrsschrift* 57:2 (1983): 257–77, speaks in more general terms about "Selbstdenken" ("autonomous thinking") in the course of the Enlightenment.
34. The following edition is used: Immanuel Kant, *Was ist Aufklärung? Aufsätze zur Geschichte und Philosophie*, hg. Jürgen Zehbe (Göttingen: Vandenhoeck & Ruprecht, 1975), pp. 55–61 (cf. Akademie Ausgabe, 8:35–42). The translations are my own.
35. Cf. the recent collections of contemporary eighteenth-century essays: Eberhard Bahr, *Was ist Aufklärung?* (Stuttgart: Reclam, 1974); Norbert Hinske, *Was ist Aufklärung? Beiträge aus der Berlinischen Monatsschrift* (Darmstadt: Wissenschaftliche Buchgesellschaft, 1973); A. Bergk, J. L. Ewald, J. G. Fichte, et al., *Aufklärung und Gedankenfreiheit: Fünfzehn Anregungen, aus der Geschichte zu lernen* (Frankfurt am Main: Suhrkamp, 1977).
36. Kant, *Was ist Aufklärung?*, p. 55: "*Aufklärung ist der Ausgang des Menschen aus seiner selbst verschuldeten Unmündigkeit. Unmündigkeit* ist das Unvermögen, sich seines Verstandes ohne Leitung eines anderen zu bedienen. *Selbstverschuldet* ist diese Unmündigkeit, wenn die Ursache derselben nicht am Mangel des Verstandes, sondern der Entschleißung und des Mutes liegt, sich seiner ohne Leitung eines andern zu bedienen. *Sapere aude!* Habe Mut dich deines *eigenen* Verstandes zu bedienen!, ist also der Wahlspruch der Aufklärung."
37. Coleman, *Harmony of Reason*, pp. 167, 181.
38. Ibid., pp. 159–61.
39. Haas, *Essay*, pp. 47–48.
40. This insistence upon the inalienable right to free speech and thought is repeated throughout the later Enlightenment. See, for example, my study, "Die gefesselte Muse? Wieland und die Pressefreiheit," *MLN* 99:3 (1984): 437–60.
41. Rohner, *Der deutsche Essay*, p. 309.
42. For a concise account of the concept of gradual evolution toward human freedom advocated in this essay and its place within Kant's overall political philosophy, see H. R. Reiss, "Kant and the Right of Rebellion," *Journal of the History of Ideas* 17:2 (1956): 179–92. More recently Barnard, "*Aufklärung* and *Mündigkeit*," pp. 288–92, draws attention to the centrality of the idea of autonomous self-direction not only for Kant's views but also as the defining characteristic of the enlightenment process itself. However, not all eighteenth-century thinkers agreed with Kant's equation of moral freedom with rationality. Herder, for example, could not accept that linkage.
43. Kant, Akademie Ausgabe, 5:321: "Der Redner giebt also zwar etwas, was er nicht verspricht, nämlich ein unterhaltendes Spiel der Einbildungskraft; aber er bricht auch dem etwas ab, was er verspricht, und was doch sein angekündigtes Geschäft ist, nämlich den Verstand zweckmäßig zu beschäftigen. Der Dichter dagegen verspricht wenig und kündigt ein bloßes Spiel mit Ideen an, leistet aber etwas, was eines Geschäftes würdig ist, nämlich dem Verstande spielend Nahrung zu verschaffen und seinen Begriffen durch Einbildungskraft Leben zu geben. . . ."
44. Just, "Der Essay," col. 1902.

3

The Style of Kant's Critique of Reason

STEPHEN F. BARKER

I. The Problem of Style and Content in Kant

Immanuel Kant stands as a giant figure in eighteenth-century thought. His long period of intellectual creativity extends through the middle and later part of the century. He led an isolated and personally uneventful life at a remote provincial university far from the centers of European culture—yet through the power and originality of his ideas he changed philosophy decisively and assured himself a central place in its history. He has come to be widely regarded as the greatest of the eighteenth-century philosophers, and many view him as the greatest philosopher of the whole modern era. His *Critique of Pure Reason*[1] is his largest, most formidable, and most influential work. Whether or not we agree with its metaphysical and epistemological doctrines, we must respect it as a crucial text in the history of modern philosophy. The thought of earlier modern philosophers can be seen as leading toward the *Critique*, while nineteenth-century philosophy must be seen as deriving from Kant's work.

Yet, despite its greatness, the *Critique of Pure Reason* is not a well-written book, and Kant himself was aware of this. He tells us in the Preface to the second edition that he cannot regard himself as possessing the talent for lucid exposition. As regards the *Critique*, he leaves to others "the task of perfecting what, here and there, in its exposition, is still somewhat defective."[2] But others never satisfactorily performed this task of polishing the expository style of Kant's first *Critique* while leaving its doctrines intact; we still have to acquire our knowledge of Kant's ideas directly from his text.

Its literary deficiencies are considerable. Occasional eloquent passages and vivid figures of speech are insufficient to overcome the turgidity and heaviness of Kant's style. His sentence structure is one negative factor:

his sentences often run on at intolerable length, with clauses so intertwined and involuted that the reader cannot keep track of their grammar (once in a while even the author loses the thread). Kant's heavy use of abstract nouns is another factor: his discussion proceeds always in abstract terms, and the reader must struggle to grasp the diffuse ballet of abstractions which Kant stages. Concrete examples are rarely offered to illustrate the abstract points. Kant's reliance upon an extensive technical vocabulary of philosophical jargon is a related factor: he borrows many technical terms from more scholastic predecessors and coins many others. He takes little care to illustrate to his readers (or to himself) what these technical terms are supposed to mean: he is content to define some of his technical terms by means of others, as though this would make everything clear. Yet another factor is Kant's notorious "architectonic," the elaborately structured logical arrangement according to which he groups his sections and subsections in a pattern of twos, threes, and fours, each part supposedly paralleling and counterbalancing others in a rigidly prescribed way. He maintains that this structure must necessarily be exactly as it is; yet there are strong signs of arbitrariness in the structure—the contents of some subsections are perfunctory or atrophied, while the contents of others struggle to burst out of the Procrustean limits within which Kant tries to confine them.

Readers of today, looking back at Kant's *Critique of Pure Reason,* may well feel a strange mismatch between the impressive quality of many of Kant's ideas and the unimpressive or even repellent quality of much of his literary expression. How can a philosopher of the first rank be so inept and unsatisfactory an expositor of his own ideas? How can ideas of such depth and originality be trapped in so clumsy and wooden a text? The contrast is extreme and perplexing.

In discussing this apparent mismatch between the thought of Kant's *Critique of Pure Reason* and its textual expression, I shall argue that the contrast is less surprising and incongruous than at first appears. Several kinds of interconnections exist between Kant's thought and his literary style; attention to these interconnections will help us see that the character of his style largely derives from the state of his thought. I hope that Kant the thinker and Kant the writer will then be seen in clearer relation to one another, making more understandable how these two aspects of his activity belong to one and the same author.

In the next section I describe the philosophical project which Kant thinks he is undertaking in the first *Critique,* and in the section after that I shall briefly consider the philosophical results which he thinks he has achieved. Then, in light of these doctrines of Kant's, I shall discuss several aspects of Kant's expository style and their interconnections with his philosophical thought.

II. Philosophy as Criticism

In the medieval world, the older and more long-established a scheme of practices or ideas was, the more it was regarded as worthy of acceptance and respect. This deferential attitude toward tradition began to be undermined in the early modern period by leading thinkers who challenged received opinions in theology and natural science, in political thought and philosophy. In the eighteenth century, with the Enlightenment, the critical examination of received opinions came to be regarded as a central task necessary for human intellectual progress.

Speaking of the eighteenth century, Kant says, "Our age is, in an especial degree, the age of criticism."[3] No longer are traditional ideas to be endorsed merely because they are traditional. Henceforth, all doctrines which present themselves for our acceptance must be subjected to independent rational scrutiny. Only if they meet the tests which reason imposes can they be entitled to receive the intellectual assent of human beings who are now autonomous in their thinking.

In his *Critique of Pure Reason* Kant is concerned with only one of what he regards as the two great aspects of human thinking. He is one of the first philosophers to make a sharp logical distinction between thought about what *is* the case and thought about what *ought* to be the case (the twentieth-century distinction between "facts" and "values" grows out of Kant's distinction). The ancients had distinguished between the active life and the contemplative life, but they did not suppose that there is any deep logical difference between knowledge about what is the case and knowledge about what ought to be the case. Kant regards this as a fundamental distinction. For him, when we think about what is the case we are seeking "theoretical" knowledge, and the task of the sciences is to amass knowledge of this type. Knowledge of what ought to be the case Kant regards as an utterly different type of knowledge. He calls it "practical" knowledge, and the task of ethical, legal, and political thinking is to formulate knowledge of this type. The *Critique of Pure Reason* is concerned with theoretical knowledge, its aim being to examine the functioning of the faculty of reason in its theoretical employment. The practical employment of reason—that is, the pursuit of practical knowledge—Kant deals with in other books, especially in his *Critique of Practical Reason*.[4]

Now, what sort of difficulty forces upon us the need for a critique of reason in its theoretical employment? There is no serious doubt concerning the ability of the human mind to achieve some theoretical knowledge. Two fields in which Kant considers that much rationally impeccable knowledge is to be found are mathematics, as begun by the Greeks, and natural science, as developed by Galileo and Newton.[5] Kant holds that in both these areas knowledge is attained by objective methods upon which all human beings must agree; this knowledge fully measures up to rational standards. However, Kant thinks that philosophers have not yet adequately explained how and why this success is achieved in mathematics and natural science. So a philosophical account is needed of how theoretical knowledge can be achieved there. Such an account will do away with the groundless doubts which some skeptical thinkers have raised concerning this knowledge. But a more serious problem concerns the field of metaphysics, the central part of traditional philosophy. Down through the centuries, metaphysicians have claimed to be able to attain universal and necessary truths, truths that are nontrivial and embody important information about the nature of reality. But in metaphysics, Kant declares, the situation is much worse than in mathematics and natural science, for metaphysics is the scene of endless unresolved controversies. In metaphysics, every claim is met by a counterclaim, and no sound rational method has been developed for settling these disagreements in an objective manner.

Kant sees two great schools of thought among his predecessors in philosophy. On the one hand, the rationalists, such as Descartes and Leibniz, glibly put forward propositions about the nature of reality; they say that their propositons are self-evident truths that reason has the inherent power to grasp. But they can offer no proof or other justification for their specific claims, and their appeal to self-evidence is ultimately sheer dogmatism. Metaphysics as they pursue it can never become a sound branch of knowledge, because their procedure is arbitrary and lacks rational support. They offer no reason why the nature of reality need conform to their ideas about it.

On the other hand are the empiricists, such as Locke, and especially Hume. They object to the dogmatism of the rationalists, and they try to substitute for it a reliance upon sense-experience. All nontrivial knowledge must be derived from sensory observations, they hold. Yet sense experience will at best yield merely probable generalizations; knowledge drawn from sense experience will lack the certainty required by metaphysics. So Kant thinks that the viewpoint of empiricism leads inevitably toward skepticism concerning the possibility that metaphysics can become a rationally acceptable field of knowledge.

Philosophy of the past has thus reached an impasse, Kant believes. The rationalists rightly see that metaphysics must make universal and necessary claims about reality, but they make their claims dogmatically. The empiricists rightly see that dogmatism is insufficient, but they move toward skepticism.

Kant's aim is to find a position in philosophy that will synthesize what is best in rationalism with what is best in empiricism, while establishing from a higher standpoint the way in which metaphysics can genuinely become rational knowledge, within limits. In order to do this, Kant conducts a critique of the human capability to have knowledge. This begins with a critical scrutiny of how the mind operates in knowing. Then the limits of what is knowable are formulated and the status of metaphysics established.

III. Results of Kant's Critical Inquiry

Kant's critical inquiry leads him to a scheme of philosophical ideas intended to provide an account of human theoretical knowledge, making clear the limits within which knowledge is possible and beyond which it is not possible. Kant thinks that characterizing these limits will explain how mathematics and natural science succeed as forms of knowledge, and it will also explain to what extent metaphysics can succeed as a legitimate field.

Crucial to Kant's results is his distinction between what he regards as the two basic faculties in the human mind. These are "sensibility" and "thought."[6] Sensibility is our passive ability to receive sensations which are forced upon us by some outer reality. Thought is the active ability to organize sensations under concepts, producing thoughts (judgments) about what is the case. Neither thought nor sensation alone will suffice, for "sensations without concepts are blind," while "concepts without sensations are empty."[7] Only when these two faculties both function within our minds can there arise within us that special kind of self-conscious awareness which is knowledge.

But this leads to a further distinction basic for Kant between "phenomena" and "things in themselves." Things in themselves are independently real beings in their own right, which do not need to be perceived or thought of by us in order to be what they are. Phenomena are things as they appear to us; they consist of patterns of passively received sensations which we in thought actively group together under concepts.

Phenomena are always necessarily spatial and temporal in form, Kant holds. Nothing can appear to us except as occupying some volume of space at some point of time. Moreover, we are able to know for certain about the character of space and time. Kant's view is that we do so in geometry (which describes space) and in arithmetic (which describes counting, the basic procedure in time). Kant insists that we possess a priori knowledge of space and time: the knowledge we have of geometry and arithmetic involves universal and necessary truths which could not be attained merely by generalizing from particular sense experiences. We possess this knowledge of space and time, Kant argues, and the only possible explanation of how we can have it is that space and time are essential forms of our human sensibility. Thus, in understanding mathematics we are understanding the fixed and fundamental character of our own minds, as regards their sensibility.

This leads to Kant's doctrine of the ideality of space and time. They are forms of our human sensibility—and nothing more than this. They are not forms to which things in themselves conform. Reality outside our human minds is neither spatial nor temporal in character. So mathematics achieves its certainty through confining itself to the study of the human forms of sensibility rather than of things in themselves. The truths it achieves hold absolutely for all possible human experiences, but they do not hold at all of things as they are in themselves.

Natural science is in a similar situation. It achieves certainty in its grasp of the laws of nature, especially the laws of mechanics, Kant says, because these laws of nature reflect the laws of thought according to which our thought-processes work in organizing our spatiotemporal sense experiences. Any spatiotemporal phenomenon that we can be aware of must conform to these laws, which our minds impose upon phenomena. But the absolute certainty here is achieved by limiting these laws to phenomena; the laws of nature, as we can know them, have no application to things in themselves.

There thus develops a deep chasm in Kant's philosophy. On the one side is the realm of phenomena, which includes all that we could possibly have scientific knowledge of. On the other side is the realm of things in themselves, which are completely unimaginable by us, as they lack all the spatiotemporal characteristics in terms of which we experience. Things in themselves cannot be studied by science, and human beings can have no theoretical knowledge of them.

Metaphysics, therefore, cannot be a field in which we gain knowledge of things in themselves. The rationalists were wrong to suppose so. However, it is possible for metaphysics to attain universal and necessary truths, if it confines itself entirely to phenomena. The "metaphysics of nature," according to Kant, can deal with some of the most general aspects of the way in which human minds arrange and structure their experience of spatiotemporal phenomena. It can establish laws about the deterministic interconnection of all events in nature, and about how all spatiotemporal events in nature must pertain to phenomenal substance, whose quantity stays always constant. Here the mind can know such principles about nature, because nature is not independently real, but is the systematic order which the human mind imposes upon its sensations.

IV. Kant's Metaphors

Turning now to Kant's writing style, let us first consider his use of metaphors. At various places in Kant's writing vivid figures of speech are developed at considerable length. Kant apparently regarded these as important to good exposition—as providing memorable decoration for the philosophical points being made. These figures of speech occur most often in introductory and concluding passages, where Kant is not making new philosophical points but is setting the stage for a new discussion or summarizing what he has completed.

One vivid metaphor is that of the voyage of discovery.[8] Kant had a lively interest in travel, even though he never did any; some of his most popular lectures at the University of Königsberg dealt with the geography and peoples of exotic regions. Since he lived in a port city and entertained sea captains at lunch, the metaphor of the voyage must have had a special meaning to him. He speaks of his philosophical undertaking as a long and dangerous sea expedition through unknown and dangerous waters, in the course of which unknown lands are to be located and their contours charted. Kant thinks of his work as having successfully completed this voyage of discovery, charting the territories of human knowledge and returning safely to make known to the rest of us these new discoveries in philosophical geography. In a further development of the metaphor, he speaks of David Hume, the empiricist, as having "run his ship ashore, for safety's sake, landing on scepticism, there to let it rot."[9] Here Kant is not denigrating Hume's work; indeed, elsewhere Kant says that Hume "first awakened me from my dogmatic slumbers."[10] It was to Hume's credit that he understood the need for such a philosophical voyage and embarked on it even though he lacked the staying power to complete it successfully.

Another of Kant's metaphors is that of territorial sovereignty.[11] This is akin to the metaphor of the voyage of discovery for both are geographical. But the metaphor of territorial sovereignty emphasizes the concept of a legal right to rule over a territory, rather than merely the geographical delineation of contours. A legal right to exercise sovereignty over a territory is a right to plenitude of power there. It is a *de jure* right, and must be contrasted with *de facto* possession, which can derive from usurpation. One has the right to sovereignty over a territory only if one derives this right from a legitimate source. The genuineness of one's title is therefore crucial. This metaphor enters Kant's discussion because he wants to speak of the human faculties as sovereign in their own territories: each faculty has its proper sphere or realm in which to rule. The faculty of thought exercises legitimate sovereignty over the realm of possible experience; this is the territory where it is entitled to rule. Here it may lay down universal laws which govern the structure of all that we can experience. Because it can do so, it can know ahead of time that all within its realm will be subject to these laws, and thus our a priori metaphysical knowledge concerning such matters as causality and substance is accounted for.

The metaphor of sovereignty is also supposed to suggest the source of the error and illusion which continually creep into philosophy: when one faculty has usurped some of the territory of another, or when one faculty tries to extend its rule beyond the legitimate boundaries of all human faculties, then confusion, misunderstanding, and error arise in philosophical thinking.[12] So the metaphor of territorial sovereignty shows that harmony among the faculties will require that each stay within its legitimate territory and not intrude upon any other.

The metaphor of sovereignty leads into the Kantian metaphor of a legal case being judged in court. Both of these types of metaphor involve the idea of legal right. However, the courtroom metaphor more vividly reflects the ongoing stages of a philosophical inquiry. The latter is compared to a legal process in which a question is brought before a judge, who hears witnesses and surveys evidence before reaching the verdict. The judge must distinguish between questions of fact ("*quid facti?*") and questions of law ("*quid juris?*"), and the record of the case and the judge's verdict will be preserved for future reference. In speaking of his critical inquiry Kant especially uses the metaphor of the courtroom: the claims of metaphysics to be able to attain knowledge are to be brought before the bar of reason, and a verdict rendered as to their legitimacy.[13] Kant pictures reason in the role of judge, presiding over this legal process. When the case is over and the claim concerning metaphysics has been adjudicated, once and for all, then the transcript of the process (the *Critique of Pure Reason* itself) is to be "deposited in the archives of Pure Reason."[14]

In a central section of the *Critique of Pure Reason*, entitled "Deduction of the Categories,"[15] Kant tries to prove that the faculty of thought has its logical patterns ("categories") which it must impose upon any sensory material of which it can have conscious knowledge. He holds that the presence of these patterns is what enables us to know a priori that in the realm of phenomena all events must be causally interconnected (the principle of determinism) and must involve enduring substance which cannot be created or destroyed (the conservation of matter). That such metaphysical principles are knowable concerning the realm of possible experience is of great importance to Kant. He calls this part of his argument a "deduction," borrowing this term from the traditional German legal usage. There, a "deduction" was a legal document purporting to establish a claim to a title of nobility, with its associated rights of ownership and rule.[16] In the still feudal political society of Germany were many princelings and many titles of nobility, great and small. Claims must often have come into conflict, and courts would have been accustomed to dealing with them. A "deduction" would trace the lineage of the claimant, showing him or her to be of legitimate descent and the true heir to the title and rights at stake. In terms of this metaphor, Kant is seeking to adjudicate the claim of human thought to achieve metaphysical knowledge through its categories. Kant's "deduction" is the attempt to exhibit the legitimacy of this claim.

While these metaphors which Kant employs decorate his exposition, their role is more than decorative, for were Kant's project not explained through metaphors like these it would be so abstract that we should scarcely be able to understand it. But do these metaphors provide us with an appropriate understanding of Kant's project? How apt are the metaphors? There are difficulties with them.

The metaphor of geographical discovery is vivid in its comparison of Hume and Kant with da Gama, Columbus, and Magellan. But we must remember that the "territory" which the philosophical traveler explores is not a real territory spread out in space which one traverses rapidly or slowly. It is an abstract logical "territory" consisting of distinctions among faculties and types of knowledge.

The metaphor of the courtroom is also vivid. But it too is potentially misleading, for it fails to bring out the full peculiarity of Kant's inquiry. According to Kant, the human mind itself, through rational thinking, is to undertake this critique or "trial" of its rational capacity to know. Thus, the same faculty which is the subject of the inquiry is to conduct the inquiry. The critical philosophy which Kant aims to develop will be a theory produced by the thinking part of the mind concerning how the thinking part of the mind operates and what its limits are. Thus, Kant's metaphor of the courtroom conjures up a most unusual "courtroom" indeed. In it, the human power of thought must play *all* the chief roles: it must be at once the judge (who presides and will render the verdict), the plaintiff (who complains against the pretensions of metaphysical knowledge), and the defendant (who stands accused of fraudulently purveying metaphysics as knowledge). In the "trial" which Kant envisages, reason sits in judgment over its accusations against itself. This is a peculiarly self-reflexive situation. In legal terms, it raises serious problems of conflict of interest: Can reason give itself a fair and impartial hearing? This self-reflexive situation vitiates the courtroom metaphor. We must not take the courtroom idea too seriously if we are to make sense of Kant's philosophy.

V. Dramatis Personae and Plot

In many ways the *Critique of Pure Reason* is an abstract and dry book. It was Kant's intention to write an austere work of technical philosophy in which fundamental problems about knowledge and reality would be attacked and solved. Nevertheless, as the book is written, there peers forth between the lines something of a narrative story. The story has a cast of characters and the rudiments of a plot. The hinted presence in this dry work of these narrative elements is surprising, but it can be explained as a consequence of the very austerity which Kant tries to practice. This austerity defeats itself, for author and reader both find themselves reading into the abstract account a more personal story.

The various faculties of the mind are the dramatis personae of the *Critique of Pure Reason*. Kant's way of writing about these faculties inevitably suggests personification of them. He did not exactly intend to personify them: he would have denied that they are persons, and he would have wanted to regard the language of personification as a merely figurative and decorative aspect of his exposition. Yet this language is deeply rooted in his text, and if he could have rewritten the book eliminating it, a very different work would have resulted. We are entitled to regard the personification of the faculties as a significant component of Kant's exposition.

The cast of characters in Kant's drama includes in starring roles three aspects of the faculty of thought: understanding, reason, and judgment. Each is an active power of the mind to arrange the material of consciousness in logical order. Because they are active in this way, the implicit suggestion is that they are to be regarded as masculine.

Of these three, understanding *(Verstand)* has to be viewed as the sober, responsible paterfamilias. It has a legitimate and useful occupation, imposing its categories upon the sensory material with which it is confronted, so as to produce knowing awareness of a spatiotemporal world of phenomena. Its word is law within the realm of possible experience, where its concepts belong. Like a good citizen, it knows its station and its duties, and does not try to range beyond its proper limits.

Reason *(Vernunft)* is the faculty of thinking in a different and much more adventurous aspect. Reason, Kant says, has an innate drive to seek completion in its explanations. But within the realm of possible experience where understanding rules, whenever we start asking for the causes of present phenomena we are led back to earlier phenomena on which they depend, and these in turn lead us back to other still earlier phenomena: we never find any first cause, or ultimate explanation, in this series. Reason is dissatisfied with this and so postulates a first cause outside the series, beyond the realm of possible experience. Thus arises the idea of God, an idea which reason frames in its quest for complete knowledge and final explanation. But to have theoretical knowledge that a God exists we would have to be able to have sense experience of Him, since concepts without sensations are empty. The idea of God is postulated in the first place as an idea of something wholly beyond the realm of possible experience; the consequence is that humans cannot have theoretical knowledge that God exists. Thus, reason has gone off on a quixotic search for the unfindable, a search which inevitably fails, but which reason by its very nature cannot abandon. This is what Kant calls the "Transcendental Dialectic"[17]—the fierce but fruitless struggle of reason to gain theoretical knowledge beyond the realm of possible experience.

If understanding is to be regarded as the sober, respectable, stay-at-home aspect of the faculty of thought, then reason is to be regarded as the errant, disturbed uncle in the family, whose ambitions are utterly beyond what he can ever achieve. He is admirable for his Faustian striving, but pitiable for his inevitable failure to achieve the goals he sets for himself. He cannot hold a solid job making a steady contribution, but always must be disrupting the equilibrium of the family with his yearning after unreachable ideal goals.

The faculty of judgment *(Urteilskraft)* is the third of Kant's aspects of the faculty of thought. Judgment is the power of the mind to subsume particular experiences under a general concept or rule. For example, if the mind has the concept of circularity, then it must rely upon its faculty of judgment to enable it to detect that a particular experience is indeed an experience of a circle. Kant does not have much to say in the *Critique of Pure Reason* about this faculty, or about how it works. He describes it as an innate gift; those in whom this power of judgment is weak have a lack which can never be made good, he says.[18] So he is thinking of judgment as a sort of male younger cousin to understanding, a cadet faculty whose power is a mysterious and inexplicable gift.

However, in his later work, the *Critique of Judgment*,[19] Kant develops his account of judgment more fully and assigns it additional responsibilities. There it emerges that judgment has a creative, important job to perform in dealing with material that is intractable to the operations of understanding. It turns out that the appreciation of beauty is the work of the faculty of judgment, as is the awareness of purposiveness in nature (teleology). So in the third *Critique* judgment comes into its own with tasks to perform in areas of human experience outside natural science, the special domain of understanding. Judgment does not compete with understanding or come into any conflict with it, but works in a quite different way in different areas. It is freer and more original in what it does, a sort of bohemian faculty, while understanding is rigid and mechanical in application of its own strict laws.

On the distaff side in Kant's drama, we encounter sensibility (or "receptivity"). This is the mind's ability to receive sensations through being affected by things in themselves. As we saw, for human beings sensibility is necessarily spatiotemporal in its form. Sensibility is the wife and helpmeet of understanding. Each is incomplete without the other. Understanding needs sensibility to provide it with material to organize; sensibility profusely produces formless material which requires the disciplinary activity of understanding to put it in order. Sensibility is richly productive, like a primal Earth-Mother; but what it produces is utterly chaotic until the firm hand of understanding is laid upon it.

So far as theoretical knowledge is concerned, sensibility and understanding are a fairly happily united couple, each doing what it does best and welcoming the other as complementary to itself. However, a coldness and distance marks their relationship. Judgment is constantly called upon to mediate between them; apparently they find direct communication with one another very difficult.

A final character, imagination, needs to be mentioned. Kant says that it is passive and partakes of the character of sensibility, but works closely under the direction of understanding. It helps judgment with the obviously difficult task of mediating between sensibility and understanding. The most important function of imagination is to create the full-blooded awareness that we have of phenomena as possessing aspects that we are not at the moment sensing. For example, in seeing what one takes to be a building, one is sensing at most the front side of its outer surface; to be aware of it as a building one must imagine it as having back surfaces and insides. The faculty of imagination must provide this awareness, but it is required to work strictly to the requirements of understanding as regards scientific laws—merely fanciful imagining is not what is called for. Kant is apparently thinking of imagination as the dutiful daughter of understanding and sensibility, a daughter who mostly forgoes fanciful reveries and devotes herself primarily to the blind labor her father orders in furtherance of his project of developing theoretical knowledge.

We may think of the *Critique of Pure Reason* as the story of this family. They have their family troubles—conflict occurs between idealistic reason and prosaic understanding, and coldness and estrangement occur between understanding and sensibility. But they have also their domestic harmony when they work cooperatively. Insofar as there is a plot in the *Critique of Pure Reason*, it has to do with how this family evolves its cooperative harmony despite the estrangement and conflict, overcoming both understanding's coldness toward sensibility and the disruption brought about by reason's ill-starred but inexpugnable drive toward ultimate reality. The resolution of these problems comes through the attainment by the family as a whole of a deeper knowledge of themselves. By learning to recognize and to accept their own capabilities and limitations, they can achieve an adequate harmony with one another. This is possible, although they all know that reason by its nature is doomed never to be able altogether to give up its yearning for theoretical knowledge of the ultimate, even after it has been forced to recognize that this can never be satisfied.

In thus describing the *Critique of Pure Reason* as though it were a soap opera, I am going beyond Kant's actual words. The drama is there only between the lines, as hinted at by the language of personification which Kant employs. While this sort of philosophical drama is only implicit in Kant's text, it will become more explicit a little later in Hegel's *Phenomenology of Mind*,[20] where the whole book is frankly written as if it were a story of the mind's progress through many stages toward ultimate self-awareness. Hegel's story differs from Kant's, though, because Hegel sees no possible barriers to a final perfect harmony within the mind, with full gratification of all its desires for knowledge. Also, for Hegel, the various faculties of the mind do not remain fundamentally separate individuals but appear only as passing phases of the basic ongoing activity of consciousness. Hegel's story is more romantic and optimistic than Kant's, but Kant's is more like real life.

VI. Correlated Difficulties of Thought and Style

The quality of writing in Kant's *Critique of Pure Reason* varies considerably. Even at his best, Kant is hardly outstanding as a stylist, and he is seldom able to keep writing at his best for long. But brief passages occur of great eloquence, good-sized paragraphs where the writing is vivid and polished, and long sections where literary difficulties at least are not oppressive. Yet there are other sections where the writing is most burdensome to a reader. The quality of the expository style is inversely correlated with the difficulty for Kant of the philosophical problems he is treating.

The Preface[21] to the *Critique* (in both editions) is readable and lively and shows Kant at his expository best. Here his writing is fluent and graceful, with striking figures of speech which students of Kant remember gratefully. Later on, the long section entitled "The Dialectic of Pure Reason"[22] is adequately written, on the whole. It deals with the logical errors into which reason falls when it leaves the realm of possible experience and tries to establish conclusions about the nature of things as they are in themselves. The ideas in this part were worked out by Kant comparatively early, and this portion of the *Critique* presumably was written some years before the publication of the book. It probably went through various drafts, and Kant may have worked a long time on revising and polishing it to make his presentation clear and readable.

Kant's sections entitled "Transcendental Aesthetic"[23] and "Transcendental Analytic"[24] are much less ingratiating as literary productions. These sections are more central to Kant's basic doctrine, and working them out seems to have given him much trouble. The Transcendental Aesthetic deals with space and time as forms of human sensibility. Its presentation is crabbed, awkward, and obscure. Kant's crucial points are tersely expressed, are not well related to the rest of the book, and make difficult going for readers. The Transcendental Analytic deals with the understanding and its categories. Here Kant is trying to work out his central thoughts about the operations of understanding and how these can yield metaphysical knowledge. His exposition is very difficult.

Within the Transcendental Analytic, one long part is especially notorious: the "Transcendental Deduction of the Categories."[25] Here Kant tries to prove the a priori necessity of the pure concepts of the understanding. He tells us that this section cost him the greatest pain and difficulty to compose,[26] and his ideas in it must have been late in reaching their final form. Here his sentence structure is at its heaviest and most awkward, his paragraphs are not well organized, and his abstract jargon is difficult to penetrate.

We can better appreciate Kant's situation if we realize that in this portion of the *Critique* he was locked in a titanic struggle with the difficulty of his philosophical thoughts. He was trying to formulate and establish an original, profound theory about the functioning of consciousness. Putting it into words was a task requiring heroic exertions.

We should also bear in mind the conditions under which Kant wrote. He worked alone; none of those who knew him and wrote accounts of his life mentions any secretary or even copyist. His habits were of legendary regularity, and he worked on his philosophical writing for only a few hours each morning, the rest of his day being reserved for lecturing, social activity, his walk, and reading. So we must suppose that with quill pen he wrote out all preliminary drafts of material and the final draft of the completed work. This was a monumental task, and we must not be surprised that he did not find time to polish his prose as much as we could wish.

Kant's philosophical ideas began to crystallize for him only in middle age, and as they did so his plans for philosophical writing became more grandiose. His plan for the *Critique of Pure Reason* grew and expanded, and he became convinced of the need to write other works to develop and complete the system of philosophy of which his first *Critique* was to be the foundation. The fear that he might not live to complete his work troubled him;[27] this must have made him write more rapidly and with less attention to style. We must suppose that this fear moved him at last to forge ahead with publishing a final draft of the first *Critique*, even though its exposition was still imperfect. To have taken additional years in refining the literary quality of this very long book would have prevented Kant from getting to the further writing on which his heart was now set. These considerations can help us to understand some of what we cannot enjoy in Kant's writing.

VII. The Architectonic Unity of Reason

The table of contents of the *Critique of Pure Reason* exhibits Kant's idea that an elaborate logical structure must be present in his philosophical material. This is the "architectonic": Kant's logical pattern of sections and subsections paralleling one another in complex array. To a twentieth-century reader the pattern looks forbidding, alien, and pointless. It seems an arbitrary and willful imposition upon the subject matter. And this bad impression is made still worse when we notice how Kant's architectonic often is out of step with the philosophical ideas which it tries to dragoon into position.

One aspect of this strain between the architectonic form and its philosophical content is that some of the headings which Kant feels bound to list end up with little material falling under them. This is especially noticeable in the final section of the book, the "Transcendental Doctrine of Method,"[28] which appears tacked on artificially. It altogether lacks the weight and interest of the earlier parallel part of the book, the "Transcendental Doctrine of Elements." Its final sections, especially the "History of Pure Reason,"[29] are strangely short and have slight content. Was Kant rushing to finish the book? If so, why did he include these sections at all?

Another way in which the strain between architectonic form and philosophical content shows itself is in those places where the ideas being treated in one section refuse to remain confined and boil over into other sections. For example, the section entitled "Antinomies of Pure Reason"[30] is supposed to be about the idea of the world as a whole; but its fourth part (the fourth antinomy) raises the question of the existence of God, a question which is supposed to be reserved for discussion in the "Critique of Speculative Theology."[31] In subtler ways, the ideas of the Transcendental Aesthetic refuse to remain separated from those of the Transcendental Analytic, and to make headway toward understanding

Kant's philosophy one must deny the sharp distinction which Kant's exposition would erect between the ideas of these sections.

What are we to make of the architectonic? We can better understand this aspect of Kant's style if we see it in relation to one of his fundamental philosophical assumptions: the transparency to itself of the mind's cognitive functioning. This doctrine is not very plausible to twentieth-century readers, who are more inclined to think of the mind as having hidden unconscious depths in which it conceals its operations from itself. But for Kant the transparency of the mind in its knowing activities is an obvious assumption. The assumption is associated with the tradition of German rationalistic philosophy,[32] and it is necessary for the type of inquiry into the mind which Kant aims to conduct.

"Transparency" is not Kant's word, but it is a suitable term for expressing this doctrine. The doctrine is that the mind can understand its own cognitive operations in a thoroughgoing fashion and can know that it has succeeded in doing so. Nothing in the cognitive functioning of one's mind can be ultimately hidden from one's self-conscious rational scrutiny. Outer things in themselves may be unknowable, and even the real nature of one's own mind, as a thing in itself, may remain unknowable. But the workings of the mind, as regards all cognitive activity, cannot be unknowable.

This doctrine of transparency underlies Kant's dedication to architectonic. If the truth about the mind's cognitive operations is all to be knowable, it must be systematic: it cannot consist of a job-lot of unrelated independent facts, for then there could never be any guarantee that one's knowledge of them was complete—one might always have overlooked some. Only if these truths about the mind all hang together in a tight logical network can we be assured that knowledge of some of these truths must in principle lead to knowledge of them all. Only then can the critique of pure reason be a task which we can be confident of being able to complete successfully.

Seen in this perspective, Kant's architectonic is a necessary aspect of the special and remarkable task of criticizing reason. Even if his architectonic classifications creak and wobble in many places, Kant will not abandon them, for he is absolutely confident that an architectonic must exist that is objectively the same for all human minds as they study their mental activity. "Pure reason," he says, "is by its nature architectonic."[33]

VIII. The Role of Examples

In his philosophical writing Kant only rarely gives examples to illustrate his philosophical points. Where examples do occur, they usually are perfunctory and are presented with little detail. This makes much trouble for the reader who is trying to grasp Kant's meaning, for Kant's abstract way of stating his points frequently leaves them floating in air. The reader must endeavor to supply illustrations and examples but often finds this difficult to do, as one cannot always divine Kant's intentions.

Kant's use of technical jargon compounds the difficulty. A barrage of technical germs occurs: *representation, intuition, phenomena, noumena, inner sense, outer sense,* and many others. Some of these terms are defined, but always only cryptically and darkly, and usually via other technical terms.[34] Such arid definitions are of only limited help to the reader. How one would like to have had varied examples and illustrations to make clearer the meanings of the technical terms.

It is on principle that Kant refrains from supplying more than perfunctory examples. Unfortunately, his view of philosophical communication is that it ought to be abstract. He scornfully says that examples are the "go-cart of judgment,"[35] implying that only children need to receive explanations in terms of examples. Mature thinkers are supposed to be able to think abstractly, and for them illustrations are to have an inessential, merely decorative function, making the prose more elegant and enjoyable perhaps, but adding nothing to its cognitive content.

The philosophical point here is deep and important, relating to communication. Is it enough, in discussing abstract matters, to rely upon abstract terms and abstract definitions? Kant probably has in mind the success of pure mathematics, where the greatest mathematicians often do the least to illustrate and explain their theorems in language accessible to the nonspecialist. These mathematicians achieve their scientific results without making concessions to the frailties of readers. Their readership is small, but their scientific eminence is high. Now, Kant himself emphasizes that mathematical thinking differs in basic ways from philosophical thinking (he supposes that mathematics has to deal with our "pure intuitions" of space and time, whereas philosophy does not);[36] but for Kant philosophy even less than mathematics need concern itself with giving examples and illustrations.

In twentieth-century philosophy it is Wittgenstein, above all, who has illuminatingly emphasized the crucial role of examples in philosophical discussion.[37] If one chooses too meager or one-sided a diet of examples, he says, one's philosophical ideas will become hopelessly distorted. Wittgenstein's view of what is involved in philosophical understanding is far more wholesome than Kant's on this matter. However, Kant's procedure in his use of examples springs from his deep-rooted conception of understanding and communication in philosophy. It is not heedlessness, carelessness, or haste which drives him to proceed as he does.

IX. Conclusion

In this chapter I have been discussing a number of the unsatisfactory aspects of Kant's expository writing. I have not argued that Kant's writing is good; no one will want to hold him up, overall, as a literary paragon to be emulated. But the weaknesses, defects, and peculiarities of his writing style can to a considerable extent be explained in terms of aspects of his thought. Some of them spring from the strain and difficulty he was experiencing in formulating his thoughts, while others are consequences of philosophical principles which he maintains. Seeing traits of Kant's style as thus associated with aspects of his thought can help us better appreciate the *Critique of Pure Reason* as the monumental intellectual achievement that it is. Also, it can help us to understand how Kant the author and Kant the thinker are very much one and the same person.

Notes

1. *Kritik der reinen Vernunft* (Riga, 1781; 2d ed., 1787). The best English translation is by Norman Kemp Smith, *Critique of Pure Reason* (London: Macmillan, 1933). I offer my own translations. Kant's *Prolegomena zu einer jeden künftigen Metaphysik, die als Wissenschaft wird auftreten können* (Riga, 1783) *(Prolegomena to Any Future Metaphysics That May Be Presented as a Science)* provides a sketch of the main conclusions of the *Critique of Pure Reason* without Kant's full arguments for them; several English translations of the *Prolegomena* are available.
2. *Critique of Pure Reason (CPuR)*, B xliii.
3. *CPuR*, A xi, note.
4. *Kritik der praktischen Vernunft* (Riga, 1788).
5. *CPuR*, B x–xiii.
6. *CPuR*, A 19 = B 33; A 50 = B 74.
7. *CPuR*, A 51 = B 75.
8. *Prolegomena*, Preface. See also *CPuR*, A 760 = B 788.
9. *Prolegomena*, Preface.
10. *Prolegomena*, Preface.
11. *CPuR*, B xv.
12. *CPuR*, A 260 = B 316.
13. *CPuR*, A xi; also A 752 = B 780.
14. *CPuR*, A 704 = B 732.
15. *CPuR*, A 84–130, B 116–69.
16. I am indebted to Professor Dieter Henrich for information on this point.
17. *CPuR*, A 293–648, B 349–676.
18. *CPuR*, A 133 = B 172.
19. *Kritik der Urteilskraft* (Berlin & Liebau, 1790).
20. G. W. F. Hegel, *Phänomenologie des Geistes* (Würzburg & Bamberg, 1807). The best English translation is by A. V. Miller, *Phenomenology of Mind* (Oxford: Oxford University Press, 1977).
21. *CPuR*, A vii-xxii, B vii-xliv.
22. *CPuR*, A 293–648, B 349–676.
23. *CPuR*, A 19–49, B 33–73.
24. *CPuR*, A 64–292, B 89–349.
25. *CPuR*, A 84–130, B 116–69.
26. *CPuR*, A xvi.

27. *CPuR,* B xliii.
28. *CPuR,* A 707–856, B 735–854.
29. *CPuR,* A 852–56, B 880–84.
30. *CPuR,* A 405–568, B 432–596.
31. *CPuR,* A 631–42, B 659–70.
32. A most helpful discussion of this tradition is found in Lewis White Beck, *Early German Philosophy* (Cambridge: Harvard University Press, 1969).
33. *CPuR,* A 474 = B 502.
34. For example, *CPuR,* A 68 = B 93.
35. *CPuR,* A 134 = B 173.
36. *CPuR,* A 714 = B 742.
37. Ludwig Wittgenstein, *Philosophical Investigations* (Oxford: Blackwell, 1953).

4

Herder's Craft of Communication

WULF KOEPKE

Johann Gottfried Herder (1744–1803) was one of the great minds of the eighteenth century, a universalist with seminal ideas. Various disciplines count him among their founders or precursors. The Age of Goethe, a high point in Germany's cultural history, considered Herder one of its outstanding representatives. However, Herder's prominence and fame is in inverse proportion to the intensity of study of his works. The standard German edition of his *oeuvre* dates to the late nineteenth century and has considerable flaws; furthermore, it is incomplete. No recent edition of his major works is available for scholarly needs.[1] The English reader has no access to most of Herder's works.[2] This creates a vicious circle: Herder finds few readers, because his books are hard to find; since he has few readers, publishers shy away from new editions.

Consequently, Herder is usually labeled with general attributes as a "stimulator" and "precursor" (*Anreger, Vorläufer*), who formulated seminal ideas that had to be developed by others in order to reveal their true significance. Some truth is in this characterization, but it is not the whole truth. Goethe, who owed much to Herder, maintained that one did not have to read Herder's works to know his ideas, because they had become absorbed into the general culture of Germany.[3] Goethe had indeed absorbed Herder's ideas, both in private conversations and by reading Herder's books, but such advice proved detrimental: Herder became a prime example for an author whose fame rested on secondhand knowledge and on short passages from selections and anthologies.

Goethe had specific reasons for advising against reading Herder. During the last decade of his life, Herder fought against the two dominant trends of the period: Goethe's and Schiller's concept of literature, called *Klassik*, and Kant and Kantianism. The earlier Romanticists, admirers of Goethe and followers of Kant and Fichte, therefore preferred not to mention Herder's name, although they owed much to him.[4]

Nineteenth-century positivism questioned Herder's universalist approach and regarded his emotional and metaphorical style as vague and unscientific. Academic scholars dedicated to objectivity and footnoted documentation thought little was to be gained from a closer reading of Herder's works. In spite of his empiricist and sensualistic tendencies, he was considered a representative of the age of "idealism" and rejected together with Schiller and Hegel.

The twentieth century has had more understanding for Herder's universalism, but it has exploited Herder for the justification of political ideologies. National Socialism used Herder's concept of the people, *das Volk*, and its ramifications for the purposes of Nazi propaganda. This may partly explain the initial reluctance of scholars in Western countries after 1945 to return to Herder research, while scholars in the German Democratic Republic and Eastern European countries have concentrated on developing a new Herder image, with some concessions to politics.[5] A revival of Herder studies in the West, however, is in the making.[6]

This very selective reception, compared to the intensive studies of Herder's contemporaries Kant, Lessing, Goethe, and Schiller,[7] is a puzzling paradox, since Herder was reader-oriented. He never produced a work as unreadable for a general audience as Kant's *Critique of Pure Reason*. Herder's first drafts usually show that his ideas were fully developed, but he rewrote his works several times to better communicate with the reader. In the preface to his magnum opus, the *Ideas for a Philosophy of the History of Mankind*, he wrote, "This invisible commerce of minds and hearts is the only and greatest benefit of the invention of book printing which otherwise would have brought as many negative as positive effects for the nations with a written literature" (13:5).[8] He was indeed convinced that the real benefit of printed books was a communication of the minds. This might lead to a universal republic of letters, on the condition that writers strive for such communication.

Herder's preoccupation with communication is evident. He was among the foremost literary critics of his day, but most importantly, a focal point of his philosophical endeavors was language. His celebrated and prize-winning *Treatise on the Origin of Language* is only the best known of his many contributions in this field, permeating his *oeuvre*. Herder was also a poet in his own right, and while his original poetry awaits an adequate scholarly and critical appraisal, his work as a translator is generally praised. Herder's translations, for example, of the Spanish *El Cid*, were his most popular works during the nineteenth century. Jean Paul Richter, one of Herder's ardent supporters, pointed out in his *School for Aesthetics* (1804) that Herder's original poetry was underestimated even then, adding that Herder was as valid a stylistic model as Goethe, Wieland, or Lessing.[9]

Herder was a Lutheran minister and educator by profession. He had to be concerned with the communication of complex ideas to simpler minds. Herder was a successful teacher and preacher,[10] which means that he had to be a good communicator. Why, then, does today's reader experience difficulty with Herder's style? Or does one?

An obvious problem with Herder is the forbidding range of his interests. He never tired of offering contributions, *Beiträge*, to historiography, literature, anthropology, linguistics, psychology, the theory of art, theology, particularly Bible studies, education, even political science. It is not easy to find the focal point in all of these concerns. Understandably, partial images emerge: Germanists and literary critics are interested in his writings on literature and his relationship to Goethe; theologians focus on his idea of Jesus Christ and his Bible studies; historians concentrate on the *Ideas* and other historical essays and biographies; linguists have their own range of interests. Herder's works themselves are often unfinished or collections of shorter essays on diverse topics. They do not so much present conclusions and results, but work in progress.

Goethe's above-mentioned remark was possibly prompted by a characteristic trait of Herder: Herder became productive through creative reception. He was stimulated, negatively or positively, by other people's writings and ideas. His works are frequently responses to specific challenges and theses. We cannot always do justice to Herder's contributions without reconstructing the status of the discussion at the time. Many writers of the eighteenth century bring us back to the polemics of two hundred years also, but Herder does it in a specific way: he subscribed to the Leibnizian idea that there is one truth, and that all our endeavors should contribute to knowledge of that truth. Nobody can claim to possess the ultimate wisdom, but a writer has to correct one's predecessors and propose new ideas; one should search for the grain of truth in all previous writings.

Furthermore, Herder was acutely aware of the limits of human langauge, in particular conceptual language. Sense data and experience, finding their immediate linguistic expression in images such as metaphors, could be more reliable guides to the truth than syllogisms. Consequently, Herder's typical discourse tried to convince the reader on two levels: through reasoning and through a system of images. Herder was addressing a reader used to discursive reasoning, but he tried to present a progression of the argument from concept to image which was more convincing than the concept. His stance runs counter to later scientific discourse. Herder was reminded of that by the famous review of the *Ideen* by his former professor Immanuel Kant[11] who observed that Herder had strayed from sober scientific discourse and reasoning into metaphorical and metaphysical speculation. Without considering

Herder's system of metaphors one can hardly do justice to his argumentation.[12]

Therefore, Herder's views on language, style, and communication must be summarized before examining his strategies and rhetorical devices. Herder was extremely suspicious of systems in terms of epistemology. In his Platonic conversations on Spinoza's philosophy, entitled *God*, Herder intended to free Spinoza's thought from its "geometrical shell," that is, from the Cartesian form in which it was presented (16:406, 432). In Herder's ambitious exegesis of Genesis, the *Oldest Document of the Human Race*, he commented sneeringly on new proofs of the existence of God by Christian Wolff and his school (6:205). Truth is accessible to human beings in direct and immediate evidence through the senses, not in long-winded and complex logical deductions. The human intellect may order and classify experience, but any system of the mind has to be verified by sense-directed experience. Herder's idea of experience may differ from that of other empiricists, but he did rely on experience.

Herder trusted the senses and he also trusted the capability of the human psyche to synthesize individual sensations into a whole. The whole, *das Ganze, Ganzheit, Gasamtheit*, is Herder's prime category. He sees all forces in nature and in history as part of a totality. The human psyche cannot be separated, as contemporary psychology seemed to do, into separate faculties *(Vermögen)* of the mind, but human capabilities, such as cognition and sensation, are interconnected and interdependent. Such a totality of forces, *Kräfte*, is presented in Herder's unpublished fourth *Critical Forest* and in his essay *Of the Cognition and Sensation in the Human Mind*.[13] These forces influence each other, and such is the nature of any organic entity in the universe. The idea of organism is crucial for Herder, for he sees life, in natural and historical terms, in accordance with the model of an organism with its relationship of parts and whole, as opposed to the idea of a mechanical apparatus. This concern is directly transferred into Herder's language: it determines major subject areas and value judgments in his imagery.[14]

All forces strive toward an innate goal, and this dynamism indicates an original order and meaning of living beings. This vitalistic psychology does not imply teleological reasoning on a metaphysical level, but it is based on the idea of *Entelechia* (the energy for realization of the self) so characteristic for Goethe. Herder agrees with much of the eighteenth century that a direct relationship must exist betweeen our organism and the world around us. In epistemological terms, a congruence must occur between our perception and cognition, and the objects perceived and known to us. Herder speaks of an analogy between the world perceived and the human senses (8:170). Without such an analogy, whether a preestablished harmony or not, perception and cognition could not be valid. It might be immaterial whether what we perceive is actually the "real" world. This last point, however, was not Herder's position: he insisted on the reality of the God-given world. Herder has been called a realist in an epistemological sense. This also pertains to language: language determines our view of reality, in a Whorfian sense. Words are not arbitrary names for objects; they represent reality.[15]

Herder's theory of the origin of human language, presented in his *Treatise*,[16] illustrates his position. He openly argues against the theory of a divine origin of human language, as proposed by Johann Peter Süssmilch, but he is equally careful not to be confused with Condillac or Rousseau. He points out that animals have language, and human beings, considered as animals, possess a natural language, *Natursprache*, an expression of various emotions through articulated sounds. Such natural sounds cannot be symbolized adequately by means of writing systems; "ach" and "oh" may be pronounced in opposite ways and mean very different things. Language is originally oral expression. All writing systems are secondary systems, and even late inventions of advanced civilizations. However, mere expression of emotions, such as fear, anger, and joy, is not human language. Human beings differ from animals not in degree, as Herder maintains against Condillac, but in kind. Human language cannot be derived from animal language. Human reason and potential for freedom instead of determination by instincts constitutes a fundamental difference and is a precondition for what Herder in his later life called *Humanität*. The compensation of the human being for its weaker instincts than animals is its *Vernunftmäßigkeit*, its potential for reasonable behavior. The capability that takes human beings beyond instincts and senses, is reflection, *Besonnenheit*. *Besonnenheit* is derived from *sich besinnen*, to think of, to recollect, to remember. The human being remembers, and thus is aware of recurring events and is able to define typical and permanent features. This is part of human nature, hence language is a human trait. A human being cannot be without language; language is only for human beings. Words are means to remember, *Merkwörter* (5:36); they define. The sheep is defined by its bleating; it is the "bleating being," *das Blöckende* (5:36–37). Herder argues against Süssmilch whose treatise contains valid and interesting arguments,[17] that God could not have taught language to human beings, if they had not already had the capability to develop and learn it, and that the language human beings speak must be human in kind. This leads Herder to state a basic belief that he was to reiterate until his *Metacritique* against Kant: there is no reason, *Vernunft*, without language, and there is no human language without reason. The Greek word *logos* indicates the common origin of the idea of word and concept, reason and word, language and cause (5:47). The famous Bible passage comes to mind.

The human being, just as the human race as a whole, learns language through hearing. The sounds of nature were transformed by human beings, and the first languages were more singing than speaking, poetry rather than prose (5:56). They were still a "lexicon of the soul," *Wörterbuch der Seele* (5:56), an emotional response to nature. Thus, the first languages are mythology, an epic poem of actions and speeches of human beings in nature. Herder considers the human being a "thinking *sensorium commune*" (5:61) and thus explains the derivation of words from sensations of other senses and their mixture. Hearing remains the "middle sense" (5:66). It is between the senses of closeness and intensity, touch and taste, and the visual sense, the sense of distance. Early languages exhibit unusual images and concentration, later languages are characterized by reasoning and logical classifications. Herder posits, together with his theory of origin, a typical development of language through history.

The human being is a "creature of language" (5:93). This would not make sense, if human beings were not destined to be social creatures for whom the development of language is as natural as it is necessary (5:112). Living in separate herds and tribes, human beings develop different languages; thus, national languages, *Nationalsprachen*, emerge (5:124). However, Herder still assumes one origin and one original habitat of the human race, and he considers similarities among languages as a guide on the way back to one original language (5:134).

The *Treatise*, although written under some constraints, since it was to be a prize essay for the Berlin Academy, exhibits essential features of Herder's procedure. He first establishes himself as an opponent of contemporary scholarship and currently held views. He does not combat one intellectual theory with another one, but rather reaches back into the psychological and historical sources of the phenomenon. He combines ontogenetic with phylogenetic arguments, and stresses the parallel between the development of the individual human being and the human race. Without reference to our own life-stages, we cannot understand the history of humanity, and vice versa. Pursuing a problem to its origin, Herder formulates natural laws: general statements arising from the nature of the phenomenon. History is determined by such natural laws, all history is natural history, just as nature is historical. Herder's celebrated historical intuition, *Einfühlung*, that initiated a new quality of historical understanding, was based on these assumptions. He studied past ages and foreign civilizations in their own right as necessary stages of a natural development, just like the stages in the development of a fruit.

The individual human being grows up in a linguistic environment which provides a basic interpretation of nature and history. In this sense, language determines thinking. However, just as *Besonnenheit* is a fundamental trait of human language, human beings can reflect on language, hence reflect on reflection and become aware of the nature of their culture. Whereas their emotions and original imagery are tied to their childhood memories, and thus to their mother tongue, human beings should enter into the spirit of other cultures and ages through foreign languages. This was the subject of Herder's first published short essay, *Concerning Diligence in Several Learned Languages* (*Über den Fleiß in mehreren gelehrten Sprachen*) of 1764,[18] and much of his first book *Fragments Concerning Recent German Literature* (*Über die neuere deutsche Literatur. Fragmente*) of 1766–67. Herder considers the intellectual universalism of the Enlightenment as shallow, since it does not take into account the deep cultural and emotional roots of linguistic expression and thus determination of human beings by their family, ethnic entity, *das Volk*, their nation. However, Herder insists on common traits and concerns of humanity, including the ability of human beings to learn other languages and understand other civilizations through them. Such learning and translations are the basis for cultural exchange that enriches each culture. As he points out in the *Fragments*, such borrowing should not be slavish imitation nor idle curiosity, but based on genuine need and interest.

Herder's concerns are typical for an age when Germans thought their national culture was lagging far behind French or English culture. In Herder's own case, these considerations were integrated into his overall view of cultural history. In a section of the *Fragments*, entitled "Of the Life-Stages of a Language" ("Von den Lebensaltern einer Sprache"), he sketches the development of a language from the poetic to the intellectual, or in Herder's term, the philosophical stage. This development parallels the human life-stages from childhood to old age. Like Rousseau, Herder hoped for renewal and rejuvenation of an aged civilization and language. In agreement with Rousseau he considered his age as old, learned, intellectual, "philosophical," and he felt it devoid of originality, poetry, vitality. While Herder's philosophy of history demanded fair and impartial appraisal of each historical period according to its premises, he had a basically negative view of his age, expressing itself in Swiftian satiric irony.[19] However, he wanted to believe in rejuvenation, and his entire work was a contribution toward that goal. Thus it was paramount to point out models for new original poetry. This was the purpose of his seminal collection of *Folk Songs*, later renamed *Voices of the Peoples in Songs* (*Stimmen der Völker in Liedern*). The collection contained translations of poems from diverse cultures and ages, including new poems by Goethe. It followed one principle: to present examples for an original poetic spirit. Herder found the same spirit in the Old Testament, as he pointed out in his *Spirit of Hebrew Poetry* (*Vom Geist der Ebräischen Poesie*) of 1782–83; he discovered it in Shakespeare, in Ossian, and in ancient Greek poetry. Hebrew poetry was a prime example for national poetry. It was poetry voicing the concerns of the entire people, and it was known to the entire nation, thus exhibiting a true patriotic spirit.

Herder felt that in his age, literature in its broader sense was divorced from public and national concerns. While the separation of the private from the public sphere was a social fact, and the poet could hardly be a public figure as in ancient society, Herder never accepted the political system of absolutism which reduced the social role of literature to flattery.[20] The renewal of poetry was tied to a renewal of a public spirit. Only a republican form of government—whatever constitutional form it might take–could give a meaningful role to literature.

Throughout the eighteenth and well into the nineteenth centuries the issue of public opinion and public speaking was on many Germans' minds. Since there were no public parliamentary debates, and the judicial system excluded most opportunities for oral exchange, public speaking was reduced to the pulpit and the theater. The debates on a "national theater" in Germany received added significance because of this potential function as a public forum for important social issues. Lutheran ministers had a hard time observing the fine lines between religious and moral issues on the one hand and social and political questions on the other, in a system where criticism was considered dangerous for the state, and where the wrong type of praise had harsh consequences.[21]

Compared to past ages, such as the heyday of Athenian democracy, the writings of a poet or philosopher could make little difference for society. Therefore, Herder pointed out the interconnections of government and higher culture and demanded a renewal of a national spirit in terms of a public spirit for the entire nation.[22] He tried to set an example in his sermons and in his educational and administrative ideas and measures.[23]

Since so much was wrong in his own time, a writer striving for a renewal, as Herder did, had to clear the way first. In his professional domain of theology and religion, Herder considered intellectual theology an obstruction on the way to true religion, to an understanding of the original word of God. True religion, he felt, is the one truth shared by all human beings. It is beyond church dogma and institutional separations.[24] While he considered himself first and foremost a Christian, his views were ecumenical rather than confined by the rules of any church.

Herder's usual strategy is determined by his understanding of his age. Current opinion was subjected to a polemical critique; this brought about the second part, the introduction to Herder's own position in intellectual terms, or as he said, "in the language of my age."[25] But Herder was never contented with this approach; he repeated his message through images, metaphors, myth, and poetry, either of his creation or quotations from others. Only through such poetic language can the minds and hearts of people be touched directly and lastingly. Herder's aim was to sow seeds, *Samenkörner,* that would grow and bear fruit, just as God's word and revelation came in the form of such suggestive myths and images, or seeds.[26]

The central Herderian image of seeds requires clearing the soil first. Hence the crucial importance of Herder's critiques. They were generally of two kinds: a polemical attack on an antagonistic or inferior adversary or, more importantly, a dialogue with an absent partner. Herder shared the fate of most German writers of his day to live in isolation, in places like Riga, Bückeburg, or even Weimar. Thus the "commerce," the communication with others, took place on paper, in private letters or in published works. Only rarely Herder found a partner like Goethe, during the conceptions of the *Ideas* and *God: Some Conversations,* or Jean Paul Richter, in the last years of his life. Usually, he communicated with absent friends, and in the case of Gotthold Ephraim Lessing, he was so grieved by the latter's untimely death that he pursued a Dialogue of the Dead with him for the rest of his life.[27]

Herder's first published works, the *Fragments* and the *Critical Forests,* were such critical assessments. Herder evaluated the *Letters Concerning the Most Recent German Literature,* a brainchild of Lessing, and continued by Moses Mendelssohn, Thomas Abbt, and Friedrich Nicolai. His first *Critical Forest* deals with a central document of eighteenth-century aesthetics, Lessing's *Laokoon.* Indeed, Lessing was so pleased with Herder's reading of his treatise, critical as it was, that he felt stimulated to write the planned second part of the book, a plan unfortunately never realized.[28] The virtue of Herder's approach was twofold: he surpassed his predecessors, like Lessing and Johann Joachim Winckelmann, in a better understanding of the specific requirements of each of the arts; and he had a superior intuition into the spirit of past ages. He saw what was proper for sculpture and for painting, for music and for writing. He also was able to do better justice to Winckelmann than Lessing, arguing that Winckelmann had spoken as an art critic and Lessing as a literary critic. In his definition of the several arts, Herder based his approach on the human senses: sculpture, for example, is developed out of the human sense of touch. Herder's aesthetic theory is most fully developed in the fourth of the *Critical Forests,* which was not published during his lifetime. It would have underscored Herder's crucial point that the arts are closely associated with human sensation and perception and have to be experienced as sense-related expression.

The same stand, leading art experience away from intellectualization, can be seen in Herder's philological art, his explanation of Homer's and Vergil's language from their time, their culture, their social conditions. Poetry has to be understood from its age and its conditions. While great art is universal and speaks through the ages, a proper understanding has to be historical. Thus it is futile to want to imitate Vergil or Sophocles; classicism of this sort is sterile. A true poet should strive to become for that poet's age what Sophocles or Vergil were for theirs. Great art can be enjoyed by later ages, but it can never be repeated.

This message directed against the academic spirit of his time, imitating Greek and Roman style without penetrating into the spirit of the ancients, informs also Herder's attacks on inferior adversaries in the *Critical Forests*, attacks that he did not enjoy. While Lessing liked to clear the German landscape of inflated mediocrities, and enjoyed a clean kill, Herder was uneasy in this terrain and sometimes stumbled, becoming personal or insulting. Shortly after moving to Weimar, he refrained altogether from such attacks.

Whereas these first writings show an untried youngster from a faraway province measuring his strength against the sharpest mind of Germany, Lessing, Herder's writings of the Bückeburg period (1771–76) were a first attempt to communicate his message. The results were unsatisfactory, at least for Herder, and he presented his ideas in a new form in the later works. *Another Philosophy of History for the Education of Mankind (Auch eine Philosophie der Geschichte zur Bildung der Menschheit)*, the first draft of Herder's philosophy of history, has found some important advocates,[29] but is generally considered inferior to the *Ideas*. Herder won the most acclaim with a little collection of occasional papers by him and Goethe that he considered not important, called *Of German Nature and Art (Von deutscher Art und Kunst)*. Exhibiting a patriotic spirit, so it seems, and due to the collaboration of Herder and Goethe, this little book has had an inordinate reputation among scholars, especially Germanists. For Herder, however, the central work of this period was his *Oldest Document of the Human Race (Älteste Urkunde des Menschengeschlechts)*. This was a commentary on the text of Genesis, trying to prove Herder's theory that the Old Testament is an ancient book of history in poetic form under divine inspiration. The *Oldest Document* does not appeal to sober minds. Robert T. Clark, Herder's most influential biographer in the English language condemned it outright: "In spite of its fructifying influence on theology and Biblical criticism, the *Document* is Herder's poorest work."[30] He echoed much of the contemporary reception, which was hostile enough so that Herder wrote ten years later, while working on the *Ideas*, on 23 August 1784, to his friend Johann Georg Hamann, "I have to speak in the language of our time, in the outward appearance of its favorite concepts, its favorite sciences, otherwise it will get thrown back into my face, like the *Oldest Document*" ("Ich muss in der Sprache der Zeit, in der Hülle ihrer Lieblingsbegriffe, und Lieblingswissenschaften reden, sonst wirft man mir alles, wie die älteste Urkunde, zurück ins Antlitz") (Br. 5:62). This rejection, as well as the value of the *Oldest Document* for Herder, indicates that central issues were at stake. Indeed, the significance of the book for comparative religion and comparative mythology is beyond doubt, although Herder's specific theses may have been proven erroneous. Genesis, for Herder, was the oldest document of early man, the original form of *Geschichte*, that is, story and history in one, divinely inspired, but in human poetic form, moreover the written record of a much earlier oral tradition. He had written this book, he wrote to Hamann in May 1774, for the sake of truth and "the dawn of God" who would, he hoped, bless the book as a "germ and dawn for *the new history and philosophy of humankind*." Religion and revelation of God should again be a "simple story and wisdom," instead of *Kritik* and *Politik*, criticism and politics (Br. 3:84). The *Oldest Document* is meant to be both an instrument and a document for the rejuvenation of humankind through the spirit of religion expressed as a poetic story *(Geschichte)*. Herder always uses the double meaning of the German word *Geschichte*, story and history. This culminates in the central metaphor for creation, dawn, the rise of the sun: "May there be light." The rising sun, a central image of the Enlightenment, takes here a new meaning. It is not simply the appearance of truth, but a metaphor for creation, birth, and the original connection between heaven and earth. It has had a lasting impact on the poetry and literature in the widest sense of the word of Herder's age. Goethe and Jean Paul Richter are prime examples, both admirers of the *Oldest Document*.[31] Herder wanted to clear away the intellectual layers of critical theology to make room for "this poor, despised, and yet so consistent, and noble story" (10:165, *Letters Concerning the Study of Theology*). God could not have revealed the Godhead in the form of a theological treatise, a "moral discourse, lectures, or sermons"; the revelation had to be seeds, *Samenkörner*, sown in different forms at different times (7:242). They had to take a form congruent with the cultural development of the human race, an idea Lessing was to develop in his seminal *Education of Mankind*, making use of Herderian thoughts.[32]

In his exegesis, Herder tries to lead the reader from this philosophical and critical age back to the origins of humanity. He tries to get as close as possible to the original text of the Bible, and progressively breaks away from the familiar translation of Martin Luther to convey the idea of the primitive, yet monumental, style and meaning of the original. The translation of the text gets progressively terser, taking away function words and isolating the main words. Herder's commentary, however, oscillates between two extremes. It sometimes comes close to that ancient Bible language, but in most parts of the *Oldest Document*, it exhibits an aggressive rhetoric. It is an attempt to win over readers presumed to be unconvinced, even hostile and unwilling to accept the author's premises. Thus Herder accumulates rhetorical questions, answers with exclamation marks, and sprinkles the text with imperatives, especially of the "let us . . ." type. The reader's attention is overexerted by too many underlined words and phrases. Most texts of Herder emphasize too many words or phrases, and thus achieve the opposite of the intended result, for they distract rather than focus the reader's attention. Such typical traits of Herder's style are particularly evident in the *Oldest Document* where he is most eager to convince the reader and most fearful he may fail. These traits come in combination with Herder's rendering of ancient poetry, and with attempts to communicate his insights in a poetic language. Clark called the *Oldest Document* "nothing but a very turgid poem,"[33] and he was correct about the poetic qualities of Herder's language, and even about their questionable taste. But the value judgment is completely false. Herder anticipates Romanticism by demonstrating that poetry can only be approached through poetry, and that a sacred text needs an exegesis in an inspired language. In his pursuit of the origins of humanity and language, God's creation that produced both of them at the same time, Herder found the phenomenon of the "hieroglyph." As Egyptian writing had not yet been deciphered, Herder presumed the hieroglyph to be a symbolic image of a whole idea. He theorized that God's instruction to human beings as told in the Bible was a combination of music and image, word and total meaning. The original hieroglyph appeared to him as follows:[34]

I
Light

II
Height of Heaven

III
Depth of Earth

IV
Lights

V
Water
Air   Creatures

VI
Creatures of the Earth

VII
Sabbath

Symbolically, the hieroglyph can be seen as follows:

$$
\begin{array}{ccc}
 & A & \\
H & & E \\
 & I & \\
O & & Y \\
 & W & \\
\end{array}
$$

The vertical relationship of heaven and earth, the contrast of light and darkness, the temporal sequence of the creation of heaven and earth and all creatures, thus space and time, are rounded and bound together in a symbolic image and form. This is not cautious, sober scholarly theory; it is a grand vision, although very stimulating for scholarship.[35] Herder, a good Lutheran, took seriously the beginning of St. John's message, "In the beginning there was the word," and *logos* was indeed word for him. Creation of human beings meant for him the communication of God's spirit through the medium of human language. The first human language, close to God, had to be concentrated, pictorial, symbolic, poetic. God was the teacher of humanity, and thus human history is, as for Lessing, a history of education, a progressive formation, *Bildung*, toward the realization of the human potential, *Humanität*. *Bildung* is progressing through reflection, memory, tradition, and the innate striving for perfectibility, *Vervollkommnung*. The medium of language is crucial for this process. It preserves the history and poetry of human beings, hidden under the later layers of language. Thus, Herder's *Oldest Document* digs into the deep layer of language itself. Through this genetic-historical approach, Herder seeks the original connection of human beings with the Godhead, as well as the original language, the first medium of communication. The reconstruction of an original language, *Ursprache*, appealed to Romanticists and Expressionists, who understood the meaning of this search. Herder was interested in the true nature of communication, of human language, as part of *Humanität*, and like Rousseau, he looked for the fundamental structures beneath the false sophistication of the philosophical age.

The *Oldest Document* was an experiment in form, message, and type of communication. Herder never repeated it in this manner, but its ingredients inform his subsequent *oeuvre:* the search for a true language and communication away from intellectual sophistry, the message of true religion, that is the divine spark of creation in human beings, the way back and forward from abstract prose to living poetry. Herder's writings after his move to Weimar in 1776 carry this message in a calmer and more poised form. He retreats from bitter polemics and employs rhetorical forms that are more urbane and less aggressive to a reader. Still, he tries to sow seeds, and thus he incessantly produced writings in diverse fields, all getting across a central message. In his new, more poised and gentle methods, Herder chose literary forms that stressed communication with the reader without imposing his positions: dialogues, letters, the short essay, and didactic poetry. Short forms are typical for this period, although it also saw the writing of his magnum opus, the *Ideas*. The short forms may be the most revealing for Herder's craft of communication.

Herder occupies a crucial position in the development of the German prose essay. As with Montaigne or Francis Bacon, Herder's form of the essay grew out of opposition to scholasticism. Herder opposed Wolffian *Schulphilosophie*, the academic form of writing, and systematic orthodox theology. If historical analysis rather than logical deduction provided the answer, the author strove to be stimulating rather than exhaustive. Like Winckelmann and Lessing, Herder rejected the label of erudite scholar, the *Gelehrte*. He wrote for a general educated audience on socially relevant topics. He personified the shift from *Gelehrsamkeit*, erudition, to *Bildung*, the self-cultivation of the self-responsible human being. Herder, like Lessing, typifies the period before the Humboldtian university when advances took place outside the strictly academic world. Paradoxically, this attitude was crucial in the inception of the new university of Humboldt, the university of *Bildung*.

Whereas Herder made no concessions to university conventions, although he came close to becoming a professor of theology in Göttingen, he stubbornly persisted in wanting to win prize essays from German academies. After he won his first prize in Berlin with his treatise on the origin of language, he kept on entering competitions. This is surprising, since in many cases, · Herder's answers to the question asked were evidently ironic, proving the question to be insufficient or even absurd, in a Socratic manner.[36] Yet he always hoped for the prize. Although such prizes brought money and recognition, Herder knew that he did not really deserve the prizes, of which he received a good number; yet he wanted to prove himself through this competition. This ambivalent attitude was motivated not only by his thirst for recognition, but also by his search for a public forum. The topics of the prize essays are revealing, insofar as they show Herder's social concerns. He wrote *On the Effects of Poetry on the Customs and Morals of the Nations in Ancient and Modern Times* (*Über die Wirkung der Dichtkunst auf die Sitten der Völker in alten und neuen Zeiten*), 1778; *On the Influence of the Humanities on the Higher Sciences* (*Über den Einfluß der schönen in die höheren Wissenschaften*), 1779; *On the Influence of Government on the Sciences and of the Sciences on Government* (*Über den Einfluß der Regierung auf die Wissenschaften und der Wissenschaften auf die Regierung*), 1780. *Of the Cognition and Sensation of the*

Human Mind (Vom Erkennen und Empfinden der menschlichen Seele), one of Herder's most important works, grew out of prize essays with different versions between 1774 and 1778. The early essay of 1774, *How the German Bishops Became an Estate of the Realm (Wie die deutschen Bischöfe Landstände wurden)*, was also intended to be a prize essay. Essays of this kind were to voice public concerns. Herder was most concerned with the interaction of culture and government. He thought about the public role of the arts and sciences, beginning with his essay of 1765, *Do We Still Have the Public and Fatherland of the Ancients?* Later, he came to reflect about the proper function of government in supporting arts and sciences. A personal angle is evident in his stubborn attempts to win the prize from the Academy of his native Prussia, and to be elected its member (he was elected in 1787). Herder's fruitless wooing of his fatherland is another example of the negative role that the glorified King Friedrich II of Prussia played for the development of German culture and literature.

Although Herder lived in Sachsen-Weimar, the state that supposedly cared most for the arts and sciences, he could not fail to notice the narrow limits imposed by financial straits, as well as by the arbitrariness of the duke and the provincialism of people in responsible positions. Long before the French Revolution, Herder was calling for a spirit of independent thinking and research, and for wider perspectives on German culture. Karl Friedrich, Margrave of Baden, entrusted Herder in 1787 with the plan for a "German Academy." Herder's draft is entitled *Plan for the First Patriotic Institute for the Communal Spirit of Germany (Idee zum ersten patriotischen Institut für den Allgemeingeist Deutschlands)*. Duke Carl August of Sachsen-Weimar did not need much time to realize that the Academy would cost too much money, and later observers have called the plan "impractical."[37] But Herder had an unwelcome choice, typical for his position and that of other forward-looking reformers of the day: he could be "realistic" and propose a plan that would be meaningless, or he could propose what he thought ought to be done, knowing it was utopian. Herder struggled with the pettiness of his environment, like Gulliver in Lilliput.

Herder's essays are contributions to the establishment of a German "Republic," envisioned as a culturally unified and politically liberalized new Germany, allowing the arts and sciences a public function, and thus giving room for public opinion and public debate. Every time he spoke out on the idea of government, he ran into barriers. With the intensification of censorship after the French Revolution and in consideration of his position as one of the highest officials of the state of Sachsen-Weimar, he felt less and less at liberty to publish his real ideas. "The best parts of my writings are those that I leave out," he said to Jean Paul Richter in 1796.[38] But he had to revise parts of the *Ideas* and withdrew his open and largely favorable commentary on the French Revolution, the first draft of his *Letters for the Advancement of Humanity.*[39] Herder's inner and outer conflict with censorship is a telling example of the constraints on free speech in the tiny German states, even at their best. Herder's essays are a document in the struggle for an establishment of public opinion in Germany.

Not all of Herder's essays are directly concerned with social issues. He was a pioneer of the biographical essay which in his case grew out of commemorative eulogies, like those on Winckelmann and Lessing. Herder was especially well suited to fulfill the demands of the biographical essay, which is to grasp and to present both the uniqueness and the typicality of the personality as well as that person's relationship with the geographical and historical environment. Other essays, particularly those collected in the *Scattered Leaves (Zertreute Blätter)*, deal with religious and literary questions. Palingenesis, or reincarnation, is a prominent topic, and Herder delighted in presenting new literary treasures or open perspectives on unknown civilizations, for example India.[40]

Herder's essays are written for an audience that he presumed sympathetic and receptive. They represent the growing cultural and social awareness of the educated middle class in Germany with its liberal spirit and concern for higher values and new ideas. The essays are concise, urbane, usually friendly, gentle even in their criticism, didactic in a mature way, stimulating, suggestive. Serious polemics did not enter Herder's writings again until the last years of his life. During the better part of his Weimar years, he could feel as a representative of the progressive educated class in Germany, an aspect of Herder's work frequently overlooked by scholars.

Parallel to the use of the essay runs the development of the letter as communicative tool. Herder's early "Provincial Letters" *To Preachers* of 1774 were protracted polemics against Enlightenment theology, especially against Johann Joachim Spalding (1714–1804). They belonged to the form of the "open letter" and had their literary model in Pascal's polemics, which provided the title. Open letters, challenging polemical statements destined for one person, but made public, were a favorite medium of the age of letter writing. Hamann, Herder's friend and mentor, never tired of them. The most notorious open letter was probably by Johann Kaspar Lavater (1741–1801), the theologian from Zurich, to Moses Mendelssohn demanding reasons why he would not convert from Judaism to Christianity.

The Letters Concerning the Study of Theology of 1780 also have a personal tone, but represent a different genre. They are didactic, a means to teach. Herder takes the role of the minister, the *Seelsorger* who gives advice to a young student of theology. It is gentle chiding and advice by an older friend to a young man feeling his way.[41] These letters do not pretend to be a systematic introduction to theology. Instead, they are "familiar letters" in the tradition of Cicero, informative but informal. They are close to sermons or speeches. They express both the personality of the letter writer and his views on the subject. Herder can never write without underlined words, rhetorical questions, and exclamation marks. But the reader is not overwhelmed. One is gently persuaded; one is told to put aside theology and turn to the Bible. One should be immersed in the text and use geographical, historical, anthropological, and psychological criteria to understand the Bible as a human text, although it deals with God's communication with the human race. Herder does not talk to a specialist about fine points; he stays with central issues and on a common-sense ground. He uses his personal approach to convince the mind and touch the heart. Herder's total commitment as a minister in its largest sense transpires through the lines and offers a model for the young man to emulate.

Herder's *Letters for the Advancement of Humanity (Briefe zu Beförderung der Humanität)*, 1793–97, offer a different approach. They were planned as a correspondence, a *Briefwechsel*, of several friends about progress and regress of humanity in several ages, especially the present (17:5), and they can be regarded as a replacement for the missing fifth part of the *Ideas*. They represent Herder's response to the American War of Independence and the French Revolution. Herder thought of introducing different correspondents so that he would not "have been responsible for any of the opinions voiced."[42] The letter becomes a form of caution and evasion of censorship at a time of upheaval. The loose form of the letter also allows free discussion of ideas. It avoids the appearance of dogmatism and permits changing the subject at will. Thus, variety and flexibility are foremost characteristics of this form. In the published version of the *Letters*, a tone of caution and uncertainty prevails. Herder hides the true meaning as much as he reveals it. One example suffices: In letter 11 of the first part, one of Herder's favorite topics is addressed: Why do modern poets produce private works and not works of public relevance, as in ancient Israel or Greece? The writer of letter 11 wishes that modern poets could bring back old times in this regard (17:63–65). Letter 12 answers with an antithesis by another correspondent: It might not be beneficial, or it may be *schädlich* (harmful, 17:67) for poets to take too strong a part in political matters. Poetry should avoid political factionalism, but express the *Geist der Zeit*, as a voice of the time (*Stimme der Zeit*) in a more general way (17:67). Thus it would be a voice of humanity in a noncontroversial way (17:65–68). Several contemporary poets are mentioned: Gottfried August Bürger, Friedrich von Stolberg, Friedrich Gottlieb Klopstock. Herder does not mention that Klopstock had written an ode in praise of the French Revolution and had been made honorary citizen of France, although he later turned away from the revolution. Instead, Herder quotes an ode by Stolberg to the Crown Prince of Denmark, expressing the hope for a just and liberal ruler (17:69–71). Letter 11 seems much more convincing than letter 12. Letter 12 voices views later expressed by Schiller in his letters *On the Aesthetic Education of Man* with which Herder strongly disagreed and which contributed to causing the deep rift between Goethe and Herder.[43] Indeed, Goethe's name is conspicuously absent from Herder's *Letters,* yet he was the most talented and prominent German writer of the day. But, in Herder's view, he failed to take a public stand for the advancement of humanity. Herder avoided polemics by not mentioning the names of Goethe and Schiller, but then his picture could not be sincere. Instead, it was full of hidden meaning and reproaches. A reading of the *Letters* provides an example for an age when only part of the truth could be said in public. The form of the letter reveals itself as half private and half public, a seemingly personal communication between friends at a time when it is dangerous or impossible to discuss public matters in public.

The form of the *Briefwechsel* is close to that of the dialogue, another favorite form of teaching and communication toward the end of the eighteenth century. Herder always saw himself in a dialogue situation, though he used the literary form of dialogue sparingly. He was not a dramatist, like Lessing, nor a novelist, like Jean Paul Richter who imagined different personalities arguing with each other. Herder wrote lyric poetry, and his dialogue partners tend to speak with one voice. They seem to agree on fundamental points; one partner enlightens the other only in a particular area. Thus Herder's dialogues are friendly conversations devoid of tensions and real conflicts. This is the case for the dialogue partners of *The Spirit of Hebrew Poetry* or the friends arguing about metempsychosis in the *Scattered Leaves.* It is particularly true for Herder's major work in the dialogue genre, *God: Some Conversations (Gott),* 1787. Herder explores an extremely touchy subject, the philosophy of Spinoza and his idea of the Godhead. The celebrated controversy on Spinoza in the 1780s had been touched off by a remark Lessing made shortly before his death, that he was at heart a "Spinozist." Spinoza was still rejected by Jews and Christians alike as an atheist and dangerous heretic. When Friedrich Heinrich Jacobi, Goethe's and Herder's personal friend, although a staunch anti-Spinozist, reported these startling remarks to his friends, including Moses Mendelssohn, Lessing's friend, they caused a stir, and Mendelssohn took it upon himself to purify Lessing from such a dark suspicion. However, Goethe and Herder were delighted. The controversy went on until Mendelssohn's death in 1786, and introduced Spinoza to the generation of the early Romanticists: Friedrich Schlegel, Friedrich Schleiermacher, Schelling, Hegel, and

Hölderlin. Herder's orthodoxy had always been questioned, and this reputation had cost him the chair of theology at the University of Göttingen in 1775. Now he was more secure, but it was still daring for a prominent church official to take sides in this controversy on pantheism and atheism.

Herder does not use the dialogue form to sharpen the debate and fuel the polemics. On the contrary, he is careful to lift Spinoza out of the realm of catchwords for censorship. In doing so, he uses what he perceived to be a Platonic dialogue. Whereas Socrates took on many forms in the eighteenth century in Germany,[44] Plato was seen in his own light. He seemed to be a visionary for a "second life" after this one, in terms of immortality of the soul and of utopia. A Platonic view was an idealistic, politically progressive, and religious view of things. Mendelssohn had given an illustrious example in his *Phädon* (1767), dialogues on the immortality of the soul. Franz Hemsterhuis (1721–90) was considered an embodiment of Platonic life and thought. Herder translated Hemsterhuis from French into German. Platonic texts of the age generally did not use the figure of Scorates, but if they did, he did not have the stinging wit and irony of Plato's Socrates.

Herder's Theophron in *God* tries to convince his friend Philolaus that his anti-Spinozist bias is unfounded. He should not trust the authority of Pierre Bayle's article on Spinoza. The main point is still to defend Spinoza against the accusation of atheism. Goethe summed up the new position when he called Spinoza in a letter to Jacobi "theissimum."[45] Herder and Herder's Theophron valiantly try to justify the concept of *Deus sive Natura* (God equaling Nature). The Godhead is not a person but a power that penetrates all creation. It is not a "soul of the world" (*Weltseele*) either.[46] Theophron has to fight two battles at once, as it turns out. Besides demonstrating the absurdity of the concept of an extramundane God, he also fights against the Kantian position that God's existence cannot be proven (16:419). Evidence exists, Theophron argues, but not of a logical kind. His convincing argument is the recitation of a poem at the end of the first conversation. The mind is brought to a point where it can be convinced by the heart.

Herder's purpose was not to do justice to Spinoza. Originally, he had planned a comparison of the philosophy of Leibniz, Shaftesbury, and Spinoza. Herder's Theophron is most concerned with freeing Spinoza's thoughts from their geometrical form, translating them from their scholarly Latin into generally accessible language. Herder considers himself a mediator, lifting from Spinoza universal truths that would be relevant for his time. Thus the interlocutors compare Spinoza to Leibniz and Shaftesbury, they argue about Jacobi's report on his conversation with

Lessing, and they finally arrive, in the fifth and last conversation, at their own definition of the Godhead. In this conversation, they are joined by the woman Theano who keeps them from losing the ground under their feet. Theano insists that philosophical language should not contradict the common usage of language nor common sense in general. The proper use of words is, as always with Herder, a prime consideration.

The partners arrive at a definition of the Godhead as the highest being (16:536), and this being *(Daseyn)* is understood in a verbal, dynamic sense. Herder likes to use infinitives as verbal nouns, expressing *energeia*, potential activity, the essence of force. The Godhead as the highest *Daseyn* involves the highest degree of necessity, *Nothwendigkeit* (16:541). Each part of the creation has its degree of inner necessity, presenting a universe of degrees of order and harmony. Arbitrariness, *Willkür*, would be at the lowest level, denoting inconsequential contingency and a chance existence. Necessity is thus the degree of divine force within the creation. "God is *before everything, and everything exists within Him;* the entire world an expression, an appearance of His ever-living, ever-working forces" ("Er ist *vor Allem und es besteht Alles in ihm;* die ganze Welt ein Ausdruck, eine Erscheinung seiner ewig-lebenden ewig-wirkenden Kräfte," 16:542). This is close to Lessing's *hen kai pan* or *Ein und Alles*, One and All, although not quite the same. The Godhead is *vor allem* (before everything), and thus not only *pantokrator, All-Erhalter* (All-Preserver, 20:153), but foremost creator who never ceases to be part of the creation and without whose living forces the creation could not sustain itself. The universe is not self-generating.

A crucial trait of creation is its striving toward *Vervollkommnung*, perfection, which is the realization of one's potential, so that each individual may reach an "in und für sich vollendete" existence (16:550–51). This is the goal of *Bildung*, leading to the realization of one's innate potential, one's entelechy. All of Herder's writings are examples for such *Bildung*. They do not simply talk about a process of formation, they make the reader undergo the process. Scholarship has mostly attributed the dominant verbal elements in Herder's language to his belonging to the *Sturm und Drang* generation.[47] But just as *Kraft* (force) remained a central category in Herder's thinking, the verbal elements did not disappear in his later writings. All of his writings show a process of thinking and clarification. Herder wants to draw the reader into this process, intellectually and emotionally. Herder was always aware that he was far from the goal; hence he appropriately labeled his works as contributions to . . . or ideas on. . . . This is conspicuously the case with his central work, *Ideas for a Philosophy of the History of Mankind*. He considered the work a preliminary collection of thoughts on the subject, a first approach, to be continued by subsequent philosophers. If the considered results of many years of thinking were designated as merely introductory, Herder must have regarded his *oeuvre* as a first step.

This feeling of insufficiency was due to a combination of factors. Herder's real subject, the philosophy of the history of humankind, was too large for any person to master in a period of rapid expansion of knowledge. Herder tried to incorporate ethnological research, the latest discoveries in the sciences, and documents of all kinds. He was forced into his universalist approach by his premise that only one truth existed, and that the divine forces were the same working in nature and history. He developed the laws of historical progression from the laws of nature. Human civilization showed the same cycles of growth, decay, and rebirth as any organism. Herder's philosophy of history replaces the linear progression favored in the earlier Enlightenment by cyclical movements he sometimes called "revolutions," adhering to the older meaning of the word—the movements of planets around the sun or similar revolving motions.[48] This organic model with its evolutions and cycles shows a tendency toward *Vervollkommnung*, self-realization, evident in the life of individuals. This may or may not be postulated for humanity as a whole or for the universe; the divine presence guarantees a positive direction.

Herder could scarcely hope to do justice to such a vast subject; he might have been more comfortable writing a gigantic didactic poem than his many diverse essays, letters, dialogues, treatises. There is a *poète manqué* in Herder. He always strove to communicate what a poet would offer: vistas, outlooks *(Aussichten, Ausblicke)* on the universe, on humanity, on creation, on the human condition in metaphysical terms. Lessing, at the beginning of the *Education of Mankind,* had pictured the author as a wanderer on the top of a hill who can see a little further than others and communicates what he sees. Herder is such a mediator between God and humanity. He has difficulties in communicating what he sees. Not so much because of the nature of his findings. He is not a mystic with extreme visions. He is not even an irrationalist, although he does not believe in the relevance of logical operations of the human mind. He believes in sense-directed experience. Knowledge occurs, he insists until his latest writings, through *Innewerden* (21:44), the inward absorption of perception. Our sensations are transformed into human knowledge through language; the synthesizing of all human forces, such as perception, volition, cognition, results in a human image of the world. The world is seen in analogy to the human being and perception, Herder insists in *Of the Cognition and Sensation of the Human Mind;* there is human truth in this analogy, and no other truth is accessible to us (8:70).

If cognition is to occur through written communication, it has to repeat the process of cognition in general. Verbal communication has to enter through the senses. Philosophical or scientific discourse that presents only the pure concept, *die reine Idee,* and thus abstracts from sensual and emotional connotations, does not produce truth, because it does not relate to reality. Reason, *Vernunft,* for Herder is derived from *vernehmen,* to perceive, hear, learn, understand. The noun *Vernunft* is not divorced from the verb, for it expresses the process of perceiving, learning, understanding. Whoever is *vernünftig* has to be open to new experience and thereby ready to abandon old ideas and systems for new insights. For Herder, an intellectual system, even if it called itself progressive, could be as closed-minded as any fanatical orthodoxy. Herder distrusted any dogma, any *Lehrmeinung,* that considered itself final and authoritative. A dogma is a human opinion about things we do not know very well and often is contrary to the universal truth that Herder called religion (20:135).

If the subject at hand and the nature of communication in an unpoetic and intellectual age presented such problems, Herder also felt impeded by the political and social conditions of his age. His thinking in processes, his didactic approach to make his audience think for itself already ran counter to authoritarian orthodoxy, both of a theological and political kind, that wanted to communicate edicts rather than ideas. Herder saw himself as a voice of public opinion; in his sermons, he dwelt on fundamental truths in a natural, simple, and common-sense way, and he used the rare occasions when the duke Carl August was present to communicate some open and bitter social points on the duties of a prince.[49] Reports concur in the assessment that Herder's sermons were effective, clear, and presented in a melodious voice that harmonized the content with the music of the language.[50]

For most of his commentary on his age, Herder was, however, restricted to written communication. He still had to address his largely anonymous audience in such a way that it could understand the message and be enlightened by it, without being repelled by too esoteric a language or too radical views. While in some of the writings of the Bückeburg period Herder seems to speak to a small circle of friends, presuming the rest of the world to be hostile, just like Pietists, he could consider himself later much more as a representative of the emerging progressive middle class. He pronounced their ideals: *Bildung,* peaceful reform, constitutional government, freedom for public opinion, reform of education, liberal church institutions. After the French Revolution, a crisis occurred that has yet to be adequately assessed. Freedom in the German states became more restricted than before; the open-minded, liberal spirit fell victim to new dogmatisms on the left and the right. For Herder, Kantian philosophy as received by the young generation represented such a dangerous dogmatism. The aftereffects of the revolution dashed Herder's hopes for the one change he had most assiduously worked for all his life: he had hoped to make art, above all poetry, meaningful again. A renewal of culture, for Herder, meant that the arts would again be the voice of the nation, speaking for the public and being perceived as its expression. During the age of absolutism, the arts had sunk into meaningless flattery of rulers. A true renewal of culture can only come from the people. The German word *Volk* that Herder liked to use, unfortunately has two meanings: it denotes the national unit, but also the social unit of the lower class. Herder considered that the true spirit of the nation lived on in the lower classes which in his day were rural. Therefore he was justified in believing *das Volk* to be the core of the nation. This *Volk*, however, was poor, without rights, and uneducated. It was unable to effect cultural or political change. Thus, although Herder collected its folksongs, he addressed *das Volk* only indirectly. Directly, he spoke to the middle class. This middle class should orient itself not toward the decadent aristocracy, but toward the healthier *Volk*.

Herder's call for a new national culture, powerfully echoed by Romanticism in the early nineteenth century, but in a very different spirit, is connected with his call for true religion, for the public significance of the arts, for freedom of expression and debate on public issues. Public opinion was just emerging in Germany, and neither governments nor the advocates of freedom were sure about the limits of freedom.[51] Herder was unsure about the appropriate response to the events after 1789. He reacted aggressively against Kant and Kantianism, he was very cautious in his political statements in public, and although he deplored Goethe's and Schiller's concept of *Klassik*, he publicly ignored it while stating his opposite position. Schiller and Goethe according to Herder, prevented a truly national culture instead of advancing it. The verdict on Herder's condemnation of *Klassik* by literary historians has been almost unanimous: Herder was wrong, and Goethe and Schiller introduced a truly national literature. But this may be questioned.[52] Yet Herder represents a type of a writer who has a difficult time defining his public role. Is he part of public opinion, and thus a voice of opposition? Or does he represent authority, and has to be careful how his words may be received by a trusting audience? While this dilemma is present for every writer and politician, it presented itself for Herder's generation as a new and problematical experience.

Herder's insistence on the whole, *Ganzheit*, universality, was not only a reaction against the fragmentation of Germany into tiny states and different social classes, but also a reaction against the prospects of specialization. Specialization, the isolation of mind, heart, and hands from each other, would dehumanize humanity. The heroic universalism of Leibniz, Herder, Goethe, and Hegel was an attempt to counteract this fragmentation and preserve the whole. Thus, for Herder, his age was not the climax of times, as the earlier Enlightenment had thought, but an age of crisis, as he stated most eloquently in *Another Philosophy*. A new direction, a renewal and rejuvenation was urgently needed, both for the nation and humanity as a whole. Herder's writings, in the last analysis, were a means to effect historical change.

In his *Diary of a Voyage*, written after his trip from Riga to Nantes in 1769, Herder still entertained grandiose projects. His image of himself was clear: he wanted to be a new Luther, a reformer ushering in a new age.[53] He wanted to become a major moral force for humanity, with religion as the basis for human affairs, and through the power of his word he wanted to change history. Luther had translated the Bible, God's word, into the language of his people, creating a common German culture by doing it. This is what Herder had in mind; he even thought of a new translation of the Bible, although he never carried out that project.

Such an image of himself may seem inflated; but Herder stands at the threshold of a new age of German culture, and his influence was pervasive, if sometimes unacknowledged. Many disciplines claim him as a precursor. However, while Herder emphasized that specialized studies had to be carried out in their own right, he insisted on a universalist framework. Any scholarly or scientific pursuit receives its justification from this framework and its ultimate purpose, which is to contribute to the advancement of humanity. In an overly specialized age, lost in subtleties and abstractions, Herder wanted to reopen a perspective on the simple truths and on primitive poetry and history as the foundation of the human spirit and its connection with the divine forces of the universe.

There is a lesson in history: whatever is gained in sophistication is lost in original insight. While the advances of the philosophical age should not be exchanged for a new barbarism, the one-sided intellectualism had to be balanced by emotional forces as a way out of the crisis of the age. The search of the origin of humanity and its primitive roots yields a perspective into the future. Humanity speaks with many voices, it is divided and even fragmented; but it was one originally, and it spoke one language, so one day, it may be reunited.

Herder was not a philosopher in the narrower sense of the word, much less an academic philosopher. It would be wrong, however, to disqualify him simply as a *Gefühlsphilosoph* (philosopher of emotion). He insisted on emotion as an essential ingredient of human communication, but his central term was *Vernunft* (Reason). Language was in the center of his thinking and writing. He was a figure standing at the crossroads of cultural history, very modern yet traditional. He was a fundamental critic of eighteenth-century intellectualism and materialism. His writings were calls to action, not of a political, but of a more subtle kind. He wanted to change history by influencing people's minds and hearts. He became a role model for philosophers like Schopenhauer, Hegel, Nietzsche, possibly Marx. Herder followed the model of Rousseau rather than that of Kant.

His achievements fell far short of his dreams and ambitions, but these were translated into the unfinished nature of his work which may have been an incentive for his successors, notably Hegel. Herder's own melodious and emotional voice, the voice of the eighteenth century, was soon drowned out by the more strident tones of the nineteenth century. Herder's name ceased to be mentioned. But he may well have achieved what he set out to do: sow seeds that will grow and bear fruit. It would be productive in Herder's own spirit to become aware of the roots of our past and pay more attention to this complex figure, his language, and his message.

Notes

1. The Volksverlag, Weimar, is offering an edition of selected works in five volumes, ed. Wilhelm Dobbek, first published in 1957. No new edition has appeared in West Germany after 1945, although some individual works are available, especially from the Reclam Verlag, Stuttgart. Compared with any other major German writer, this can only be called utmost neglect.

2. Cf. Gottfried Günther, Albina A. Volgina, Siegfried Seifert, Herder-Bibliographie (Berlin/Weimar: Aufbau Verlag, 1978), pp. 199–204; the majority of items are from the earlier nineteenth century. Since most of the recent translations are doctoral dissertations, they indicate some academic interest.

3. Goethe to Eckermann, 9 November 1824. Goethe felt that times had progressed beyond Herder, thanks in part to Goethe's own work. Herder would have objected to such a linear view of progress.

4. Friedrich Schlegel set the example by praising Lessing and being silent on Herder. Even the last of the Romanticists, Heinrich Heine, mentioned Herder only in one short sentence, but was eloquent and specific on Lessing and Goethe.

5. This is evident in Herbert Lindner, Das Problem des Spinozismus im Schaffen Goethes und Herders (Weimar: Arion, 1960). A recent comprehensive overview of new trends is provided by Herder-Kolloquium 1978, ed. Walter Dietze (Weimar: Hermann Böhlau, 1980).

6. One outcome of several Herder sessions in the United States is Johann Gottfried Herder: Innovator through the Ages, ed. Wulf Koepke, Modern German Studies, vol. 10 (Bonn: Bouvier, 1982).

7. Very active societies and yearbooks are devoted to these writers and philosophers, but not to Herder.

8. Quotations are from the only standard edition, Sämtliche Werke, 33 vols., ed. Bernhard Suphan (Berlin: Weidmann'sche Buchhandlung, 1877–1913), with volume and page numbers. The letters are quoted from the new edition Briefe. Gesamtausgabe 1763–1803, edited by a team directed by Karl-Heinz Hahn (Weimar: Hermann Böhlau, 1977–), designated "Br." with volume and page numbers. Translations are mine.

9. Jean Paul Richter, Vorschule der Ästhetik, Werke, ed. Norbert Miller (Munich: Carl Hanser, 1963), pp. 99, 451–56.

10. Rudolf Haym, Herder. Nach seinem Leben und seinen Werken, reprint (Berlin: Aufbau-Verlag, 1958), 1:100; 2:374–405.

11. Kant's central statement may be that he attributed to Herder "not indeed a logical accuracy in the definition of the concepts or a careful differentiation and consistency in his principles, but a large view not staying long (with details), a sagacity in finding analogies and using them with a daring imagination, connected with a skill to make his subject that he still keeps in a shadowy distance, attractive through emotions and sensations" ("nicht etwa eine logische Pünktlichkeit in Bestimmung der Begriffe oder sorgfältige Unterscheidung und Bewährung der Grundsätze, sondern ein sich nicht lange verweilender vielumfassende Blick, eine in Auffindungen von Analogien fertige Sagazität, im Gebrauche derselben aber kühne Einbildungskraft, verbunden mit der Geschicklichkeit, für seinen immer in dunkeler Ferne gehaltenen Gegenstand durch Gefühle und Empfindungen einzunehmen.") *Kants Werke. Akademie-Textausgabe*, reprint (Berlin: Walter de Gruyter, 1968), 8:45. What Herder states as laws of human history, Kant affirms, "übersteigt offenbar alle menschliche Vernunft" ("evidently transcends all human reason," 8:55). Herder and Kant had different concepts of *Vernunft* and of epistemology.

12. Cf. Walter Moser, "Herder's System of Metaphors in the *Ideen*," *Johann Gottfried Herder: Innovator through the Ages*, pp. 102–24; Michael M. Morton, "Herder and the Possibility of Literature: Rationalism and Poetry in Eighteenth-Century Germany," op.cit., pp. 41–63.

13. Robert T. Clark, *Herder: His Life and Thought* (Berkeley and Los Angeles: University of California Press, 1955), defines this as "Vitalistic Psychology" (pp. 218–28). It may be appropriate to reexamine the vitalistic interpretation of Herder's concept of *Kraft* and his idea of the organism in view of recent concepts.

14. Cf. Moser, "Herder's System of Metaphors in the *Ideen*," and Edgar B. Schick, *Metaphorical Organicism in Herder's Early Works* (The Hague: Mouton, 1971).

15. James W. Marchand, "Herder: Precursor of Humboldt, Whorf, and Modern Language Philosophy," *Johann Gottfried Herder: Innovator through the Ages*, pp. 20–34, and Werner de Boor, *Herders Erkenntnislehre in ihrer Bedeutung für seinen religiösen Realismus* (Gütersloh: Bertelsmann, 1929).

16. On the abundant literature on this subject, cf. *Herder-Bibliographie*, pp. 443–49 and 513–15; cf. also Haym, *Herder*, 1:429–39.

17. Bruce Kieffer, "Herder's Treatment of Süssmilch's Theory of the Origin of Language in the *Abhandlung über den Ursprung der Sprache*: A Re-evaluation," *Germanic Review* 53 (1978): 96–105.

18. Cf. Michael M. Morton, *Herder's "Über den Fleiss in mehreren gelehrten Sprachen,"* (Diss. University of Virginia, 1982).

19. Herder's nickname in the Strassburg circle was "Swift," and Goethe's account in *Poetry and Truth* stresses this point, although attributing it entirely to personal motifs.

20. Some examples among many: 2:364; 8:418; 9:369.

21. A telling and realistic example provides the point of departure for Friedrich Nicolai's very popular novel *Leben und Meinungen des Herrn Magisters Sebaldus Nothanker* (1773–76): Nothanker had preached a sermon on the virtue of dying for one's fatherland!

22. Although Herder's ideas on nation and *das Volk* spawned the nationalistic movements in Eastern Europe and were used to justify German nationalism, even the Nazi movement, he evidently had different things in mind, and his works had to be used very selectively for such political purposes, disregarding the real thrust of his thought.

23. Cf. Haym, *Herder*, 2:374–411. The tone was already set by Herder's early speech in Riga, "Do We Still Have the Public and Fatherland of the Ancients?" ("Haben wir noch das Publikum und Vaterland der Alten?"), 1765.

24. "Dogmas separate and embitter; religion unites; for in the hearts of all people it is only One" ("Lehrmeinungen trennen und erbittern; Religion vereinet: denn in aller Menschen Herzen ist sie nur Eine") 20:125.

25. Br. 5:62; to Hamann, 23 August 1784.

26. 7:242 (*An Prediger*) is one of many examples.

27. Cf. my article, "Herders Totengespräch mit Lessing," in *Aufnahme—Weitergabe: Literarische Impulse um Lessing und Goethe*, ed. J. McCarthy and A. Kipa (Hamburg: H. Buske Verlag, 1982), pp. 125–42.

28. *Johann Gottfried Herder im Spiegel seiner Zeitgenossen. Briefe und Selbstzeugnisse,* ed. Lutz Richter (Göttingen: Vandenhoeck & Ruprecht, 1978), p. 61.

29. Notably Friedrich Meinecke, *Die Entstehung des Historismus. Werke* (Munich: R. Oldenbourg, 1963), 3:386–410, especially p. 408. Meinecke defines the earlier work as the highest achievement, the later as the most influential (431).

30. Clark, *Herder,* p. 164. The influence of Clark in the English-speaking world is inordinate.

31. On Jean Paul, cf. my *Erfolglosigkeit. Zum Frühwerk Jean Pauls* (Munich: W. Fink, 1977), pp. 236–42; cf. also Goethe's letter to Gottlob Friedrich Ernst Schönborn, 8 June 1774, *Goethes Werke,* Weimarer Ausgabe, Section 4, 2:173.

32. Clark, *Herder,* p. 286, links it specifically to *Another Philosophy.*

33. Ibid., p. 167.

34. 6:292; Clark, *Herder,* p. 166.

35. Ulrich Faust, *Mythologien und Religionen des Ostens bei Johann Gottfried Herder* (Münster: Aschendorff, 1977); Thomas Willi, *Herders Beitrag zum Verstehen des Alten Testaments* (Tübingen: J. C. B. Mohr–Paul Siebeck, 1971).

36. Clark, *Herder,* pp. 131–32; such ironies were not always understood, sometimes not even by Hamann.

37. Ibid., p. 353.

38. Jean Paul Friedrich Richter, *Briefe,* ed. E. Berend (Munich: Georg Müller, 1922), 2:206.

39. Cf. Br. 5:115, 10 March 1785, to Karl Ludwig von Knebel; and Br. 5:121, to Hamann, 23 April 1785. On Goethe's advice, Herder changed the section on government. On the *Letters,* cf. the first collection in its original form, 18:305–29, and the *Schlußbericht,* 18:518–37.

40. For Herder's crucial role in the discovery of Indian culture, cf. A. Leslie Willson, *A Mythical Image: The Ideal of India in German Romanticism* (Durham, N.C.: Duke University Press, 1964).

41. The addressee was Johann Georg Müller, a Swiss student of theology and frequent guest at Herder's home. Müller became the editor of the first edition of Herder's complete works.

42. Cf. Richard Critchfield, "Revolution and the Creative Arts: Toward a Reappraisal of Herder's Defense of the French Revolution," *Johann Gottfried Herder: Innovator through the Ages,* pp. 190–206.

43. Cf. Goethe's letter to Schiller of 26 October 1794, in praise of the *Aesthetic Education,* where he mentions Herder's dislike; *Goethes Werke,* Weimarer Ausgabe, Section 4, 10:202–3 (Weimar: Hermann Böhlau, 1892).

44. Benno Böhm, *Sokrates im 18. Jahrhundert. Studien zum Werdegange des modernen Persönlichkeitsbewußtseins* reprint (Neumünster, 1968).

45. *Goethes Werke,* Section 4, 7:62; letter dated 9 June 1785.

46. Cf. my article, "Truth and Revelation: On Herder's Theological Writings," *Johann Gottfried Herder: Innovator through the Ages,* pp. 138–56.

47. Eric A. Blackall, *The Emergence of German as a Literary Language, 1700–1775,* 2d ed. (Ithaca: Cornell University Press, 1978), pp. 451–81; the second edition also contains a concise review of recent literature on Herder and language, pp. 555–57.

48. Günter Arnold, "Wandlungen von Herders Revolutionsbegriff," *Herder-Kolloquium 1978,* pp. 164–72.

49. Br. 4:258–59, Herder's letter to Hamann, 10 March 1783, contains Herder's account of Wieland's report on the reactions to Herder's sermon on a prince's birthday.

50. One of the strange fates of Herder editions is that the sermons are largely unpublished. On the selection presented in Suphan's edition, vols. 31 and 32, cf. Hans Dietrich Irmscher, "Der handschriftliche Nachlaß Herders und seine Neuordnung," *Herder-Studien,* ed. Walter Wiora (Würzburg: Holzner-Verlag, 1960), p. 10, where he points out that the selection made before World War I reflected a deference to the rulers of Sachsen-Weimar.

51. Fritz Valjavec, *Die Entstehung der politischen Strömungen in Deutschland, 1770–1815* (Munich: R. Oldenbourg, 1951).

52. Herder had to be wrong, in the eyes of Germanists, since he fell back on positions of the Enlightenment. In spite of sound recent scholarship on this issue in the German Democratic Republic, the question needs to be examined further.

53. 4:362; he wanted to be influential "not through the written word, through wars of the pen, but in real life, through *Bildung*" ("nicht schriftlich, nicht durch Federkriege, sondern lebendig, durch Bildung," 4:364).

5

Reading Philosophical Poetry:
A Hermeneutics of Metaphor for Pope's
Essay on Man

HARRY M. SOLOMON

The ontological status of figurative language, especially of metaphor and analogy, is the key question involved in the interpretation of philosophical poetry like Alexander Pope's *An Essay on Man* (1733–34). The abiding mutual hostility of the philosophic and poetic approaches to language makes even formulation of the question difficult. Although according to Douglas Berggren, metaphor "has always been one of the central problems of philosophy," philosophers usually dismiss it as "nothing more than a stylistic ornament, superimposed on cognitive discourse for emotive purposes, or else a mere illustrative comparison whose possible meaning and truth could emerge only when the metaphor was reduced to literal statements."[1] For the philosopher, therefore, figurative language is superfluous discourse—a marginal otherness which the propositional rigor of philosophic discourse seeks to eliminate. As John Richetti argues, "contemporary philosophical readers separate the chaff of persuasive tone and matter from the logical kernel."[2]

This tradition of translating metaphor into literal statement has a prestigious pedigree in English philosophy. Following Francis Bacon, Hobbes in *Leviathan* warns against the absurdities encouraged by the inclusion of analogical language in propositional discourse, especially the "use of metaphors, tropes, and other rhetorical figures, instead of words proper." In *An Essay Concerning Human Understanding* Locke similarly advises, "if we would speak of things as they are, we must allow that all the arts of rhetoric . . . all the artificial and figurative application of words eloquence hath invented, are for nothing else but to insinuate wrong *ideas*, move the passions, and thereby mislead the judgment."

Paul de Man astutely characterizes this abiding fear of "the disfiguring power of figuration":

> Metaphors, tropes, and figural language in general have been a perennial problem . . . for philosophic discourse. . . . It appears that philosophy either has to give up its own constitutive claim to rigor in order to come to terms with the figurality of its language or that it has to free itself from figuration altogether. And if this latter is considered impossible, philosophy could at least learn to control figuration by keeping it, so to speak, in its place, by delimiting the boundaries of its influence and thus restricting the epistemological damage that it may cause. This attempt stands behind recurrent efforts to map out the distinctions between philosophical, scientific, theological, and poetic discourse.[3]

Deconstructionists like Derrida and de Man have exposed the inability of philosophers to make this binary opposition of figurative to literal language operate consistently within their own texts.[4] Other literary theorists, however, and most theologians embrace the suggestion that they are playing different language "games" than the scientist and the philosopher.[5] Some go so far as to condemn "mixed modes of writing which enlist the reader's feeling as well as his thinking," calling instead for "a spell of purer science and purer poetry."[6]

From such a binary perspective, philosophical poetry is the most impure, the genre most insistent on the union of the figurative and the propositional. Speaking of *An Essay on Man* shortly after its publication, theologian J. P. de Crousaz laments, "Mr. Pope's Physics smell of the Poet."[7] Pope's metaphorical use of language in *An Essay on Man*, a recent critic similarly objects, is just "the sort of thing that gets poets a bad name with philosophers."[8] Philosophers, as Richard Rorty argues, would rather dispense with writing and its dangerous use of figurative language altogether and just *show*, like physics.[9] Only a literal or empirical "steno-language," with univocation and with a clear distinction between symbol and referent, seems suitable for philosophic discourse, Philip Wheelwright complains.[10] For most philosophers metaphor is a kind of contamination.

In what follows, I argue that this hostility to figurative languge has led both philosophers and literary critics to systematically distort and thereby misread *An Essay on Man*. I argue against the usual practice of interpreting Pope's metaphors either as analogical arguments for the existence of God or as empirically adequate descriptions of reality. As corrective I propose a concept of regulative metaphor, analogous to Kant's concept of regulative ideas, to describe Pope's use of figurative language in the *Essay;* and I illustrate this concept with a reading of one of Pope's most important and most frequently misinterpreted metaphors.

I. The Misreading of Metaphor as Analogical Argument

It is because "Poetry and Metaphysics . . . are generally considered as two kinds of writing inconsistent with each other," Pope's early advocate Du Resnel insists, that Pope's combining of "the Extasies and Flights of the Poet, and the Nicety and cool Argumentation of the abstracted Reasoner" in the *Essay* is so exceptional.[11] Pope's success in uniting the poetic and the philosophic uses of language was initially much praised; but perhaps because there was no critical idiom adequate to characterize his accomplishment, this praise was sometimes conducted in terms which distort the ontological status of his figurative language and which ultimately led to misinterpretation and to the discrediting of the "argument" of the poem. Notably, when William Warburton in 1742 praises Pope's "Art of converting Poetical Ornaments into Philosophic Reasoning; and of improving a *Simile* into an *Analogical Argument*,"[12] he situates discussion of Pope's use of figurative language in a context of contemporary religious argument which does nothing to aid interpretation of the *Essay.*

Yet Warburton's characterization of Pope's figurative language as analogical argument usefully reveals the impasse that Pope faced in his attempt to unify "Poetry and Metaphysics." In the years immediately preceding the publication of Pope's *Essay* a heated controversy emerged concerning analogical versus empirical reasoning.[13] Both sides agreed in Lockean fashion that we have not "the *Least glimmering* Idea of things purely Spiritual" and that all real knowledge comes from sensation and reflection. In contrast to the empiricists, however, analogists like Peter Browne and George Cheyne saw an avenue to metaphysics in "the noble art of just analogy." Having earlier in *The Procedure, Extent, and Limits of Human Understanding* (1728) treated "of the *Ideas* of *Sensation,* as the only *Original* Materials for the Mind of Man to work upon," Browne proceeds to "discourse more fully and particularly of that *Divine Analogy* to which we owe the greatest Enlargement of human Understanding; and without which the Nature and Properties of God . . . would be as utterly inconceivable to us as if they had no Existence." If we cannot analogize from empirical observation to metaphysical properties, John Balguy similarly insists, we are "cutting the knot" that links us to the divine.[14]

If a priori, arguments on necessary being are discredited, then no possibility exists of metaphysical or religious thought without analogy.

In fact, empiricists like Pope and his friend Bolingbroke, to whom the *Essay* is dedicated, dismissed both Samuel Clarke's "high priori" argument and physicotheological analogizing. Bolingbroke questions both the anthropomorphizing and the mysterious tendencies latent in analogy as metaphysical methodology. The tendency to construct a cosy anthropomorphic metaphysics by analogizing from what God ought to do for man to what God has actually done makes any analogical argument suspect. If, on the other hand, we deanthropomorphize the analogy by insisting that metaphysical statements differ essentially from empirical statements (as God or the ultimate nature of reality differs from the human perspective, for example) not only in degree but in kind, then the propositional status of the analogy is suspect. If man can no more comprehend God than a blind man can perceive light, what ontological status can analogy pretend to?

For this reason, Bishop Peter Browne elaborately distinguishes metaphorical from analogical reasoning, insisting that theologians' analogies reveal real similarities while poets' metaphors have no cognitive significance. Yet when Browne affirms that God is "out of the reach of all human Imagination,"[15] the empiricists object to the equivocal propositional status of an utterance which is and is not a description, which does and yet does not tell us what God is. The subsequent objections of the Logical Positivists are identical: if you make religious or metaphysical assertions in an altogether different sense from that in which you assert them of finite beings, you are making statements "to which you can, *ex hypothesi*, assign no intelligible content."[16] To eighteenth-century empiricists all such analogizing is "hypothesis" and, hence, anathema. In the "General Scholium" to Book III of the *Principia* Newton insisted that he framed no hypotheses: "for whatever is not deduced from the phenomena is to be called an hypothesis; and hypotheses, whether metaphysical or physical . . . have no place in experimental philosophy." In essays addressed to Pope, Bolingbroke tirelessly speaks against any hypothesis not tied directly to empirical observation. This general revulsion from hypothesis, especially in the form of analogical argument, is a marked characteristic of Pope's age, and extended to a wholesale discrediting, as in Condillac's *Traité des systèmes*, of all attempts to use empirical knowledge to construct a metaphysical system.[17]

Douglas White is correct to argue that Pope, in the *Essay* and elsewhere, ridicules system making that goes beyond the evidence of immediate experience.[18] Yet, paradoxically, Pope is most frequently criticized as a faulty system-maker and the *Essay* is trivialized and dismissed by praising its beauty as poetry while disparaging its allegedly inconsistent metaphysical argument. This pattern of misreading results in large part from treating Pope's metaphors as unequivocal metaphysical analogies, despite the repeated warnings in the *Essay* against the license of anthropomorphic hypothesis and the frequent admonitions against exceeding the limits of human reason.

II. Metaphor as Regulative Hypothesis

Before interpreting Pope's figurative languge, we must understand that he like the metaphysician uses metaphor to solve a problem; and, consequently, his usage can best be understood and assessed if that problem is acknowledged.[19] As author of a philosophical poem Pope was faced with both a logical and an empirical impasse. Perhaps nothing was clearer to Pope's age than the inadequacy of human reason to understand the ultimate nature of reality. As Locke emphasized, finitude and infinity are both intellectually incomprehensible. Kant's antinomies are not sudden personal revelations but his codification of the conflicting axioms of an age. The "high priori" road was closed. Similarly, no access to the noumenal through the phenomenal existed, despite the hocus-pocus of analogy. Our ideas extend no farther than our impressions, Hume writes. Since we have no impressions of the noumenal we can formulate no meaningful metaphysical ideas. "What can we reason," Pope says in the *Essay*, "but from what we know?" Without an unquestioned dogma or direct supernatural revelation, to neither of which Pope defers, metaphysics seems impossible.

Yet, as Dorothy Emmet argues, while the transcendent may be beyond our intellectual categories that does not mean it is entirely beyond our experience.[20] That Kant read Pope's *Essay* admiringly to his students is suggestive, for Kant and Pope shared a metaphysical temperament. As ably as Hume, Kant exposes the rational inadequacies of the physicotheological argument but insists, paradoxically, that it deserves respect. Like Pope, Kant was not satisfied to assert dogmatically the entire impossibility of "philosophical theology," no matter how problematic, because to do so falsified experience. For Kant as for Pope the noumenal was implicit in ethics; ethics was, in Pope's metaphor, the "God within the mind." Like Kant, Pope is responsive equally to the immensity and awesome order of the physical universe outside humanity and to the moral law within. Pope's problem as poet and as philosopher was to synthesize realms of experience without distortion—to do justice to the moral intuition without distorting our empirical knowledge. "We live in a Critical Age," Bishop William Sherlock writes in 1694, "which will not allow us to speak intelligibly of God because we lack Words sufficiently to distinguish between the Motions and Actings of the Divine Mind and the Passions of Creatures."[21] Pope's challenge was to create a language able to move beyond the rational and empirical impasses without lapsing into poetic "pseudo-statement," the purely subjective alternative to the moral and emotional barrenness of scientific description.

Faced with experiential antinomies which resisted, like Kant's phenomenal and noumenal realms, any satisfactory logical unification, Pope's solution was to use metaphor regulatively rather than as analogical argument. This concept of regulative metaphor is similar to Kant's concept of regulative ideas. In the *Critique of Judgment* and in *Lectures on Philosophical Theology* Kant explains that adopting a teleological model which is, strictly speaking, logically unjustified is sometimes productive, if we understand the model as serving only a regulative or heuristic function in organizing and facilitating our knowledge. In other words, Kant argues, we are justified in viewing reality *as if* it were purposive so long as we are careful not to confuse our hypothesis with a mysterious, objective property of reality apart from our model. In this way we order and synthesize our experience. For Kant these Transcendental Ideas, including the teleological model, are purely methodological; they are regulative rather than constitutive. God is, thus, a metaphorical or analogical construct of reason functioning regulatively. While the teleological model is not necessitated either logically or empirically, Kant nonetheless insists that it is intellectually inevitable.

The modern pervasiveness of such provisional metaphorical models is clear in the currency of such phrases as root-metaphor, scientific paradigm, and hermeneutic circle. To attribute an analogous regulative use of metaphor to Pope is fitting. Although contemporaries like Newton and Hume denounced groundless speculative hypotheses, they assumed the necessity of working hypotheses.[22] Moreover, the hypothetical if-leap is something Pope himself calls attention to in a letter to his friend John Caryll. Not identifying himself as the author of the *Essay,* Pope observes that "Nothing is so plain as that the author quits his proper subject, *this present world,* to insert his belief of *a future state* and yet there is an *If* instead of a *Since* that would overthrow his meaning."[23] Although each of the "if" structures in *An Essay on Man* requires individual interpretation, Pope acknowledges the deliberately equivocal and hypothetical status of the utterance; and he acknowledges the logical impropriety of moving from the empirical or phenomenological ("his proper subject") to the metaphysical or noumenal.

The traditional role of the poet in Pope's day was as perceiver and communicator of significant similarities and differences in nature and in human experience. Figurative language synthesized disparate but significantly similar realms of experience. Extrapolating from Epistle II of the *Essay* one may distinguish these realms as (1) the intellectual (Reason), (2) the emotional (Passion), and (3) the ethical (God within the

Mind). Pope's divisions anticipate Hume's organization of *A Treatise of Human Nature* (1739) into books (1) Of the Understanding, (2) Of the Passions, and (3) Of Morals. Each of these faculties or realms of experience asks something of the poet or philosopher who would avoid distorting human experience. As Kant suggests in the *Critique of Pure Reason*, human beings want to know (1) what they may believe (may know as certain), (2) what they may hope (may desire with the possibility of fulfillment), and (3) what they should do (may do ethically). Pope's self-imposed task, then, is simultaneously (1) to argue and to give evidence, (2) to inspire or depress, and (3) to mandate moral action. To the Horatian admonition that poetry must simultaneously move the emotions and improve the morals of the reader, the philosophical poet adds an obligation to characterize external reality as accurately as human faculties allow.

Regulative metaphor is the primary means by which Pope does justice to these different logical and experiential claims. Metaphor holds in tension two or more descriptions of reality so that they become complementary. The sensuous analogy of the noumenal which Kant finds in the Aesthetic Ideas of genuine poetic and religious figurative language prefigures Philip Wheelwright's insistence on the "ontological status of radical metaphor." Through the tension of metaphor the poet achieves, he argues, a transcendence of either-or distinctions, "an ontological overlapping by which emotionally congruent things, qualities and events blend into oneness." To any one faculty in isolation this oneness will appear paradoxical; and, indeed, there is something "mysterious" about both Kant's Aesthetic Ideas and Wheelwright's claim of ontological status for radical metaphor. Yet if we view reality, as distinguished from human perceptions of reality, as coalescent, to use Wheelwright's term, then envisioning sharp lines between kinds of experience may be merely the attempt of each faculty to claim priority for its own perceptions— either the logical, the emotional, or the ethical. The limitation of reality to one of our philosophical categories is distortion; while all categories try to refer to reality, to the extent that each makes a univocal statement from its point of view, that statement is inevitably inadequate. Neither the field nor the particle model of quantum mechanics is adequate alone. Metaphor overcomes this desiccation of reality by holding such potentially complementary descriptions in a fructifying tension. Regulative metaphor, however, makes no unbracketed ontological claims. The faculties united are limited human faculties still. A "Chaos of Thought and Passion," as Pope asserts in Epistle II, we are never more than "darkly wise." Clearly unequal to what he calls the "empyreal Sphere" of metaphysics, human beings have "too much knowledge for the Sceptic side." The philosophic poet's role is to create the richest description of reality available to human perception.

As Douglas Berggren argues, metaphor is indispensable for integrating diverse phenomena and perspectives without sacrificing their diversity. Myth in metaphysics or misinterpretation in poetry occurs when the tensive metaphor is read in terms of its constituent elements. This enervates the tension by ignoring the regulative function of the metaphor and treating it instead as rhetorical artifice—mere illustration or ornament. Most criticism does this by distinguishing between the tenor and the vehicle of a metaphor. By identifying the tenor as the reality and the vehicle as the arbitrary sign which represents it, critics give priority to the tenor and praise the poet or philosopher in proportion to the rhetorical effectiveness of the vivifying though ontologically insignificant vehicle. This translation of tensive metaphor into univocal utterance distorts because it relaxes the tension among perspectives by ascribing reality to one alone.

III. The Mismapping of Metaphor as Empirical Statement

Incalculable damage is done by misinterpreting Pope's metaphors in the *Essay* as literal, constative statements, for this is the preliminary to putting his statements in their argumentative place. The situational metaphor is deliberate, for most critics of *An Essay on Man* are argumentative contextualizers, ambitious to paraphrase the propositional content of the metaphor and then assess it in an exclusively logical or logocentric context, to adopt the fashionable deconstructionist term. Typically this process takes two forms in criticism of *An Essay on Man*: either (1) the critic stipulates the logical proposition affirmed by a metaphor and then constructs the rational presuppositions and implications of that proposition, or (2) the critic places the metaphor in its presumed place in the history of ideas.

An early representative of the first kind of misreading is Crousaz's discovery of fatalism in the metaphor "of a Universe, formed with a mutual Dependence of one Part upon another, in the manner of a Machine." This "grand and magnificent" rhetoric, the Swiss theologian objects, vivifies an "Idea" which leads to "very destructive Consequences." Similarly, a recent critic finds in "the asserted transcendence of the system as a whole over the isolated functioning of any parts" a danger of "turning God into a sadistic mechanic." Equally malign consequences are drawn by the 1751 author of *Common Sense* from Pope's metaphor,

> All are but parts of one stupendous whole,
> Whose body Nature is, and God the soul.

Interpreted in the narrow context of the debate over God's immanence or transcendence, the anonymous author reads the utterance as a denial of God's transcendence and, consequently, as atheistic and fatalistic. Thus, Pope's argument as deduced from his metaphor places him among those "pretending to philosophy, who . . . talk much indeed of God, but mean such a one, as is not really distinct from the animated and intelligent universe."[24] This either-or argumentative flight from tensive metaphor produces just the mythic metaphysical "extremes of doctrines seemingly opposite" which Pope desired to "steer betwixt," as he specifically says in the Design which begins the Essay. To situate Pope's "doctrine" in either of the antinomies that God is transcendent or God is immanent ignores his explicit methodolgy and reduces metaphor to mere vivification of logical statement.

Perhaps no metaphor has been more frequently misinterpreted than Pope's use of the venerable chain of being. As Pope told Joseph Spence, he initially adopted the metaphor of the "scale of beings" because of its currency with admirers of the Spectator where it was one of Addison's "cant words."[25] In the Essay the metaphor is assumed as a formula familiar to his audience, and is used to create a sense of awe, what Bacon calls "broken knowledge," in the face of nature's multifarious unity. As Wheelwright correctly notes, metaphor most powerfully embodies the "responsive awe" humans feel in the presence of the irreducible mystery of reality. Instead of interpreting Pope's use of the chain of being as regulative metaphor, however, critics have charted the dangerous consequences of the syllogisms deducible from its presumed argument. Pope is frequently charged with "Cosmic Toryism," with using the chain of being as a "metaphysical sanction" to keep people within their social class. The metaphor, another critic asserts, supports a necessitarian doctrine of social submission. Most critics are like Crousaz in sifting through the infection of the poetry in order to reach the nuggets of paraphrasable dogma. However, as Samuel Johnson objected when translating Crousaz's tendentious attack, their mistake is to have "too great an Inclination to draw Consequences"; and critics who read Pope's use of the chain of being metaphor as intended to sanction submission to one's social superiors misinterpret him as advocating that "enormous faith of many made for one" which he attacks throughout the Essay.[26]

Interpretation of the chain of being metaphor also illustrates the second typical misreading of Pope's metaphor: situating it in the history of ideas. Arthur O. Lovejoy's placement of Pope is the definitive example of this method of reading. For Lovejoy, Pope's Essay is a marginal chapter in the story of a bad idea. The metaphor was never more popular, Lovejoy argues, than in the eighteenth century, a theme expatiated upon by such authors as Addison, King, Bolingbroke, Pope, Haller, Thomson, Akenside, Buffon, Bonnet, Goldsmith, Diderot, Kant, Lambert, Herder, and

Schiller. The metaphor was so congenial and adaptable, another scholar writes, that it could be accepted by people of very "varied philosophical opinions." This should give critics pause. When writers with radically differing philosophical orientations use the same metaphor, caution and discrimination are necessary in interpreting each occurrence of the metaphor, for a metaphorical meaning becomes explicit only when analyzed in the context of its use by each individual author, since the "same metaphor may acquire various, even contrasting, meanings in different writers."[27] Yet Lovejoy's summary of Pope's *Essay* is an unsubtle conflation where similarities to others are stressed and differences ignored. Pope is made to sound like an amalgam of Soame Jenyns and the Leibnizian Pangloss in Voltaire's *Candide*.

In Lovejoy's ambitious survey where Pope is viewed as a marginal, literary echo of writers of philosophic prose like Leibniz, King, Shaftesbury, and Bolingbroke, this distortion is understandable. Unfortunately, the same habit of mind is bequeathed, because of Lovejoy's deserved reputation, to scholars writing exclusively on Pope. "Once we have recognized this way of thinking as natural to its time," a recent critic writes of Pope's use of the chain of being metaphor, "limited as that time was by certain habits of religious thought, political institutions, social customs, and a restricted knowledge of the world outside Europe, we can see how the social divisions that keep every man in his place were seen at the time as sacred." This is not what Pope says in the *Essay* nor what he believed. Instead, this view is representative of the "patronizingly supercilious" dismissal of Pope as philosopher which F. E. L. Priestley, the author of the only first-rate essay on Pope's use of the great chain metaphor, finds endemic in criticism on Pope.[28]

Both usual ways of reading Pope's metaphors evade interpretive responsibility. Situating the metaphors within systems outside the poem, critics assess them in that extratextual context. The first method extends the metaphor by placing it in a propositional context of its own presumed argumentative presuppositions and implications. Figure is thus reduced solely to rational argument. This elaborate propositional construct replaces the metaphor for purposes of assessment. The second method situates the metaphor in the history of ideas, paying insufficient attention to its distinctive use in a particular text. Such readings emphasize Pope's self-admittedly cant generic formula and ignore his doctrinal uniqueness.

IV. A Hermeneutics of Regulative Metaphor

Situating a metaphor outside the text or restating a metaphor by paraphrase or structural description is inadequate interpretation. Even if a single universally valid hermeneutics of metaphor were impossible, any interpretive methodology must be structured by the possibilities of meaning in language. Additionally, the methodology should be able to acknowledge the intentions of the author and the shared expectations for the literary genre. In philosophical poetry the expected conjunction is between constative and emotive uses of language, between philosophy narrowly conceived and poetry narrowly conceived. Pope expressly adds the directive or ethical use when he says in the Design, "If I could flatter myself that this Essay has any merit, it is in steering betwixt the extremes of doctrines seemingly opposite, in passing over terms utterly unintelligible, and in forming a *temperate* yet not *inconsistent*, and a *Short* yet not *imperfect* system of Ethics." These three uses of language correspond to the tripartite self of Epistle II: reason, passion, and the moral sense, or *ego*, *id*, and *superego* in Freudian terminology. Additionally, and especially in regulative metaphor, language has a performative aspect. The poet must hold these three descriptions of reality—(1) the logical or the constative, (2) the emotive, and (3) the ethical or the directive—in a satisfying tension that makes them complementary rather than contradictory. Thus, in interpreting Pope's metaphors we should ask: (1) What is asserted as fact? (2) What attitude is urged? (3) What action is mandated? and (4) What is the generative tension among these speech acts that makes them complementary rather than contradictory?

The interpretive categories themselves suggest appropriate evaluative criteria. (1) The strong logical or propositional component of philosophical poetry constitutes a convenant between poet and reader not to retreat into the subjectivism of purely evocative metaphor. This compact similarly warrants the reader in going beyond interpretation to evaluation of metaphor in order to determine whether the metaphor is a rich description of reality or simply a creation of the aesthetic imagination attempting to make its perspective dominant. In its propositional aspect the metaphor should square with and embody what we know. The suggestiveness characteristic of poetic language should not contradict empirical evidence, and some specifiable degree of factual similarity must warrant the metaphor. Although the metaphor may interpret empirical experience, it should not lose sight of what Dorothy Emmet calls the world's matter-of-factness. (2) In its emotive aspect the metaphor should be subjectively important, should reflect a feeling of appropriate emphasis. The metaphor should feel significant. (3) In its directive function, the metaphor should sanction ethical action. (4) In its performative aspect the metaphor should simultaneously activate the reader's intellectual, emotional, and ethical realms of experience and juxtapose them in a tension which is more adequate to our experience of reality than any single perspective in isolation. Although the metaphor should convince, move, and dispose the reader to moral action, the definitive characteristic of regulative metaphor is its capacity to harmonize these three or more worlds of experience without doing injustice to what Murray Krieger describes as the Manichaean complexity of the "raging existential world." Consideration of the performative aspect of the metaphor must, therefore, assess the success of the metaphor in resisting deconstruction into description solely in logical, emotional, or ethical terms. The metaphor should hold in tension, as coalescent, three or more perspectives on reality. The generative richness of this juxtaposition determines its value.

Empirical description pretends to absolute objectivity and eschews hypothesis altogether; but, as Emmet observes, any description of reality "which attempts an estimate of the significance of events, whether philosophical or theological, cannot be merely empirical."[29] Through metaphor the poet or metaphysician seeks a synoptic vision adequate to harmonize the diverse worlds of human experience. The metaphors used function as regulative hypotheses. They are imaginative models, and they are the key to adequately characterizing the writer's perspective. Therefore, the resolution of metaphor or any other variety of figurative language into propositional statement is the reverse of an adequate interpretive method. The philosophic poet's vision is hermeneutically inseparable from the poet's metaphor, for it is through the metaphor that what Berggren calls a stereoscopic vision is achieved. The assessment of a poet's metaphor, therefore, is an assessment of the adequacy of that poet's philosophic vision. And this vision is richer in proportion to its comprehensiveness: the number of experiences—intellectual, emotional, ethical—which the metaphor makes complementary. A regulative poetic metaphor may, like a metaphysical analogy or rootmetaphor, remain open. It may indicate recalcitrant aspects of reality which resist inclusion or categorization, but the metaphor should have an aesthetically satisfying comprehensiveness which has implications for our intellectual, emotional, and ethical responses to reality. The aesthetic or rhetorical and the philosophic thereby come together because the master harmonizer of the propositional, emotive, ethical, and performative uses of language simultaneously achieves the most comprehensive, synoptic description of reality.

V. An Interpretation of God as the Soul of the World

Natural theology was, among other things, an attempt to connect "our ordinary everyday discourse about the world or even our scientific discourse on the one side, and theological discourse on the other."[30]

This is also one motivation of the scientist Robert Boyle's establishment of a lectureship to promulgate discoveries in natural philosophy which would reinforce supernatural philosophy. One of the metaphors that Pope uses to "go betwixt" those contradictory modes of discourse illustrates regulative metaphor at work. In the penultimate section of Epistle I Pope characterizes reality, in the outraged words of the author of *Common Sense*, as "a prodigious great Animal":

> All are but parts of one stupendous whole,
> Whose body Nature is, and God the soul;
> That, chang'd thro' all, and yet in all the same,
> Great in the earth, as in th' aethereal frame,
> Warms in the sun, refreshes in the breeze,
> Glows in the stars, and blossoms in the trees,
> Lives thro' all life, extends thro' all extent,
> Spreads undivided, operates unspent,
> Breathes in our soul, informs our mortal part,
> As full, as perfect, in a hair as heart;
> As full, as perfect, in vile Man that mourns,
> As the rapt Seraph that adores and burns;
> To him no high, no low, no great, no small;
> He fills, he bounds, connects, and equals all.

Few analogies were more frequent in Pope's age in sermon or theological treatise than the comparison of God's relationship to the physical universe to that of the soul's animation and direction of the body. Its use as metaphor was warranted by the general consensus of pagan and Christian alike, as Ralph Cudworth argued earlier in *The True Intellectual System of the Universe* (1678). However, because of the pantheistic implications which antagonists could draw from the immanent metaphor, most authors were carefully equivocal, calling on the difference between literal description and analogy adapted to human capacities. So problematic was the immediate involvement of the deity in the operations of the creation that Newton in the *Principia* pointedly affirms God's transcendence as a being who "governs all things, not as the soul of the world, but as Lord over all." Pope was aware of the animistic or Spinozist tendencies of the metaphor, for which he was subsequently denounced. Pope wrote in the same letter to Caryll cited earlier that at the end of Epistle I the anonymous author of the *Essay* "uses the Words *God*, the *soul* of the *World*, which at first glance may be taken for heathenism, while his whole paragraph proves him quite Christian in his system, from *Man* up to *Seraphim*."

In adopting the metaphor of God as the soul of the world Pope is consciously "steering betwixt" an atheistic (heathen) and a theistic

(Christian analogy) description of reality. He also recognizes the semantic tyranny of "God-talk" and the danger, cited by Thomas F. Merrill, "when utterances of one language-game are interpreted according to the rules appropriate to another."[31] Thus Pope is eager to know what Caryll makes of the metaphor so that he may judge his figurative effectiveness, part of which consists in dissociating himself from the rhetorical confines of the immanent-transcendent, atheist-Christian controversies. Pope's nineteenth-century editor Reverend Whitwell Elwin, like Crousaz over a century earlier, denounces Pope's equivocal diction which, he argues in discussing the *Essay*, fits equally impiety and religious belief. Yet, as the letter to Caryll makes clear, Pope intends this figural ambiguity or undecidability to frustrate critical attempts to situate his metaphor in the history of ideas and thereby reduce it to just another vivification of the immanent or the transcendent arguments.

Within the Epistle the metaphor is unmistakably regulative for two contextual reasons. First, Pope has unequivocally and repeatedly stated the impossibility of comprehensive metaphysical understanding. Second, Pope has already metaphorically characterized the nature of reality in mechanical terms which, if taken as an ontologically adequate description, would contradict description in terms of an organic metaphor. But, as Douglas White astutely notes, Pope was "not satisfied with the mechanical description alone."[32] Pope proceeds, therefore, to provide a complementary organic description. Contextually, he is indicating that these and other metaphors may productively organize our appreciation of the universe but none can be a fully adequate description. Misinterpretations ignore this regulative bracketing by treating the metaphor either as empirical description or as analogical argument.

In applying the proposed criteria for interpreting regulative metaphor, the first question to ask is

(1) What does Pope's metaphor actually assert? An awesome energy animates and orders the universe into one organic unity. All parts of the universe participate in this energy and order but none is more privileged. Beyond this, the propositional implications of the metaphor are problematic and provocative. What is a reader to make of the word "God" when its tendency to semantic control of the utterance is undercut by the impersonality of the world-soul which does not distinguish between a hair or heart, a world-soul which, in an earlier metaphor linked to this by a shared allusion to Matthew 10:29–31,

> sees with equal eye, as God of all,
> A hero perish, or a sparrow fall,
> Atoms or systems into ruin hurl'd,
> And now a bubble burst, and now a world.
>
> (I, 87–90)

(2) What attitude does the metaphor urge? The unity of creation reinforces a feeling of connectedness in the individual whose existence is animated by the same force which "Glows in the stars, and blossoms in the trees." Also, the sense of being part of a universal order is encouraged. Both identifications of the individual with the universal life-force involve an appropriate and exhilarating depersonalization. Involvement in the godhead is common to all creation. Consequently, our exhilaration coexists with a recognition that, although unique, we are not accorded privileged treatment by "God." The tension achieved by Pope's appropriation of the figurative language used in Matthew underscores this undecidability of the cosmic significance of human life:

29 Are not two sparrows sold for a farthing? and one of them shall not fall on the ground without your Father.
30 But the very hairs of your head are all numbered.
31 Fear ye not therefore, ye are of more value than many sparrows.

Paradoxically, Pope's metaphor mortifies and exhilarates us simultaneously. Above all, we are encouraged to contemplative wonder at the immensity and variety of reality which is somehow united by a common energy. The sublimity of the metaphor, as Joseph Warton noted in 1782, encourages our awe.[33]

(3) The ethical actions mandated by the metaphor have clear links to other metaphors in the *Essay*, especially the earlier parts-whole metaphor which contrasts those perspectives and the later chain of love metaphor which emphasizes the connectedness of the part to the whole. Since the part cannot contemplate the whole, since man's limited faculties are inadequate to grasp the scheme of things entire, man should recognize the vanity of insisting on a fully adequate, exclusively logocentric or empirical model of reality. The search for a coherent metaphysical model is vain not only because a mind which is categorically phenomenal ("What can we reason, but from what we know?") cannot pretend to the noumenal ("Why Heav'n has made us as we are"), but also because the very attempt is presumptuously anthropocentric ("All quit their sphere, and rush into the skies"). The metaphor of God as the soul of the world reasserts the recurrent motif of Epistle I that, despite his egotism, man is not the sole reason for reality's being, that the ecology of the universe has "no high, no low, no great, no small." Thus, Pope's metaphor anticipates his later denunciation of the "enormous faith of many made for one," which is simply a politicizing of man's metaphysical anthropomorphism. By stressing that "All are but parts of one stupendous whole," the metaphor simultaneously mandates the eschewal of anthropocentric metaphysics and encourages a sense of

solidarity with all creation which anticipates the later chain of love metaphor:

> Slave to no sect, who takes no private road,
> But looks thro' Nature, up to Nature's God;
> Pursues that Chain which links th' immense design,
> Joins heav'n and earth, and mortal and divine;
> Sees, that no being any bliss can know,
> But touches some above, and some below;
> Learns, from this union of the rising Whole,
> The first, last purpose of the human Soul;
> And knows where Faith, Law, Morals, all began,
> All end, in LOVE of GOD, and LOVE of MAN.
>
> (IV, 331–40)

The recognition of our connectedness with all reality, of our sharing of a common soul, is both an ethical ground and a call to respect and relish all things rather than insensitively to "destroy all creatures for our sport or gust." As John Sisk acknowledges, human beings move toward inhumanity when they begin to doubt that "they have a vital connection with the force that moves the heaven and all the stars, when they begin to doubt that their sense of justice has some ground in the order of things."[34] Pope's metaphor establishes that universal consanguinity.

(4) The generative tension among these uses of language grows out of the dual derivation of the metaphor (heathen/Christian) that Pope alludes to in his letter to Caryll. As theological God-talk the metaphor of God as the soul of the world is redolent with revelatory power. As scientific description the metaphor is also heuristically suggestive in accounting for our sense of connectedness. The tension between "God" in theological language and "God" as scientific cipher alters both terms. God, in Pope's metaphor, is no longer the solicitous father-figure in Matthew who numbers the hairs on our head, nor is God an alien cosmic energy. Instead, "God" functions as a regulative metaphor correlating nature's order, animation, and connectedness with our subjective rational, passionate, and ethical experiences.

In "steering betwixt" theological use of analogy and scientific description, Pope's metaphor is a third force linking two worlds of discourse. His stereoscopic metaphor straddles the epistemological gap between Kant's transcendental and empirical standpoints. Pope's synoptic vision fuses realms of experience. His figurative fable of identity, to adapt Northrop Frye's phrase, captures a sense "of lost rapport with nature which logic, reason, and the dualistic differentiation of consciousness have destroyed."[35]

Viewing his metaphor either as reifiable or as a kind of alogical "su-

preme fiction" is equally disintegrative to Pope's poem. If philosophical
poetry is merely a construct of fictive pseudo-statements serving to tell
the anthropoid ear only what it wants to hear, then such poetry is trivial.
If, on the other hand, metaphors are read as metaphysically accurate and
adequate descriptions then the poet becomes a megalomaniacal myth-
maker whose utterances are revelations. Regulative metaphor, in contrast, is propositionally responsible and always hypothetical. Pope
acknowledges in his letter to Caryll that the author of *An Essay on Man*
cannot move into the metaphysical realm without quitting his proper
sphere. Yet, he adds in justification, "there is an *if* instead of a *Since*."
Pope uses metaphor to organize experience hypothetically but recognizes that he cannot ontologically warrant his construct. The poet as-
pires, as Francis Bacon says, "to give some shadow of satisfaction to the
mind of man in those points wherein the nature of things doth deny it."
Bacon's metaphor of shadow is inappropriately disparaging, for as a
recent theologian acknowledges, "It is . . . not a scandal but something
every hearer of poetry should understand, that all the statements theologians make about God are similitudes, as it is written, *per speculum in
enigmate* [through a glass darkly]." Similarly, writing in 1709, William
King cautioned theologians "to remember, that the Descriptions which
we frame to our selves of God . . . are not taken from any direct or
immediate Perceptions that we have made of him" and are consequently
analogies seen "thro a Glass darkly."[36] Pope characterizes man as being
"darkly wise" (II, 4), ambitious for but estranged from apodictic certainty
regarding his "being's end and aim." Although critics insist otherwise,
Pope knows that the philosophic poet can organize humanity's multiple
experiences only provisionally; conditioning Pope's figural language is
always "an *if* instead of a *Since*."

Notes

   1. Douglas Berggren, "The Use and Abuse of Metaphor," *Review of Metaphysics* 16:1
(1962): 236.
   2. John J. Richetti, *Philosophical Writing: Locke, Berkeley, Hume* (Cambridge: Harvard
University Press, 1983), p. 17.
   3. Paul de Man, "The Epistemology of Metaphor," *Critical Inquiry* 5 (1978): 29,13.
   4. Jonathan Culler, *On Deconstruction* (Ithaca: Cornell University Press, 1982), pp. 147ff.
   5. Gerald Graff, *Poetic Statement and Critical Dogma* (Chicago: University of Chicago
Press, 1980), pp. xiff.
   6. I. A. Richards, *Creation and Discovery* (Chicago: Henry Regnery, 1955), p. 3.
   7. J. P. de Crousaz, *A Commentary Upon Mr. Pope's Four Ethic Epistles, Intitled An Essay on
Man* (London: E. Curll, 1738), pp. 36, 64.
   8. A. D. Nuttall, *Pope's "Essay on Man"* (London: George Allen and Unwin, 1984), p. 84.
   9. Richard Rorty, "Philosophy as a Kind of Writing: An Essay on Derrida," *New Literary
History* 10 (1978): 156.
   10. Philip Wheelwright, *The Burning Fountain* (Bloomington: Indiana University Press,
1954), pp. 52ff.

11. J. P. de Crousaz, *A Commentary on Mr. Pope's Principles of Morality, or Essay on Man* (London: A. Dodd, 1739), p. 302.

12. William Warburton, *A Critical and Philosophical Commentary on Mr. Pope's Essay on Man* (London: John and Paul Knapton, 1742), p. 137.

13. This context is provided by Douglas H. White in *Pope and the Context of Controversy: The Manipulation of Ideas in "An Essay on Man"* (Chicago: University of Chicago Press, 1970), pp. 77–81.

14. Peter Browne, *The Procedure, Extent, and Limits of Human Understanding* (London, 1728), p. 473; Peter Browne, *Things Divine and Supernatural Conceived by ANALOGY with Things Natural and Human* (London: William Innys, 1733), p. 1; John Balguy, *The Law of Truth: or, The Obligations of Reason Essential to All Religion* (London: John Pemberton, 1733), p. xii.

15. Browne, *Human Understanding*, pp. 132–46, 86.

16. E. L. Mascall, *Existence and Analogy* (London: Longmans, 1949), p. 87.

17. Norman Hampson, *The Enlightenment* (Baltimore: Penguin, 1968), pp. 76–77; Peter Gay, *The Enlightenment: An Interpretation* (New York: Norton, 1966), 1:132–41.

18. White, *Pope and the Context of Controversy*, p. 82.

19. See Karl Popper, *Conjectures and Refutations* (London: Routledge, 1972), p. 199; and Friedel Weinert, "Tradition and Argument," *Monist* 65:1 (January 1982): 88–105.

20. Dorothy M. Emmet, *The Nature of Metaphysical Thinking* (London: Macmillan, 1957), p. 205.

21. William Sherlock, *A Discourse Concerning the Divine Providence* (London, 1694), p. 348.

22. James Noxon, *Hume's Philosophical Development* (Oxford: Clarendon Press, 1975), p. 91.

23. *Correspondence of Alexander Pope*, ed. George Sherburn (Oxford: Clarendon Press, 1965), 3:354.

24. Crousaz, *Commentary on Mr. Pope's Principles of Morality*, p. 207; *Common Sense a Common Delusion . . . Mr. Pope's Essay on Man*, 2d ed. (London: T. Reynolds, 1751),p. 10; Robert Boyle, "A Free Inquiry into the Vulgarly Received Notion of Nature," *The Works of the Honourable Robert Boyle*, ed. Thomas Birch (London, 1772), 5:183.

25. Joseph Spence, *Anecdotes, Observations and Characters of Books and Men*, ed. Bonamy Dobrée (Carbondale: Southern Illinois University Press, 1964), p. 114.

26. Arthur O. Lovejoy, *The Great Chain of Being* (Cambridge: Harvard University Press, 1936), p. 206; Kenneth MacLean, *John Locke and English Literature of the Eighteenth Century* (New Haven: Yale University Press, 1936), pp. 145–46; Crousaz, *Commentary on Mr. Pope's Principles of Morality*, p. 123; White, *Pope and the Context of Controversy*, p. 153.

27. Daniel J. Wilson, "Arthur O. Lovejoy and the Moral of *The Great Chain of Being*," *Journal of the History of Ideas* 41:2 (1980): 249–65; Lovejoy, *Great Chain of Being*, 183–84; MacLean, *John Locke and English Literature*, pp. 145–46; Guiseppa Saccaro-Battisti, "Changing Metaphors of Political Structures," *Journal of the History of Ideas* 44:1 (1983): 31.

28. Yasmine Gooneratne, *Alexander Pope* (Cambridge: Cambridge University Press, 1976), p. 107; F. E. L. Priestley, "Pope and the Great Chain of Being," *Essays in English Literature from the Renaissance to the Victorian Age*, ed. Millar MacLure and F. W. Watt (Toronto: University of Toronto Press, 1964), p. 213.

29. Emmet, *Metaphysical Thinking*, p. 202. The criteria of importance and matter-of-factness as well as comprehensiveness and openness in metaphysical analogies are discussed by Emmet on pp. 195–202.

30. John Macquarrie, *Thinking about God* (New York: Harper, 1975), p. 137.

31. Thomas F. Merrill, *Christian Criticism: A Study of Literary God Talk* (Amsterdam: Rodopi, 1976), p. 10.

32. White, *Pope and the Context of Controversy*, p. 41.

33. Joseph Warton, *An Essay on the Genius and Writings of Pope* (London: J. Dodsley, 1782), 2:77.

34. John P. Sisk, "The Tyranny of Harmony," *American Scholar* 46 (1977): 204.

35. Northrop Frye, *Fables of Identity* (New York: Harcourt, Brace, 1963), p. 141.

36. Austin Farrer, *Reflective Faith: Essays in Philosophical Theology*, ed. Charles C. Conti (London: SPCK, 1972), p. 32; William King, *Divine Predestination and Fore-Knowledg, Consistent with the Freedom of Man's Will* (London: J. Baker, 1709), pp. 5, 14.

6

Style as Philosophical Structure: The Contexts of Shaftesbury's *Characteristicks*

ROBERT MARKLEY

Shaftesbury has traditionally proved a difficult writer for both literary critics and philosophers. Most of his commentators have taken his self-proclaimed status as a "philosopher" as both the beginning and logical conclusion of their attempts to interpret his work: Shaftesbury is located within the historical traditions of philosophic thought and his "ideas" examined and explicated as disinterested contributions to the history of knowledge. These efforts, however, have led most of his critics to neglect a good portion of his writing, concentrating (albeit understandably) on the *Inquiry Concerning Virtue* and the *Letter Concerning Enthusiasm*. They ignore or dismiss the stylistic and literary traditions which influenced Shaftesbury, and, by emphasizing the timeless, "philosophical" aspects of his work, neglect its social, political, and ideological assumptions and values.[1] Their concerns, in this regard, pay homage to the success of one important aspect of Shaftesbury's program as a writer: the championing of a disinterested philosophic language that is both morally instructive and aesthetically pleasing.

There are however, problems with this traditional, ahistorical perception of Shaftesbury's thought—and, as John Richetti has argued, with the ways in which we approach much late seventeenth- and early eighteenth-century philosophy.[2] Shaftesbury's concern with the realm of ideas cannot—by his own account—legitimately be divorced from the stylistic and historical contexts of his work. Repeatedly in *The Characteristicks*, Shaftesbury calls attention to the historical situation of his writing: he satirizes his detractors, develops elaborate defenses of his previous work, footnotes his classical authorities, offers his opinions on contemporary developments in art, politics, and religion, and does what he can to advance his aristocratic social, aesthetic, and philosophical judgments. Seen in this light, his very "disinterestedness," his appeals to—and for—the ahistorical realms of beauty and truth are themselves ideological constructs, the products of a complex interaction of social, philosophical, and stylistic traditions. Shaftesbury often seems as concerned with his literary strategies, his "style," as he is with his "ideas." Unlike many of his critics, he sees "philosophy" as a strategic and polemical discourse designed to inculcate in his readers a decidedly aristocratic sense of virtue. In this respect, the pretext that his language follows *"The Simple* Manner . . . endeavouring only to express the effect of Art, under the appearance of the greatest Ease and Negligence" (1:257)[3] is crucial to his self-perception as both a writer and philosopher. The "natural," disinterested mode of philosophical discourse that Shaftesbury advocates, then, is an end as well as a means. For our purposes, a study of the relationships between Shaftesbury's style and his thought becomes an examination of the interests—historical, social, literary, and critical—that the author uses to promote philosophic disinterest.

I

Underlying the diverse literary forms of Shaftesbury's *Characteristicks* are two major seventeenth-century stylistic traditions: Jonsonian "humour" and Fletcherian "wit" or, as other critics have termed them, the "self-consuming" and the "self-satisfying," the Senecan and the "scientific," or the two plain styles.[4] The Jonsonian tradition (derived from the example of Ben Jonson's poems and prose comedies)[5] is essentially Horatian and satiric; it emphasizes the moral utility of language, taking as its model the classical ideal of instruction and delight. It acknowledges the ideal possibility of an objective language which embodies moral truth, but concentrates most of its energy on anatomizing the seemingly irrevocable corruptions of human speech, or probing, through the author's often tortuous progress toward self-knowledge, the moral complexities of the individual consciousness. In contrast, the Fletcherian tradition (an outgrowth of the Cavalier aesthetic of the 1620s and 1630s) reifies aristocratic speech—what Dryden calls "the language of gentlemen"[6]—into both a stylistic and social ideal. Language embodies a code of gentlemanly behavior and values that makes the creation of an "objective" or "natural" discourse both a means and an end. Style, in short, becomes a measure of social worth, a badge of aristocratic self-definition.

Theoretically, then, Jonsonian humour and Fletcherian wit offers writers of the late seventeenth century two seemingly distinct stylistic opinions, two different philosophical traditions on which to draw. In practice, however, these traditions interact dialectically to produce a Cavalier, or Royalist, or aristocratic, prose style that conflates moral virtue and the external manifestations of "good breeding"—a key phrase for writers from Fletcher and James Shirley in the seventeenth century to Shaftesbury and Pope in the eighteenth. The result, for writers of the Restoration period, is a nearly fanatic concern with stylistic propriety, with making one's writing conform to aristocratic standards of verbal decorum.[7] As Brian Corman has shown, even a self-professed Jonsonian like the playwright Thomas Shadwell subordinates his satiric concerns to the stylistic prerogatives of Fletcherian wit comedy.[8] In trying to reconcile the often contradictory demands of "wit" and "humour," late seventeenth-century writers frequently blur the distinctions between them; in Shaftesbury's writings, for example, the terms often become interchangeable. William Congreve (to take only one example from among Shaftesbury's contemporaries) in the "Prologue" to his comedy *Love for Love* (1695) asserts his claims as both a satirist and a gentleman:

> Since *The Plain Dealer's* scenes of manly rage,
> Not one has dared to lash this crying age.
> This time the poet owns the bold essay,
> Yet hopes there's no ill-manners in his play:[9]

The falling off in these lines from the satiric "rage" of William Wycherley's play to Congreve's worries about "ill-manners" suggests something of the dilemma that confronts late seventeenth-century writers who must try to reconcile morality and stylistic decorum. As Jonson's prose comedies had demonstrated early in the century, the language of satire is inherently unstable; it inevitably participates in the corruption it condemns.[10] Or, to define the problem in Augustinian terms, the language of moral reflection must always be inadequate to the celebration of a deity who, by definition, cannot be understood or encompassed linguistically: this is the dilemma that confronts the anti-Ciceronian writers of the sixteenth and seventeenth centuries, from Montaigne and Bacon to Robert Boyle and Isaac Newton.[11] Almost by definition, the languages of satire and moral reflection work against the linguistic stability sought by an aristocratic discourse that prides itself on what Shaftesbury, Congreve, and Dryden refer to—unabashedly—as its own "perfection."

In one respect, Shaftesbury's *Characteristicks* may be read as an eighteenth-century attempt to resolve the crises of seventeenth-century prose style, to unite the languages of satiric morality and aristocratic manners. In practice, however, Shaftesbury's championing of "*The Simple* Manner" as "the strictest Imitation of Nature" (1:257) assumes stylistic values that emphasize aristocratic authority and verbal grace rather than the kind of epistemological inquiry which characterizes the writings of his seventeenth-century predecessors, notably Bacon. In the *Letter Concerning Enthusiasm*, Shaftesbury insists, "Justness of Thought and Stile, Refinement in Manners, good Breeding, and Politeness of every kind" (1:10) are "naturally" and irrevocably related; and he reiterates this point throughout his writings. This assumption prevents him from acknowledging the instability of classical or Jonsonian satire, its tendency to call into question even those values it seeks to affirm. In Shaftesbury's writings, the "self-consuming artifacts" of epistemological questioning give way to the reification of moral values—virtue, truth, and even aesthetic beauty—as idealized, ahistorical absolutes.[12] This process, the appropriation of traditional moral categories by a language of aristocratic authority, defines the stylistic construction of Shaftesbury's thought.

II

Throughout the *Characteristicks* Shaftesbury describes his prose style as "simple," straightforward, and unambiguous. This description suggests an almost Lockean conception of language as a transparent, utilitarian medium; and, to be sure, language, for Shaftesbury, always reflects what he sees as stable social values and timeless moral and aesthetic truths. Yet, at the same time, the act of writing—the dramatic presentation of self—fascinates Shaftesbury in a way that puzzled Locke. Style in *The Characteristicks* is part revelation, part complex game. It does not simply convey or passively reflect objective ideas but demonstrates, even embodies, the values it upholds.

Shaftesbury's prose style usually assumes one of three basic forms: the satiric, the self-consciously philosophical or analytic, and, in *The Moralists*, the rhapsodic. In defending his "variety of STILE," Shaftesbury calls these modes the "*Comick, Rhetorical,* and . . . the *Poetick* or *Sublime;* such as is the aptest to run into Enthusiasm and Extravagance" (3:285). Although diction and syntax vary widely among these styles, they are different strategies to the same or similar ends—demonstrating that good writing and "Good Breeding" are inseparable. Part of this demonstration is the idealizing of gentlemanly discourse as it appears in his texts. For Shaftesbury, "the appearance of the greatest Ease and Negligence" (1:257) defines a conscious stylistic program that attempts to bring philosophic discourse within the realm of polite conversation. Shaftesbury refers casually to his *Letter Concerning Enthusiasm* as "a sort of idle Thoughts, such as pretend only to Amusement, and have no relation to Business or Affairs" (1:3); but, in the first of his *Miscellanies*, he takes pains to defend his *"Concealment of Order"*: "the *Art* was to destroy every . . . Token or Appearance [of order], give an *extemporary* Air to what was writ, and make the *Effect* of Art be felt, without discovering the *Artifice*" (3:21–22). Style, realized as its own ideal, becomes ironically self-effacing. In defending himself against charges that his writing is unsystematic, Shaftesbury claims that he has been "sufficiently *grave* and *serious*, in defense of what is directly contrary to Seriousness and Gravity. I have very *solemnly* pleaded for *Gaiety* and GOOD-HUMOUR: I have declaim'd against *Pedantry* in learned Language, and oppos'd *Formality* in Form" (3:129). This kind of irony, a deliberate dissociation of content from form, emphasizes that language can be manipulated in various ways to produce different kinds of self-presentation. In this respect, Shaftesbury sees style (to borrow Dryden's metaphor) not as the man but as his clothing.

The studied artlessness of Shaftesbury's prose, though, is consciously crafted, drawing on diverse stylistic traditions and assuming diverse syntactical forms. In much of his writing, his stylistic models are the Roman satirists, Horace, Juvenal, and Persius. All three are quoted throughout his work; Horace is cited more than twice as often as all other writers—ancient and modern—combined. Shaftesbury frequently strives for a Horatian ideal of conversational ease and pointed wit. His language often tries to create its own sense of satiric authority:

> We may defend Villany, or cry up Folly, before the World: But to appear Fools, Mad-men, or Varlets, to *our-selves;* and prove it to our own faces, that we are really *such,* is insupportable. For so true a Reverence has every-one for himself, when he comes clearly to appear before his close Companion, that he had rather profess the vilest things of himself in open Company, then hear his Character privately from his own Mouth. So that we may readily from hence conclude, That the chief Interest of *Ambition, Avarice, Corruption,* and every sly insinuating *Vice,* is to prevent this Interview and Familiarity of Discourse which is consequent upon close Retirement and inward Recess. (1:173–74)

Shaftesbury's target in this passage is a staple of much seventeenth- and eighteenth-century satire: the kind of monstrous hypocrisy that deludes the individual even as he or she tries to dupe "the World." Stylistically, his prose is closer to, say, Jonson's than to Swift's in its subtle but significant disruptions of balanced rhetorical structures. The syntax of this passage is deliberately fragmented; what could be read as one leisurely sentence breaks into three. The emphasis is less on the logical development of the author's thought than on the cumulative rhetorical force of a series of aphoristic clauses structured around strong, unambiguous verbs. The intransitive verbs—"is"—in the first and third sentences carry the weight of universal decrees. In essence, Shaftesbury creates an authoritative satiric voice by his refusal to particularize. The generalizing tendency of his imagination transforms personal observation into what he calls elsewhere "a simple, clear, and *united View*," unbroken "by the Expression of any thing peculiar, or distinct" (1:143). In this respect, then, Shaftesbury presses the idiosyncratic language of satire into the service of promoting universal "truths." Its assertions about human "Villany" and "Folly" describe a satiric world distinct from the author's ideal realm of philosophical self-examination and self-knowledge.

Elsewhere, however, Shaftesbury assumes different stylistic strategies. In the *Inquiry Concerning Virtue*, his language becomes more self-consciously "philosophical," his syntax more complex and periodic, than in his other writings. The satiric, Horatian mode of Jonson and the English satirists is replaced by the stylistic model of Locke's philosophical writings. Citations of classical authorities largely disappear; atypically, Shaftesbury becomes less ironic than descriptive:

> Thus the several Motions, Inclinations, Passions, Dispositions, and consequent Carriage and Behaviour of Creatures in the various Parts of Life, being several Views or Perspectives represented to the Mind, which readily discerns the Good and Ill towards the Species or Publick; there arises a new Trial or Exercise of the Heart: which must either rightly and soundly affect what is just and right, and disaffect what is contrary; or, corruptly affect what is ill, and disaffect what is worthy and good. (2:30)

This sentence is carefully constructed around a central antithesis: "Good" versus "Ill." Clauses and phrases precisely balance or oppose each other; the verbs "affect" and "disaffect" are contrasted to achieve a logical as well as rhetorical closure. The syntax is relaxed, almost leisurely; Shaftesbury avoids the terse, epigrammatic statements that characterize his prose in other essays. In this passage, as throughout the *Inquiry*, he is rhetorically persuasive rather than satirically assertive.

In *The Moralists*, Shaftesbury attempts to articulate straightforwardly a coherent, idealistic philosophy in the person of Theocles. The dialogue form in which this essay is cast allows the author the opportunity to juxtapose the languages of wit and analytic philosophy. In turn, these modes are set against the "enthusiastic" language of Theocles' "Meditations," set pieces best described as deliberately rhapsodic excursions into Vergilian hyperbole. Theocles' first "Fit" (his own term) is a cross between what he calls "a sensible kind of Madness, like those Transports . . . permitted to our *Poets*" and "downright Raving" (2:346–47):

> Ye Fields and Woods, my Refuge from the toilsom World of Business, receive me in your quiet Sanctuarys, and favour my Retreat and thoughtful Solitude.—Ye verdant Plains, how gladly I salute ye!—Hail ye blissful Mansions! Known Seats! Delightful Prospects!! Majestick Beautys of this Earth, and all ye Rural Powers and Grace!—Bless'd be ye chaste Abodes of happiest Mortals, who here in peaceful Innocence enjoy a Life unenvy'd, tho Divine; whilst with its bless'd Tranquility it affords a happy Leisure and Retreat for Man; who, made for Contemplation, and to search his own and other Natures, may here best meditate the Cause of Things; and plac'd amidst the various Scenes of Nature, may nearer view her Works. (2:344)

As Theocles' comments suggest, this passage verges on self-parody; it both takes itself seriously and draws our attention to its excessive rhetoric. Its diction, tone, and subject set it apart from the language that Shaftesbury employs to characterize his more rational (and imaginatively limited) "dialogist," Philocles. It is, in short, very much a set speech or, to borrow one of Shaftesbury's favorite terms, a "Performance."

This passage marks itself, then, as the stylistic equivalent of Shaftesbury's "Enthusiasm," the dialectical opposite of the author's satire. Near the end of *The Moralists*, after several more rhapsodies, Theocles reaches the climax of this hyperbolic mode: "all sound *Love* and *Admiration* is ENTHUSIASM: the Transports of *Poets*, the Sublime of *Orators*, the Rapture of *Musicians*, the high Strains of the *Virtuosi*; all mere ENTHUSIASM! Even *Learning* it-self, the Love of *Arts* and *Curiositys*, the Spirit of *Travellers* and *Adventurers*; *Gallantry, War, Heroism*; All, all ENTHUSIASM!" (2:400). "ENTHUSIASM" here, as Stanley Green notes,[13] exemplifies the joy and idealism of Shaftesbury's philosophy. His style in this case reaches an extreme of authorial assertion. The range of eighteenth-century arts and sciences are comprehended by a single word: the capitalized abstraction—part cry of joy, part expression of awe, part command—becomes the linguistic representation of what Shaftesbury calls "the Good and Perfection of *the* UNIVERSE, [the deity's] *all-good* and *perfect Work*" (2:374). Language here yearns to transcend itself, to transcend the social conditions of its mundane existence and ascend to the realm of a mystical perfection.

III

Throughout his writings, Shaftesbury insists on the power of forms to affect the reader, viewer, or beholder, whether for good or ill: "beautiful forms beautify; polite polish. On the contrary, gothic gothicize, barbarous barbarize."[14] Style, then, is an affective process as well as a reflection of a writer's values; it polishes the reader's manners as it incites the reader to virtuous actions. In his defense of *Advice to an Author*, Shaftesbury maintains that although "his pretence has been to *advise Authors*, and polish *Stiles* . . . his Aim has been to correct *Manners*, and regulate *Lives*" (3:187). This "pretence" is less a deception than an unambiguous strategy. Shaftesbury's "literary" advice becomes a means of correction and regulation; the plural *"Lives"* suggests that he has more in mind than self-improvement. Language, in other words, embodies and deploys a system of values; it does not passively reflect a moral or aesthetic order but attempts to define and shape what "order" itself may be.

Shaftesbury appropriates the languages of satire, analytical philosophy, and rhapsodic praise as part of a larger, and at times explicit, effort to make the language of philosophy an active social force rather than merely a vehicle of scholastic definition and debate. His stylistic practice is often frankly polemical. He has, as he says, little interest in the "Magnificent Pretension" of trying to define *"material* and *immaterial Substances"* and distinguish "their *Propertys* and *Modes"* (1:289); in an important passage, he describes the purpose of his efforts as an appeal to "the grown *Youth* of our polite World . . . whose *Relish* is retrievable, and whose *Taste* may yet be form'd in *Morals;* as it seems to be, already, *in exteriour Manners* and *Behaviour"* (3:179). The significance that Shaftesbury places on this ideological aspect of his writing is implicit in his general definition of philosophy: "To *philosophize*, in a just Signification, is but To carry *Good-Breeding* a step higher. For the Accomplishment of Breeding is, To learn whatever is *decent* in Company, or *beautiful* in Arts: and the Sum of Philosophy is, To learn what is *just* in Society, and *beautiful* in Nature, and the Order of the World" (3:161). Polished language, *"Good Breeding," "*Manners," social grace, aesthetic perfection, natural harmony, and universal order form a natural progression in Shaftesbury's mind. Stylistically, the transition from one to the next is as smooth as the unfolding of his syntax.

The ease with which Shaftesbury equates stylistic decorum and aristocratic virtue reflects the insistent idealism which characterizes his perception of writing. Again and again in *The Characteristicks*, Shaftesbury emphasizes that the true artist, "tho his Intention be to please the World . . . must nevertheless be, in a manner, *above it;* and fix his Eye upon that consummate *Grace*, that Beauty of *Nature*, and that *Perfection* of Numbers" which allows him to maintain "at least the *Idea of* PERFECTION" (2:332) in his work. This ideal perfection, if unattainable, still guides "those Artists who . . . study the Graces and Perfections of *Minds*" and become "real Masters" who are "themselves improv'd, and amended in their *better Part*" (2:206) by their own endeavors. The "Moral Artist" who "can describe both *Men* and *Manners* . . . is indeed a second *Maker:* a just PROMETHEUS, under JOVE"; his art demonstrates "the Harmony of a Mind" (2:207). This kind of idealistic outburst goes beyond the often defensive rhetoric that characterizes many conventional Restoration apologies for "modern" literature. Shaftesbury's concern with "the *Idea* of PERFECTION," his idealizing of the poet as "a second *Maker*," translates historical literary opinion into a system of absolute aesthetic and moral values that finds its ultimate expression in the bold statement that "all *Beauty is* TRUTH" (1:142).

This equation, however, is more problematic than it first seems. Shaftesbury's idealization of the artist, his celebration of the "study of the Graces and Perfections of *Minds*," reflects an ideological bias against writers who do not fit his conception of what art and literary style should be. His comments on two significant figures in his literary past, Shakespeare and Seneca, are suggestive of both his indebtedness to the conventional critical prejudices of his era and his more radical attempts to define language as an ideological construct.

IV

In general, Shaftesbury's criticism of English poets reveals his resistance to much of his literary heritage. His tastes are often narrowly conservative, if not downright derivative; he tends to repeat familiar charges rather than analyze specific texts or writers. The "stammering Tongues" of his forerunners, he says, "have hitherto spoken in wretched Pun and Quibble. Our *Dramatick* SHAKESPEAR, our FLETCHER, JOHNSON, and our *Epick* MILTON preserve this Stile. And even a latter Race, scarce free of this Infirmity, and aiming at a false *Sublime*, with crouded *Simile*, and *mix'd Metaphor*, (The Hobby-Horse, and Rattle of the MUSES) entertain our raw Fancy, and unpractis'd Ear" (1:217). This criticism, if extreme, is nonetheless characteristic of much seventeenth-century literary thought; William Cartwright, Dryden, and Thomas Rymer, among others, had earlier made similar arguments.[15] Like these critics, Shaftesbury sees Shakespeare's achievement as a triumph of natural wit over the primitive, nearly barbaric nature of his dramatic language: "Notwithstanding his natural Rudeness, his unpolish'd Stile, his antiquated Phrase and Wit, his want of Method and Coherence, and his Deficiency in almost all the Graces and Ornaments of [dramatic] Writing; yet by the justness of his MORAL, the Aptness of many of his *Descriptions,* and the plain and natural Turn of several of his *Characters,* he pleases his Audience, and often gains their Ear; without a single Bribe from Luxury or Vice" (1:275). Shaftesbury's criticism of Shakespeare's "natural Rudeness" and "antiquated" language reveals both social and aesthetic prejudices that turn the dramatist into an intuitively virtuous country bumpkin. Shaftesbury's easy dismissal of his predecessor's dramatic language is largely a function of his own rhetoric of aristocratic exclusion. This is criticism by snob appeal. Yet, at the same time, Shaftesbury's praise of Shakespeare's moral authority suggests that the example of natural virtue can be instructive for eighteenth-century readers and audiences. Shakespeare and his contemporaries have "broken the Ice for those who are to follow 'em"; their eighteenth-century successors will "polish our Language, lead our Ear to finer Pleasure, and find out the true *Rhythms,* and harmonious Numbers, which alone can satisfy a just Judgment, and *Muse-like* Apprehension" (1:218). The implication in Shaftesbury's criticism of Shakespeare is that although morality and virtue remain the same in every era, the languages in which they are cast can be consciously and deliberately improved.

Language, for Shaftesbury, is therefore a social and political as well as a cultural artifact; it necessarily reflects the ideological conditions under which it is produced. At several points in his writings, he contrasts the literary products of "English liberty" (post-1688) with those of French, Italian, or ancient Roman "tyranny." He is particularly severe on Seneca. He prefaces his attack on "the random way of *Miscellaneous* Writing" (3:24) with an account of Seneca's influence as a writer: "We own *the Patriot,* and *good Minister:* But we reject *the Writer.* He was the first of any Note or Worth who gave credit to that *false* Stile and Manner [of miscellaneous writing]. He might, on this account, be call'd in reality *The Corrupter* of ROMAN *Eloquence*" (3:22). Yet given the "horrid Luxury and Effeminacy of the *Roman* Court . . . there was no more possibility of making a Stand for Language, than for Liberty" (3:23). Seneca, the honest statesman, is corrupted by the court in style rather than in personal morality. Though noble and patriotic, he writes "with infinite Wit, but with little or no Coherence; without a Shape or Body to his Work; without a real *Beginning,* a *Middle,* or an *End*" (3:24–25). Seneca, then, becomes both the victim of an artistically stifling and morally repressive society and the perpetrator of a kind of linguistic corruption that reaches down to modern times. In this manner, his "*false* Stile" reflects the tyranny of the Roman Empire's aggression; "by their unjust Attempts upon the Liberty of the World," says Shaftesbury, the Romans "justly lost their own. With their Liberty they lost not only their Force of

Eloquence, but even their Stile and Language it-self" (1:219). Literary style in this passage is perceived as historically determined, the product not of an individual consciousness but of a politically corrupt ideology. The aesthetic shortcomings of Seneca's miscellaneous writing, in short, reflect the disorder and irrationality which Shaftesbury sees as the inevitable result of tyranny.

As his remarks on Shakespeare and Seneca indicate, Shaftesbury, as critic, combines an acute sensitivity to the ideological nature of writing with an almost naïve belief in idealistic, ahistorical standards of literary value. His discussions of the history of language and style, whether Roman, British, or Greek (see 3:138–41), are, even by early eighteenth-century standards, fanciful, less attempts at historical reconstruction than assertions of his faith in the near-sanctity of classical tradition. If Shaftesbury is less hostile to received knowledge than Locke, he is also inclined to judge historical figures solely by the standards of contemporary aristocratic "breeding." He praises Menander, for example, by observing that "he join'd what was deepest and most solid in Philosophy, with what was easiest and most refin'd in Breeding, and in the Character and Manner of a Gentleman" (1:255). The vocabulary Shaftesbury employs to describe a comic playwright of the fourth century B.C. is reminiscent of the language that he uses throughout the *Characteristicks* to discuss his aesthetic and social ideals of writing and behavior. Menander is, in effect, imaginatively re-created as an English gentleman of the eighteenth century, an historical embodiment of values that Shaftesbury finds congenial. The implication is that the standards of art and breeding—like virtue itself—remain unchanged from era to era; what differ are merely the forms of corruption or barbarism that lead Seneca and Shakespeare to fall short of the stylistic ideals of polished wit, verbal grace, and aesthetic unity.

Shaftesbury's remarks on Shakespeare and Seneca, then, are less significant as original evaluations of his literary past than as demonstrations of the moral and aesthetic bases of his thought. Criticism, in his mind, is no mere parasitic commentary on primary texts but a dialectical attempt to distinguish between true and false standards of language, art, and morality. As a form of original discourse it mediates between the languages of poetry and philosophy; it complements—even rivals— creative art. Shaftesbury defends the critic's prerogatives to judge and improve the language—and manners—of his age. He "condemn[s] the fashionable and prevailing Custom of inveighing against CRITICKS, as the common Enemys, the Pests, and Incendiarys of the Commonwealth of Wit and Letters . . . on the contrary, they are the *Props* and *Pillars* of this Building; and without the Encouragement and Propagation of such a Race, we shou'd remain as GOTHICK *Architects* as ever" (1:235–36).

For Shaftesbury, critics as well as poets must be the legislators of any civilized race; they are the guardians of a classical learning which prevents one from falling prey to the trap of cultural relativism. In distinguishing between *"Criticks by Fashion"* and *"just Naturalist[s] or Humanist[s],"* Shaftesbury offers his own attack on literary fashion-mongering: "They who have no Help from Learning to observe the wider Periods or Revolutions of Human Kind, the Alterations which happen in Manners, and the Flux and Reflux of Politeness, Wit, and Art; are apt at every turn to make the present Age their standard, and imagine nothing barbarous or savage, but what is contrary to the Manners of their own Time" (1:271–72). Criticism offers a defense against novelty by promoting a cyclical view of literary history as the ongoing struggle of "Learning" against mere fashion. In this respect, Shaftesbury's praise of the ancients, like Ben Jonson's a century earlier, is an attempt to return to—and revitalize—what he sees as broadly Horatian standards of instruction and delight.

V

Shaftesbury's defense of criticism and the role of the critic is, at heart, a justification of his ambitions to perfect the English language as a medium for an aristocratic discourse of liberty and culture. The number of pages he devotes to a metacritical commentary on his previous work indicates how crucial the designation "critic" is to his self-perception as a writer. He sees the critic's task as an almost heroic undertaking, distinct from the kind of carping that, in his mind, characterizes his detractors: "To *censure* merely what another Person writes; to *twitch, snap, snub up,* or *banter;* to torture *Sentences* and *Phrases,* turn a few Expressions into Ridicule, or write what is now-a-days call'd an *Answer* to any Piece, is not sufficient to constitute what is properly esteem'd a WRITER, or AUTHOR in due form. For this reason, tho there are many ANSWERERS seen abroad, there are few or no CRITICKS or SATIRISTS" (3:271). Shaftesbury's linking of "CRITICKS" and "SATIRISTS" virtually erases traditional generic distinctions between critical and creative writing, between secondary and primary forms of discourse. Like satire, criticism participates in the radical, creative activity of trying to generate its own linguistic authority. The critical act, in this sense, becomes an attempt to establish one's authority and to reassert the "authority" of aristocratic and neoclassical values. For Shaftesbury, then, to write is to create an authoritative discourse, to redefine the traditional "authority" of language itself.

Like John Wilkins a generation earlier, Shaftesbury is intent on creating an authoritative, "natural" discourse that remains distinct from biblical tradition. Language, in his mind, imitates nature itself; it is not, as it is for Boyle, an imperfect refraction of a perfect biblical Logos.[16] Throughout the *Characteristicks*, Shaftesbury argues implicitly and explicitly that literary language is always historically mediated; it has no metaphysical existence beyond the limits of the printed page. His theistic enthusiasm—the direct contemplation of nature—therefore takes precedence over the written authority of the Bible. "The best Christian in the World," he states, "who being destitute of the means of *Certainty*, depends only on History and Tradition for his Belief in these Particulars [i.e., miracles], is at best but *a Sceptick-Christian*. He has no more than a nicely critical *Historical Faith*, subject to various Speculations, and a thousand different *Criticisms* of Languages and Literatures" (3:72). Biblical language, in this respect, cannot be distinguished from the "Criticisms" it inspires. It is a literary, and therefore historical, work; it can lay no real claim to being the mystical origin of language, the divine Logos. By inserting the Bible into the tradition of "a thousand different *Criticisms* of Languages and Literatures," Shaftesbury effectively rejects the logocentric assumptions that underlie Western linguistic theory from Augustine through the anti-Ciceronian prose stylists of the seventeenth century. One task Shaftesbury sets for himself is to relocate the origins—the authority—of critical or philosophical language.

In an important passage in the *Advice to an Author*, Shaftesbury contemplates what he perceives as the similarities between the origins of poetry and philosophy.

> 'Tis pleasant enough to consider how exact the resemblance was between the Lineage of *Philosophy* and that of *Poetry*; as deriv'd from their *two* chief Founders, or Patriarchs; in whose Loins the several Races lay as it were inclos'd. For as *the grand poetick* SIRE was . . . allow'd to have furnish'd Subject both to the *Tragick*, the *Comick*, and every other kind of genuine Poetry; so *the Philosophical* PATRIARCH, in the same manner, containing within himself the several Genius's of Philosophy, gave rise to all those several Manners in which that Science was deliver'd. (1:253–54)

The imagery in this passage—patriarchal and deliberately sexual—parodies the biblical rhetoric of both creation and procreation. Homer and Aristotle become nearly mythic, rather than merely historical, figures, containing "inclos'd" within themselves all of their subsequent poetic and philosophical progeny. These "Patriarchs" are truly originary; they stand at the beginning—or before—literary-historical time. The "several Manners" of poetic and philosophical discourse are similarly original.

They are not redefined or invented by subsequent generations of writers but exist embryonically within the works of Homer and Aristotle. For Shaftesbury, then, the role of the poet or philosopher is to develop, explicate, or (as Pope said of poets who must follow in the footsteps of Homer) paraphrase an authoritative discourse which already exists.

Philosophy, criticism, and poetry are, for Shaftesbury, languages of regeneration. They assert the timeless truths of order and harmony that structure both the natural and social worlds. To write is to enter into a dialectical relationship with literary or philosophical tradition, to revitalize classical authority, even as that authority justifies one's own writing. Shaftesbury's *Characteristicks*, in this respect, is less the articulation of a self-consciously original system than a celebration of what the author sees as his position within the classical tradition of his "Patriarchs." The literary dimensions of Shaftesbury's work are ultimately defined by the goals of his "performance" as an author—to demonstrate the values of an aristocratic culture that, in itself, remains essentially unchanged by the stylistic forms in which it is described.

Notes

1. One important exception has appeared since this chapter was written, Lawrence Klein, "The Third Earl of Shaftesbury and the Progress of Politeness," *Eighteenth-Century Studies* 18 (1984–85): 186–214. Klein demonstrates that in *The Characteristicks*, "Shaftesbury was self-consciously engaged in 'polite' literary performance, a phenomenon he construed in many" ideologically determined ways (p. 208). Klein's reading of Shaftesbury might be set against John Andrew Bernstein in *Shaftesbury, Rousseau, and Kant: An Introduction to the Conflict between Aesthetic and Moral Values in Modern Thought* (Rutherford, N.J.: Fairleigh Dickinson University Press, 1980). Robert Voitle's recent biography, *The Third Earl of Shaftesbury, 1671–1713* (Baton Rouge: Louisiana State University Press, 1984), though generally disappointing in its treatment of Shaftesbury's thought, raises valuable points about the relationship between his published work and his private philosophical "exercises" (see especially pp. 160–62). For representative views of Shaftesbury's aesthetic theories see Ernest Tuveson, "The Significance of Shaftesbury," *ELH* 20 (1953): 267–99; A. Owen Aldridge, "Lord Shaftesbury's Literary Theories," *Philological Quarterly* 24 (1945): 45–64; Robert Marsh, *Four Dialectical Theories of Poetry: An Aspect of English Neoclassical Criticism* (Chicago: University of Chicago Press, 1965), pp. 18–47; R. L. Brett, *The Third Earl of Shaftesbury: A Study in Eighteenth-Century Literary Theory* (London: Hutchinson, 1951); Stanley Grean, *Shaftesbury's Philosophy of Religion and Ethics: A Study in Enthusiasm* (Athens: Ohio University Press, 1967); Robert W. Uphaus, "Shaftesbury on Art: The Rhapsodic Aesthetic," *Journal of Aesthetics and Art Criticism* 27 (1969): 341–48; Pat Rogers, "Shaftesbury and the Aesthetics of Rhapsody," *British Journal of Aesthetics* 12 (1972): 244–57; Jerome Stolnitz, "On the Origins of 'Aesthetic Disinterestedness,'" *Journal of Aesthetics and Art Criticism* 20 (1961): 131–43; Dabney Townsend, "Shaftesbury's Aesthetic Theory," *Journal of Aesthetics and Art Criticism* 41 (1982): 206–13.

2. John Richetti, *Philosophical Writing: Locke, Berkeley, Hume* (Cambridge: Harvard University Press, 1983).

3. All quotations, cited parenthetically in the text by volume and page, are from the sixth edition of *Characteristicks of Men, Manners, Opinions, Times*, 3 vol. (London, 1737–38). This edition, which follows the authoritative second edition closely, includes the late, but significant, "Letter Concerning Design."

4. On seventeenth-century literary style see especially Stanley Fish, *Self-Consuming Artifacts: The Experience of Seventeenth-Century Literature* (Berkeley: University of California Press, 1972); *"Attic" and Baroque Prose: Essays by Morris W. Croll*, ed. J. Max Patrick et al. (Princeton: Princeton University Press, 1966); and, for a critique of traditional categories of stylistic description, Paul Arakelian, "The Myth of a Restoration Style Shift," *Eighteenth Century: Theory and Interpretation* 20 (1979): 227–45.

5. On the structure and historical significance of Jonson's prose see Jonas Barish, *Ben Jonson and the Language of Prose Comedy* (Cambridge: Harvard University Press, 1960).

6. The phrase occurs repeatedly throughout his work; see, for example, his reference to the comic style of Beaumont and Fletcher in W. P. Ker, ed., *The Essays of John Dryden* (Rpt., New York: Russell and Russell, 1962), 1:80–81.

7. See, for example, Dryden's remark in "Defense of the Epilogue," *Essays* 1:167–73. On Shaftesbury's aristocratic ideology, see Bernstein, *Shaftesbury, Rousseau, and Kant*, pp. 13, 55.

8. Brian Corman, "Thomas Shadwell and Jonsonian Comedy," in Robert Markley and Laurie Finke, eds., *From Renaissance to Restoration: Metamorphoses of the Drama* (Cleveland, Ohio: Bellflower Press, Case Western Reserve University, 1984), pp. 126–52.

9. Herbert Davis, ed., *The Complete Plays of William Congreve* (Chicago: University of Chicago Press, 1967), p. 214.

10. See Barish, *Jonson and the Language of Prose Comedy*, passim.

11. On Boyle and Newton, see Robert Markley, "Objectivity as Ideology: Boyle, Newton, and the Languages of Science," *Genre* 16 (1983): 355–72.

12. On Shaftesbury's aesthetic theory, see Rogers, "Shaftesbury and the Aesthetics of Rhapsody," pp. 244–57; Uphaus, "Shaftesbury on Art," pp. 341–48; Townsend, "Shaftesbury's Aesthetic Theory," pp. 206–13.

13. See Grean, *Shaftesbury's Philosophy*, especially pp. 19–36.

14. Benjamin Rand, ed., *Second Characters, or the Language of Forms* (Cambridge: Cambridge University Press, 1914), p. 123.

15. See Cartwright's commendatory verses in John Fletcher and Francis Beaumont, *Comedies and Tragedies* (London, 1647), Sig. d4r–d4v; Dryden, *Essays* 1:79–83; and Rymer, "Tragedies of the Last Age," in Curt Zimansky, ed., *The Critical Works of Thomas Rymer* (New Haven: Yale University Press, 1956), especially pp. 38–39.

16. See Boyle's *Some Considerations Touching the Style of the Holy Scriptures* (London, 1661). On the significance of Boyle's influence on the language theories of Locke and other philosophers, see Hans Aarsleff, "Leibniz on Locke on Language," rpt. in *From Locke to Saussure: Essays on the Study of Language and Intellectual History* (Minneapolis: University of Minnesota Press, 1982), pp. 42–83.

7

"A Philosophic Wanton": Language and Authority in Wollstonecraft's *Vindication of the Rights of Woman*

LAURIE A. FINKE

After the publication in 1792 of Mary Wollstonecraft's *Vindication of the Rights of Woman*, Horace Walpole, in a letter to Hannah More, described its author as one of "the philosophizing serpents we have in our bosom," and later as a "hyena in petticoats." A review of William Godwin's *Memoirs of the Author of "Vindication of the Rights of Woman"* in *European Magazine* describes Wollstonecraft posthumously as a "philosophic wanton."[1] Although *Rights of Woman* was not everywhere viewed with such loathing, a woman philosopher in the eighteenth century, as these remarks suggest, could be dismissed as unnatural, a perversion of nature. Dr. James Fordyce in *Sermons for Young Women* writes, "You yourself, I think, will allow that war, commerce, politics, exercises of strength and dexterity, abstract philosophy, and all the abstruser sciences are most properly the province of men. I am sure those masculine women, that would plead for your sharing any part of this province equally with us, do not understand your interests."[2] Just as women lacked the physical strength to wage war, so the argument went, they lacked the mental dexterity, the ability to reason abstractly, required of a philosopher. Any woman who could pretend to such abilities must be unsexed, a "masculine woman."

Clearly, however, "philosophy" is what Wollstonecraft thought she was writing in *Vindication of the Rights of Woman* and what so many of her contemporaries vilified her for attempting to write. A philosopher, Wollstonecraft writes elsewhere, "dedicates his existence to promote the welfare, and perfection of mankind, carrying his views beyond any time he chooses to mark."[3] In *Rights of Woman*, she claims, "Rousseau exerts himself to prove that all *was* right: a crowd of authors that all *is* now right: and I, that all will *be* right" (p. 15).[4] The *Vindication of the Rights of Woman* is Wollstonecraft's utopian vision of what woman's place should be in a perfected society. Her feminism, in this respect, is inseparable from the philosophy of egalitarianism that made her a staunch supporter of the ideals of the French Revolution.

On the surface, then, Wollstonecraft locates her concept of philosophy—her philosophic project—within the context of eighteenth-century attempts to define the nature of human beings within society. In *Rights of Woman*, Wollstonecraft begins with the premise that all human beings, women included, are rational and that through the exercise of reason the lot of mankind, and womankind, can be improved. Chapter 1 argues that "the perfection of our nature and capability of happiness, must be established by the degree of reason, virtue, and knowledge, that distinguish the individual, and direct the laws which bind society," and that "from the exercise of reason, knowledge and virtue naturally flow" (p. 12). The first part of *Rights of Woman* argues that denying women the capacity to reason has led to what she calls their "state of degradation" (chapter 1–4). For Wollstonecraft, this "natural" state of degradation is institutionalized by the male "authorities" who have written on women, a phenomenon she analyzes in chapter 5, "Animadversions on Some Writers Who Have Rendered Women Objects of Pity, Bordering on Contempt." This chapter is crucial in Wollstonecraft's argument. It examines the writings on women not only by philosophers like Rousseau, but also, and as importantly, by popular educators and conduct-book writers. At first, Wollstonecraft's use of such materials seems incongruous, at odds with her claims of philosophic seriousness. But, in her mind, the rationality that argues for the subjugation of women cannot be divorced from the social institutions that shape the lives of both men and women. For Wollstonecraft, neither philosophy nor reason can be timeless, ahistorical, or natural but must develop from an "early association of ideas"—that is, from the socializing process of education. In the last five chapters of *Rights of Woman*, Wollstonecraft sets out to dismantle the notion that philosophy and reason are the purveyors of timeless truths. By including chapters on social distinctions, on the family, on national education, and on the concepts of modesty and morality, Wollstonecraft examines the ways in which the attitudes and expectations that perpetuate the subjugation of women are encoded in the languages of the family, of the schools, and of philosophy itself.

Yet, even though the critics, both her contemporaries and ours, have perceived in *Rights of Woman* well-defined intellectual categories—history, politics, education, philosophy—the work has never found a comfortable niche in the history of eighteenth-century ideas. Her husband, William Godwin, calls it "a very unequal performance and eminently deficient in method and arrangement." Mary Hays notes in her memoirs of Wollstonecraft that "in perspecuity and arrangement it must be confessed to be defective." Even its most recent critics, while admitting its undeniable power, harp on the same flaws its original critics were so fond of pointing out. Ralph Wardle writes condescendingly of it: "the book is tedious. Did she write it in six weeks? Then would she have spent six years on it! . . . Its worst fault is its lack of organization." Eleanor Flexner argues that Wollstonecraft's "lack of education is also shown in her inability to organize material, to follow a consistent train of thought, or to avoid digressions when they are largely irrelevant and in her habit of loose organization. She is incapable either of the coherent organizaiton of ideas or of avoiding repetition."[5]

This criticism, however, faults Wollstonecraft for her disregard of philosophic authority and for not conforming to what most would acknowledge as the rhetorical rules of philosophic discourse: a commitment to a coherently expressed and logical argument, the dispassionate weighing of alternatives, and the objective observation of the world.[6] The charges of Wollstonecraft's lack of organization criticize her—paradoxically—by the very standards she is bent on attacking. Preoccupied with her breaches of philosophic and stylistic decorum, her critics largely fail to identify the alternatives posed by her writing because they have not done justice to her radically subversive argument. A more sympathetic critic writes, the "unevenness of the book, its unclear organization, its repetition of arguments, have less to do with Wollstonecraft's lack of formal education—she can be formidable in argument when she allows herself to be—than with her attempt to bring about a bloodless revolution."[7] The idiosyncrasies of her style that have been criticized in the past are part of a deliberate rhetorical strategy by which Wollstonecraft attempts to forge—out of a hostile philosophic tradition—an alternative language that embodies her thinking about her sex, a feminine rhetoric.

Wollstonecraft's style wavers between strategies of assimilation and strategies of rebellion, between conservative philosophic language and a radical attempt to call into question its assumptions and values. This stylistic tension reflects tension in her argument between traditionalist and revolutionary views of the nature of women. As Virginia Woolf notes, Wollstonecraft's arguments in Rights of Woman are at once original and clichéd; they are, she states, "so true that they seem now to contain nothing new in them."[8] Wollstonecraft accepts without question some stereotypic notions of women. She never questions the nurturing role given women by society; women ought to be given rights, she argues, primarily to make them better mothers. "When I treat of the peculiar duties of woman," she writes, "as I should treat of the peculiar duties of a citizen or father, it will be found that I do not mean to insinuate that they should be taken out of their families, speaking of the majority" (p. 63). Later she writes, "As the care of children in their infancy is one of the grand duties annexed to the female character by nature, this duty would afford many forcible arguments for strengthening the female under-standing, if it were properly considered" (p. 151). These statements are characteristic of most of Wollstonecraft's argument. She accepts as bio-logical facts the social imperatives that limit women (with some excep-tions) to roles as wives and mothers.

Yet, without making Wollstonecraft into a twentieth-century feminist, we can perceive a more radical tendency toward asserting the political independence and rights of women. Her argument is frequently cast in economic terms: "How many women thus waste life away the prey of discontent, who might have practised as physicians, regulated a farm, managed a shop, and stood erect, supported by their own industry, instead of hanging their heads surcharged with the dew of sensibility, that consumes the beauty to which it at first gave lustre" (p. 149). Passages such as these work against the stereotypes that Wollstonecraft generally accepts. If women are to be better mothers and wives, they must have at least the choice of alternative ways of living. In this respect, her argument is often forthrightly egalitarian and feminist. Nowhere is Wollstonecraft's propensity to radical thought more evident than in her penultimate chapter on the reform of national education.

> If marriage be the cement of society, mankind should all be educated after the same model, or the intercourse of the sexes will never deserve the name of fellowship, nor will women ever fulfill the pecu-liar duties of their sex, till they become enlightened citizens, till they become free by being enabled to earn their own subsistence, indepen-dent of men; in the same manner, I mean, to prevent misconstruction, as one man is independent of another. (P. 165)

Education, in Wollstonecraft's mind, becomes inseparable from an equality of opportunity for the sexes. Although she is careful to sub-sume "education" within the framework of traditional sex roles, the implication of her argument is: women must be given greater political and economic freedom to exercise their rights in new and potentially disruptive (at least for her critics) ways.

This tension between the conservative and radical elements of her argument informs and structures Wollstonecraft's prose in *Rights of Woman*. Indeed, the conservative elements of her argument result from her conscious stylistic decision to write from within a philosophic tradition. "Yet, because I am a woman, I would not lead my readers to suppose that I mean violently to agitate the contested question respecting the inequality or inferiority of the sex; but as the subject lies in my way, and I cannot pass it over without subjecting the main tendency of my reasoning to misconstruction, I shall stop a moment to deliver, in a few words, my opinion" (p. 8). The apologetic tone of these remarks (and many like them) reveals the anxieties Wollstonecraft experienced as a woman writing for a living. She must avoid the appearance of being too radical; she must not appear violent or overly passionate. Instead, to gain her audience's acceptance, she must appropriate masculine models of writing while, at the same time, effacing her sexual identity. Characteristically, Wollstonecraft attempts to outdo her male counterparts in their own style, to demonstrate her rationality, objectivity, and evenhandedness. She identifies herself in her writing with men, referring, in this passage to women as "the sex" and in others simply as "them." She distances herself throughout *Rights of Woman* from her "despised femininity" by dismissing "pretty feminine phrases" (p. 9), "pretty superlatives," and "false sentiments" (p. 10) from her self-consciously masculine style.

These decisions reflect Wollstonecraft's belief that she is writing for an unsympathetic audience—she conceives of and addresses her readers primarily as men, not as other women.[9] She also writes within a paternalistic philosophic tradition that excludes women as both writers and subjects. To enable herself to write, Wollstonecraft adopts the combative rhetorical pose of patriarchal discourse—even as she simultaneously subverts it. She must work within the confining strictures of a rhetoric that is aggressively masculine. Rhetoric, Walter Ong argues, "developed in the past as a major expression on the rational level of the ceremonial combat which is found among males and typically only among males at the physical level throughout the entire animal kingdom." As a result, "until the romantic age, academic education was all but exclusively focused on defending a position (thesis) or attacking the position of another person."[10] Philosophic discourse in the eighteenth century was tied to this peculiarly martial concept of rationality. As a woman, Wollstonecraft could not hope to be published without appropriating the trappings of this rhetorical pose, however incongruous it might seem for her sex. For this reason, she is stridently argumentative in asserting her thesis:

In this work I have produced many arguments, which to me were conclusive, to prove that the prevailing notion respecting a sexual character was subversive of morality, and I have contended, that to render the human body and mind more perfect, chastity must more universally prevail. . . . (P. 4)

> I have repeatedly asserted, and produced what appear to me irrefraga-
> ble arguments drawn from matters of fact, to prove my assertion, that
> women cannot, by force, be confined to domestic concerns. . . . (P. 5)

She "contends" and "proves" arguments, drawn from "fact," that are
"irrefragable" and "conclusive"; the verb "contending" in the first passage possesses all the force of its primary connotation of combat. The
first four chapters are full of such self-conscious references to her argument: she speaks of disputes and proofs, of "simple truths," of "unequivocal axioms," and of "reason," a word that can be found at least
once on virtually every page of *Rights of Woman*. The militant tone of her
language is partly the result of the warmth with which she writes, but it
is also calculated to establish her credentials as an aggressive, even
masculine reasoner, and to enlist the sympathies of heretofore hostile or
indifferent male readers by proving herself one of them and not merely a
woman.

   The value Wollstonecraft places on such a "masculine understanding"
is evident in her praise of Catherine Macaulay, who for Wollstonecraft
was "an example of intellectual acquirements supposed to be incompatible with the weakness of her sex. In her style of writing, indeed, no sex
appears, for it is like the sense it conveys, strong and clear" (p. 105). Like
Macaulay, Wollstonecraft, in appropriating a masculine rhetoric, must
efface herself as a speaking subject and her sexual identity along with it.
Again and again in *Rights of Woman*, she tries to ensure her objectivity by
creating a fictional vantage point that allows her to stand outside of her
feminine experiences.

> Let me now as from an eminence survey the world stripped of all its
> false delusive charms. The clear atmosphere enables me to see each
> object in its true point of view, while my heart is still. I am calm as the
> prospect in a morning when the mists, slowly dispersing, silently
> unveil the beauties of nature, refreshed by rest. (P. 110)

In dedicating herself to describing the truth, she assumes what one critic
has called an "ideal, disembodied state" that allows her to transcend her
femininity. Her "Miltonic disinterestedness" creates the illusion that she
speaks from outside the "false delusive charms" of the world, from
beyond the historical circumstances that led her to compose *Rights of
Woman*.[11]

   On the surface, therefore, Wollstonecraft's treatise attempts to conform to the rhetorical rules of logical argument, rules developed by and
for men. It asserts and supports a thesis, attacking its opponents by
rational argument. Its prose attempts to be, like Macaulay's, "strong and

clear." Furthermore, she impresses the reader with her objectivity, visible in the transparency of her prose.

> Animated by this important object, I shall disdain to cull my phrases or polish my style;—I aim at being useful and sincerity will render me unaffected; for, wishing rather to persuade by the force of my arguments, than dazzle by the elegance of my language, I shall not waste my time in rounding periods, or in fabricating the turgid bombast of artificial feelings, which, coming from the head, never reach the heart.—I shall be employed about things, not words!—and, anxious to render my sex more respectable members of society, I shall try to avoid that flowery diction which has slided from essays into novels, and from novels into familiar letters and conversation. (P. 10)

This passage accomplishes two purposes. First, it distances Wollstonecraft's writing from the more trivial kinds of women's writing—novels, letters, and the like—and identifies it more closely with masculine writing; it purports to be forceful, not flowery. Second, and more importantly, it does what all philosophic writing since Plato must do. It creates the fiction that its rhetoric—the rhetoric of rational discourse—does not really exist, that the prose is simply a vehicle, a "mirror of nature," which conveys unmediated truth. Wollstonecraft's sincerity, and hence the truth of her argument, are assumed by her concern with "things," not "words." She, rather ingenuously, disdains "rounding periods," "the turgid bombast of artificial feeling," and "elegant" language. Such a ploy is intended to prevent the reader from considering the role language and rhetoric must necessarily play in shaping a truth and hence the possibility that truth is much more subject to the writer's perspective and position within a particular historical and social context than many philosophers would like to believe.[12]

Wollstonecraft's insistence on the disinterestedness of her prose, and hence its truth, is one reason she is so often criticized when she fails to live up to her standards. Yet this rhetorical strategy proves much more problematic for a woman philosopher than for her male counterparts. Wollstonecraft recognizes the problems implicit for her writing in the masculine models she adopts. The illusion of complete objectivity is necessary, but it does not suit her purposes beyond establishing her ability to reason as effectively as a man, thus establishing her authority, because it reinforces as truths masculine notions of women and ensures the secondariness of women. Her attack on patriarchy requires that she question all "artificial structure[s]" (p. 78) that repress women as subjects; one of the most powerful of these structures is writing. She must appropriate the apparently disinterested rhetoric of masculine authority for her own purposes because there is no other language in which she can write; but she must simultaneously subvert it, exposing it as an arbitrary fiction, a prejudice that keeps women in their place. She must fashion out of patriarchal discourse a language in which to inscribe her subjectivity and experience as correctives to the masculine authorities on women she has read. Her task is not easy.

In *Rights of Woman* experience—Wollstonecraft's experience—is constantly bumping up against the authority of the written word. The opening paragraph illustrates this productive tension between what becomes in *Rights of Woman* two kinds of rhetoric: that of the philosophic authorities she has read, and that of her experiences as a woman.

> After considering the historical page, and viewing the living world with anxious solicitude, the most melancholy emotions and sorrowful indignation have depressed my spirits and I have sighed when obliged to confess, that either nature has made a great difference between man and man, or that the civilization which has hitherto taken place in the world has been very partial. I have turned over various books written on the subject of education, and patiently observed the conduct of parents and the management of schools; but what has been the result?—a profound conviction that the neglected education of my fellow-creatures is the ground source of the misery I deplore; and that women, in particular, are rendered weak and wretched by a variety of concurring causes, originating from one hasty conclusion. (P. 7)

The first sentence is a microcosm of Wollstonecraft's style. The tone of the first clause is judicious. Words such as "considering" and "viewing" create the impression of a thoughtful observer, while "anxious solicitude" gives just the right sense of distance objectivity. The speaking subject, if not totally suppressed, stands out of the situation she surveys. "Historical page" imparts weight and authority to the prose, both because it is a circumlocution for "books" and because it invokes "authority." The rationality and disinterestedness of the first clause, however, give way in the second to a personal emotion of gothic intensity, conveyed by words and phrases such as "melancholy," "sorrowful indignation," "depressed," and "sighed." The second sentence repeats the same pattern. The dispassionate phrases "turned over" and "patiently observed" are followed in the second clause by "profound conviction," "neglected education," "misery," and "weak and wretched," all of which she "deplores." The contradictions of Wollstonecraft's life—her belief in the Enlightenment ideal of reason as opposed to the passionate intensity of her life—are embedded in her prose. Each sentence begins objectively, but the façade is quickly dropped. The pose of objectivity itself is called into question. The reader is, with the writer, drawn into a subjective experience of womanhood. The paragraph climaxes in an extended simile describing woman as created—and perverted—by man, a hothouse flower, "planted in too rich a soil," whose "strength and usefulness are sacrificed to beauty" (p. 7). Wollstonecraft's strategy in this introductory paragraph enables her to consider herself—a woman—as both subject and object. It enables her to adopt the masculine rhetoric of eighteenth-century philosophy and at the same time to subvert it, questioning its truths about women.

The clash between masculine and feminine rhetorics or strategies of writing repeats itself throughout *Rights of Woman*. The effect is less that of a single style (however various), than of a variety of competing styles, each of which makes different claims on the reader's attention. The extremes of Wollstonecraft's styles testify to the perspicuity of Mary Hays's remark that "the high masculine tone, sometimes degenerating into coarseness, that characterizes this performance, is in a variety of parts softened and blended with a tenderness of sentiment, an exquisite delicacy of feeling, that touches the heart, and takes captive the imagination."[13] As Wollstonecraft appropriates and experiments with various kinds of masculine rhetorical poses, she demonstrates just how difficult it is for a woman, even a woman of superior sense, to get outside of the language of men, to create a language capable of expressing feminine desire and experience.

In *Rights of Woman*, Wollstonecraft strives for stylistic effects appropriate to the philosophic seriousness of her argument. Her language is often elaborately structured, even ponderous, given to rhetorical flourishes that are intended as much to create a tone of weighty disinterestedness as to further the specifics of her argument.

The stamen of immortality, if I may be allowed the phrase, is the perfectibility of human reason; for, were man created perfect, or did a flood of knowledge break in upon him, when he arrived at maturity, that precluded error, I should doubt whether his existence would be continued after the dissolution of the body. But, in the present state of things, every difficulty in morals that escapes from human discussion, and equally baffles the investigation of profound thinking, and the lightning glance of genius, is an argument on which I build my belief of the immortality of the soul. Reason is, consequentially, the simple power of improvement; or, more properly speaking, of discerning truth. (Pp. 52–53)

Both the diction and syntax contribute to the impression of philosophic authority that Wollstonecraft tries to create in this passage. She relies heavily on abstract, Latinate nouns such as "stamen," "immortality," "perfectibility," and "dissolution" to create a sense of stasis. Her first sentence delays, through a long series of dependent clauses, her main point that perfection logically precludes existence since the purpose of existence is to strive for perfection. The reader is asked to follow the sentence's, and indeed the whole passage's, movement hypotactically through a series of logical connectives—"if," "for," "when," "but," and "consequentially." The passage as a whole attempts to command assent by convincing the reader of the objectivity, the orderliness, and hence the truth of its argument. The characteristics often associated with philosophic discourse—seriousness, abstraction, and logical connection through subordination (cause and effect)—all figure prominently here in Wollstonecraft's style.

Yet even in this passage, so thoroughly serious about itself as philosophy, Wollstonecraft characteristically undercuts its masculine fictions of objectivity and certitude. Many of the dependent clauses create seemingly unnecessary hedges: "if I may be allowed the phrase," "I should doubt," "I build my belief," and the subjunctives "were" and "did." The author, in one sense, heaps qualification upon qualification, creating a rhetoric that both asserts and questions its own beliefs. The result is a language that distrusts the authority of philosophic discourse, and distrusts the ability of language to proceed logically to a discovery of truth. Her philosophic style, in this regard, insists not merely on its own authority but on the ambiguities that inhere in the assumptions philosophy traditionally makes about its claims to authoritative discourse.

Wollstonecraft's distrust of the language that she employs results in radical shifts in style and tone. Her philosophic prose is experimental, given to pushing the decorum of philosophic language to its extremes. Chapter 7, "On Modesty," begins with an exaggerated apostrophe.

Modesty! Sacred offspring of sensibility and reason!—true delicacy of mind!—may I unblamed presume to investigate thy nature, and trace to its covert the mild charm, that mellowing each harsh feature of a character, renders what would otherwise only inspire cold admiration—lovely!—Thou that smoothest the wrinkles of wisdom, and softenest the tone of the sublimest virtues till they all melt into humanity;—thou that spreadest the ethereal cloud that, surrounding love, heightens every beauty, it half shades, breathing those coy sweets that steal into the heart, and charm the senses—modulate for me the language of persuasive reason, till I rouse my sex from the flowery bed, on which they supinely sleep life away! (P. 121)

This passage is one often counted among the inflated excesses of Wollstonecraft's style. Mary Poovey, for instance, discusses it at some length, noting that the "artificial and abstract rhetoric" enables Wollstonecraft to distance herself from her volatile emotions, in this case from her sexuality.[14] For Poovey, Wollstonecraft's "dematerialization" of her subject is proof of her ideological commitment to the repression of female sexuality. Poovey is right, and others have commented on Wollstonecraft's almost pathological denial of female sexuality.[15] Yet the passage's excesses border on parody and, considered in the context of the chapter's style, they have a quite different effect.

The language of this passage is a parody of feminine discourse as a man would conceive it. It mocks the docile, acutely feminine voice of countless gothic heroines. It echoes woman's weakness and dependence. To lend some authority to the prose, she borrows a nearly biblical phraseology, replacing the more common "you" with "thou" and "thy" and employing the feminine verb ending *-est* in "smoothest," "softenest," and "spreadest." Her abstract diction forgoes the pursuit of philosophical truth for clichés: "mellowing," sublimest," "wrinkle of wisdom," "ethereal cloud," "coy sweets," and "flowery bed." The paragraph's climax conjures up the image of a Sleeping Beauty or a gothic heroine, passively, even docilely, awaiting the arrival of her savior—and her despoiler.

Wollstonecraft underscores the ironic mockery of her prayer to Modesty to "modulate for me the language of persuasive reason" when in the next sentence this is precisely what happens: she "modulates" her style to a different kind of language.

> In speaking of the association of ideas, I have noticed two distinct modes; and in defining modesty, it appears to me equally proper to discriminate that purity of mind, which is the effect of chastity, from a simplicity of character that leads us to form a just opinion of ourselves, equally distant from vanity or presumption, though by no means incompatible with a lofty consciousness of our own dignity. (Pp. 121–22)

The straightforward language of this sentence is as serious as the previous one is purplish. Despite its length, it has a plainness lacking in the previous passage, and even in the more philosophic sections of Wollstonecraft's prose. Its insistence on logical divisions and classifications coincides with its simplicity of diction and style. It must be read, then, as the antithesis of the preceding paragraph, even as it asks the reader to compare rhetorical strategies. Taken together, these two passages define the difference between what Wollstonecraft sees as a feminine style foisted upon women by men and what she sees as a truly philosophical style, one which, in effect, subsumes the differences between masculine and feminine in its pursuit of general truths.

Wollstonecraft's attempts to rewrite philosophic discourse, to move from a prose characterized by its reliance on masculine models to one which can convey her experience and observations, are the basis for her efforts to create a style free from the tyranny of masculine ideology. But her success at circumventing—or subverting—the ideologies of patriarchy and middle-class morality is necessarily mixed. To criticize the system, Wollstonecraft must write from within it; she must borrow one language in order to create a new one. Her attempts to deal with feminine experience are often undermined by a language that verges on bourgeois sentimentality. The long passage below suggests the difficulty of her task:

> Cold would be the heart of a husband, were he not rendered unnatural by early debauchery, who did not feel more delight at seeing his child suckled by its mother, than the most artful wanton tricks could ever raise; yet this natural way of cementing the matrimonial tie, and twisting esteem with fonder recollections, wealth leads women to spurn. To preserve their beauty, and wear the flowery crown of the day, which gives them a kind of right to reign for a short time over the sex, they neglect to stamp impressions on their husbands' hearts, that would be remembered with more tenderness when the snow on the head began to chill the bosom, than even their virgin charms. The maternal solicitude of a reasonable affectionate woman is very interesting, and the chastened dignity with which a mother returns the caresses that she and her child receive from a father who has been fulfilling the serious duties of his station, is not only a respectable, but a beautiful sight. So singular, indeed, are my feelings, and I have endeavoured not to catch factitious ones, that after having been fatigued with the sight of insipid grandeur and the slavish ceremonies that with cumberous pomp supplied the place of domestic affections, I have turned to some other scene to relieve my eye by resting it on the refreshing green every where scattered by nature. I have then viewed with pleasure a woman nursing her children, and discharging the duties of her station with, perhaps, merely a servant maid to take off her hands the servile part of the household business. I have seen her prepare herself and children, with only the luxury of cleanliness, to receive her husband, who returning weary home in the evening found smiling babes and a clean hearth. My heart has loitered in the midst of the group, and has even throbbed with sympathetic emotion, when the scraping of the well-known foot has raised a pleasing tumult. (Pp. 142–43)

In this pasasage, Wollstonecraft confronts a subject of almost exclusive concern to women—breastfeeding. While such a subject might occupy the attention of, say, a medical book on obstetrics, in the context of a philosophic work such as *Rights of Woman* purports to be, its inclusion appears ludicrously incongruous, even tasteless. Yet Wollstonecraft's treatment of the subject is less tasteless than overly sentimental, less radical than fraught with the values of conservative bourgeois ideology. The passage employs a clichéd poetic diction to defuse a potentially embarrassing subject, one perhaps too closely allied with female sexuality, a subject Wollstonecraft generally prefers to ignore in *Rights of Woman* as potentially dangerous or highly disturbing. Her choice of imagery, euphemisms, and circumlocutions in this passage disembody her subject, rendering it nonthreatening and safe. Nowhere is there any hint of the physical suggested by the word "breastfeeding." Instead, "the child" is "suckled by its mother." Images like "stamp impressions," "snow on the head," and "chill the bosom" distance the writer from her body and perhaps from her desires and experiences. The entire passage basks in the kind of sensibility and flowery diction of which she has earlier been so critical and which she had hoped to avoid: "virgin charms," "maternal solicitude," "caresses," "smiling babes," "throbbed with sympathetic delight," and "pleasing tumult" create safe emotionalism that allows the writer to assume a position of both superiority and alienation. This passage, rather than confronting the feminine as a potentially creative and liberating, although disturbing, force, endorses the middle-class virtues of economy and cleanliness which have kept women in the state Wollstonecraft deplores.

Wollstonecraft's failure here is instructive. In this passage she demonstrates just how difficult it is to deal with female experience within the context of a philosophic discourse that was created to treat only masculine experience. She can appropriate either the vocabulary of the medical textbook or that of the sentimental novel, but either way she falsifies the experience. Breastfeeding was a subject Wollstonecraft felt very strongly about. It symbolized for her one way in which woman could be at once creative and powerful, and nurturing without being rendered powerless and secondary. For her, it must be a fit subject for philosophy if philosophy were ever to become truly egalitarian. Yet, the philosopher's insistence on reason must deny the emotional nature of the mother-child relationship, while the only language available to Wollstonecraft with which to describe this female experience is the flowery diction of sentimentality. The stylistic dilemma this passage creates for Wollstonecraft is crucial to understanding the so-called flaws of *Vindication of the Rights of Woman*. Wollstonecraft must constantly move between two poles, between a masculine posture of confrontation and a feminine strategy of indirection, between reason and emotion.[16]

"We reason deeply, when we forcibly feel," Wollstonecraft writes in *Letters Written during a Short Residence in Sweden, Norway, and Denmark*.[17] As my analysis of this passage suggests, reason and passion, for Wollstonecraft, cannot exist as mutually exclusive modes of thought. She attacks the eighteenth century's bifurcation of emotion and reason and its concomitant devaluation of emotion as feminine.[18] Emotions are not the sole prerogative of the female. Indeed, in their present state, she argues, women do not experience true emotion: "Women are supposed to possess more sensibility, and even humanity, than men, and their strong attachments and instantaneous emotions of compassion are given as proofs; but the clinging affectation of ignorance has seldom any thing noble in it, and may mostly be resolved into selfishness . . ." (p. 188). Nor are men purely rational creatures, like Dean Swift's "insipid Houyhnhnms" (p. 58). Their so-called rational arguments slide as easily into sentimentality and emotion as a woman's. According to Wollstonecraft, Rousseau's errors all arise from "sensibility": "When he should have reasoned he became impassioned" (p. 90). Neither reason nor emotion can be the exclusive province of either sex, nor can the two function independently: "the passions should unfold our reason" (p. 14).

Accustomed as they are to the elegant dialectics of eighteenth-century philosophy—in which reason opposes passion; slavery tyranny; power powerlessness; body spirit; male female—little wonder Wollstonecraft's critics feel so ill as ease with her prose and have accused her of pointless digressions. Central to her critique of patriarchal culture is her challenging a rhetoric that can so neatly dispose of contradictions by creating such rigid dichotomies, often in the service of oppression. All such oppositions imply the valorization of one term to the exclusion of the other; the powerful are privileged over the powerless, the objective over the subjective, reason over emotion, and male over female. Generally, the lesser of each pair is regarded as feminine and devalued accordingly. Wollstonecraft forges a new rhetoric to counter the oppressive power of this confrontational rhetoric by conflating oppositions, collapsing one term into the other. This strategy has the effect of robbing the one term of its privileged masculine status and revaluing the other. Elissa Guralnick has pointed out that, in *Rights of Woman* "oppressed woman-kind serves . . . not merely as a figure for oppressed and impoverished mankind, but as a figure for all men, high as well as low, who are implicated in social and political contacts which condone inequality of wealth, rank, and privilege."[19]

Woman is, at once, a figure for both oppressed and oppressor, for in Wollstonecraft's mind, woman is *both* tyrant and slave. Women, "sometimes boast of their weakness, cunningly obtaining power by playing on the *weakness* of men; and they may well have more real power than their masters" (p. 40). Her strategy, throughout *Rights of Woman*, exposes the neat dialectics of patriarchy as tools of oppression. The long digressions in chapter 1, for instance, on the monarchy, the army, and the clergy illustrate for many critics Wollstonecraft's tendency to lose track of her argument. In their minds, the abuses of power she finds in these institutions have nothing to do with her argument about the rights of woman. For Wollstonecraft, however, they are precisely the point; they are examples of that "arbitrary power" (p. 15) that keeps women from exercising their rights and duties as citizens. She attacks all institutions "in which great subordination of rank constitutes its power" (p. 17).

> It is impossible for any man, when the most favorable circumstances concur, to acquire sufficient knowledge and strength of mind to discharge the duties of a king, entrusted with uncontrouled power; how then must they be violated when his very elevation is an insuperable bar to the attainment of either wisdom or virtue; when all the feeling of a man are stifled by flattery, and reflection shut out by pleasure! Surely it is madness to make the fate of thousands depend on the caprice of a weak fellow, whose very station sinks him *necessarily* below the meanest of his subjects. But one power should not be thrown down to exalt another—for all power inebriates weak men; and its abuse proves that the more equality there is established among men, the more virtue and happiness will reign in society. (P. 16)

Central to Wollstonecraft's argument here is the belief that power *is* powerlessness and tyranny *is* slavery. This passage suggests that the institution of monarchy is a figure for this paradox. It oppresses not only the "common mass of mankind" (p. 37), but the monarch as well, who becomes enslaved to flatterers and sycophants. By usurping all power for itself, the monarchy itself is powerless. By tyrannizing over others, a king is himself enslaved; his very station "sinks him *necessarily* below the meanest of his subjects." Repeatedly in *Rights of Woman*, Wollstonecraft attacks the divine right of kings along with the divine right of husbands (p. 41). But women, too, are like kings—their power springs from their weakness and their weakness springs from their power. "A king is always a king—and a woman always a woman" (p. 56): both exercise their right to enslave others to the detriment of their own freedom.

The clergy and the military provide Wollstonecraft with two more analogies for the woman who is both slave and despot. "Blind submission" (p. 18) is the lesson of the clergy, while the army is "a chain of despots, who, submitting and tyrannizing without exercising their reason, become dead weights of vice and folly on the community" (p. 17). Indeed, soldiers become feminine in their tyrannical servility.

> As for any depth of understanding, I will venture to affirm, that it is as rarely to be found in the army as amongst women; and the cause, I maintain, is the same. It may be further observed, that officers are also particularly attentive to their persons, fond of dancing, crowded

rooms, adventures and ridicule. Like the *fair* sex, the business of their lives is gallantry.—They were taught to please and they only live to please. (P. 24)

The language here and in other passages (pp. 17, 39) emasculates army officers; it works to reduce the distinctions between male and female, showing that, rather than being biologically innate, many result from social prejudice and early training.

As Wollstonecraft's argument develops, the oppression of women attaches itself to so many other social issues that eventually it encompasses all forms of oppression. Yet, as Elissa Guralnick has pointed out, she rarely compares women to the "truly abject."[20] Instead, Wollstonecraft links women to the powerful and privileged, arguing that "wealth and female softness equally tend to debase mankind" (p. 51). Repeatedly, the rich, like military officers, are emasculated:

> . . . the whole female sex are, till their character is formed, in the same condition as the rich: for they are born . . . with certain sexual privileges, and whilst they are gratuitously granted them, few will ever think of works of supererogation, to obtain the esteem of a small number of superior people. (P. 57)

> . . . women, in general, as well as the rich of both sexes, have acquired all the follies and vices of civilization and missed the useful fruit. (P. 60)

> The comparison with the rich still occurs to me; for, when men neglect the duties of humanity, women will follow their example; a common stream hurries them both along with thoughtless celerity. Riches and honours prevent a man from enlarging his understanding, and enervate all his powers by reversing the order of nature, which has ever made true pleasure the reward of labour. (P. 64)

Wollstonecraft so frequently reiterates the comparison between women and the rich that it becomes less a flaw in her argument—a pointless digression or tedious repetition—than an essential element in it. She realizes that the edifice of male privilege has been built upon the bifurcation of masculine and feminine virtue. Metaphoric emasculation, the collapsing of the dichotomy between male and female, is one of the tools she uses to dismantle the "artificial structure" of power, exposing it as an ideological formation and not the natural order of things.

Wollstonecraft defines power in what many cultural critics would call ideological terms.[21] Underlying and uniting all the digression and repetition in *Rights of Woman* is an attack on an ideology of male power that has hardened into absolute authority.

Power, in fact, is ever true to its vital principle, for in every shape it would reign without controul or inquiry. Its throne is built across a deep abyss, which no eye must dare to explore, lest the baseless fabric should totter under investigation. (P. 150)

Ideological power is all the more difficult to question precisely because its foundations are nearly invisible. For Wollstonecraft, power inheres not in any single institution or individual, but in what Foucault calls the "deployment" or discursive formation of languge and belief.[22] Therefore, her attack on masculine prerogatives is an attack on the language in which they are cast. The rhetorical tools of eighteenth-century philosophic discourse—its fictions of dispassionate objectivity and rational oppositions—support the conservative ideology upon which both aristocratic and masculine privilege are based. Wollstonecraft's efforts, like those of her predecessors, the architects of the French Revolution, to construct a counterideology of the rights of man and woman necessitates a counterdiscourse. The "flaws" in Wollstonecraft's style, in this context, become the vehicles for her philosophic program that embraces the so-called feminine values of subjectivity and emotionalism and that looks forward to Romanticism with its valorization of intuition, passion, and the imagination over reason.

Wollstonecraft's counterideology takes the form of a confrontation with her philosophic fathers, the authorities on women she has read. She realizes that the authority of books, of the written word, powerfully perpetuates the myths of male superiority and female weakness precisely because it is a discourse controlled by—and for—men.

I must therefore venture to doubt whether what has been thought an axiom in morals may not have been a dogmatic assertion made by men who have coolly seen mankind through the medium of books. . . . (P. 110)

Ralph Wardle has noted that in *Rights of Woman* Wollstonecraft alludes to more works by other authors than in any of her other books, and although she refers to a few works by women, the majority of the texts she discusses are by men. The list is extensive. She refers not only to authorities on women's education—Rousseau, Talleyrand, Knox, Dr. James Fordyce, Dr. John Gregory—but also to works on political theory, linguistics, philosophy, and literature. She cites or quotes passages from the Bible and works by Shakespeare, Milton, Pope, Locke, Hume, Richardson, Swift, Johnson, Lord Monboddo, Adam Smith, Butler, Gay, Boswell, Dryden, Cowper, and Edward Young.[23] This list suggests not so much the extent of her indebtedness to other writers (or the gaps in her education), but the anxiety a woman writer must necessarily feel when confronted by the burden of so many authorities who have coopted the power to impose upon her their fictions about femininity. Insofar as women are educated by men, they share men's culture. But they must, by virtue of their sexual difference, confront their predecessors differently, see in them different values, and react differently to their own images in men's writing. Wollstonecraft's program of extensive citation demonstrates how masculine discourse has created and perpetuated the weaknesses of women. She devotes her entire fifth chapter to writers who, in her words, "Have Rendered Women Objects of Pity, Bordering on Contempt." She insists that it is not the power of individuals, or even institutions, that has kept women from assuming equal citizenship with men, but the power of the written word.

Two writers who epitomize for Wollstonecraft the power of masculine discourse to oppress women, the power of the father to stifle his daughters, are Rousseau and Milton. Rousseau represents, for Wollstonecraft, the masculine deployment of discursive power against women in education and philosophy. She devotes almost half of chapter 5, "Animadversions on Some Writers," to her argument with Rousseau's ideas on the education of women. On the surface, the education of children—whether boys or girls—does not seem weighty enough for philosophic debate; but Wollstonecraft recognizes, in reading Rousseau's comments on the education of Sophia, the subtle ways in which the unequal relationships inherent in institutions like schools underlie and undercut the theoretical equality of men claimed by philosophy.[24] She examines and questions the disciplinary "technologies" (the term is Foucault's) of education advanced by Rousseau—the separation of children from their parents (p. 158), the separation of the sexes (pp. 79, 165), and the physical constraints imposed upon schoolgirls (pp. 82, 162)—that invisibly perpetuate the unequal relationships between the sexes. Because men and women are not "constituted alike in temperament and character," Rousseau argues, they should not be educated alike.

> . . . the education of the women should always be relative to the men. To please, to be useful to us, to make us love and esteem them, to educate us when young, and take care of us when grown up, to advise, to console us, to render our lives easy and agreeable: these are the duties of women at all times, and what they should be taught in their infancy. (P. 79)

Rousseau, Wollstonecraft argues, maintains an arbitrary distinction that he claims is based on "the natural order of things": "the effect of habit is insisted upon as an undoubted indication of nature" (p. 81). Such trivial activities as a young girl's playing with dolls, her fondness for dress, even her capacity for needlework form the basis of Rousseau's system of female education, providing at the same time both the proof of woman's unfitness for masculine endeavor and the means of her exclusion from it. The very triviality of these activities allows Rousseau to maintain as "natural" social conventions and "narrow prejudices" (p. 92) more powerfully than any tyrannic authority imposed from above because they are so thoroughly and invisibly inculcated in young girls as "habits of thinking" at an early age.

Wollstonecraft perceptively grasps the problems inherent in Rousseau's thoughts on the education of women for his vision of a perfected society. His ideas, which Wollstonecraft discusses at length, support rather than subvert the unequal distribution of power throughout society. Hence Rousseau is a "partial moralist" (p. 84) whose notions endorse and perpetuate the very vices he wishes to correct. Wollstonecraft protests:

> I now appeal from the reveries of fancy and refined licentiousness to the good sense of mankind, whether, if the object of education be to prepare women to become chaste wives and sensible mothers, the method so plausibly recommended in the foregoing sketch, be the one best calculated to produce those ends? Will it be allowed that the surest way to make a wife chaste, is to teach her to practise wanton arts of a mistress, termed virtuous coquetry. . . . (P. 90)

Far from being a rationalist and an egalitarian whose first wish is to perfect mankind, Rousseau is a sensualist whose licentiousness supports the status quo under the guise of rationality. Rousseau is not a philosopher, but a "poetic writer" who "skillfully exhibits the objects of sense, most voluptuously shadowed or gracefully veiled—And thus making us feel whilst dreaming that we reason, erroneous conclusions are left in the mind" (p. 91).

Yet it is Milton, the philosophic poet, even more than Rousseau, the poetic philosopher, who represents for Wollstonecraft the coopting of creative energy by men. Sandra Gilbert and Susan Gubar note that *Rights of Woman* "often reads like an outraged commentary on *Paradise Lost*."[25] If Wollstonecraft's domineering "poetic father" troubles her imagination—and incites her rebellion—more than her "philosophic father," Rousseau, it is because of the mythic power of "the institutionalized and elaborate metaphoric misogyny Milton's epic expresses" (*Madwoman*, p. 189), buttressed by the full weight of biblical authority, by "Moses's beautiful poetic cosmogony." Indeed, Gilbert and Gubar argue that most women writers have been all too aware of Milton's intimidating presence. Virginia Woolf remarks in *A Room of One's Own* that literate women had to "look past Milton's bogey, for no human being could shut out the view" (*Madwoman*, p. 188). If *Paradise Lost* is more incapacitating for Wollstonecraft than Rousseau's "wild chimeras" (p. 39), it is because the book itself "constitutes the essence of what Gertrude Stein has called patriarchal poetry" (*Madwoman*, p. 188). So intimidating is Milton's presence for Wollstonecraft that she cannot confront him directly as she does Rousseau, but only indirectly, through allusions and footnotes. Her reading of *Paradise Lost* suggests that to assert her independence and the possibility of her creativity, requires the ultimate act of rebellion against masculine authority:

> I will simply declare, that were an angel from heaven to tell me that Moses's beautiful, poetical cosmogony, and the account of the fall of man were literally true, I could not believe what my reason told me was derogatory to the character of the Supreme Being: and, having no fear of the devil before mine eyes, I venture to call this a suggestion of reason, instead of resting my weakness on the broad shoulders of the first seducer of my frail sex. (P. 79)

In the end, Milton's "bogey" is his theology. Although he did not create the myth of origin that is the heart of Western patriarchy, he gave it a poetic force that has, as Harold Bloom has argued, made *Paradise Lost* an inhibiting text for all his successors. It is particularly intimidating for the woman writer. His history of woman defines her as secondary—"He for God only, she for God in him"—and Other, a "fair defect of nature." By making the ultimate act of creation the sole act of a "Father," Milton defines creativity itself as a masculine act. Therefore, to be able to write, Wollstonecraft must identify herself closely not with the feminine and submissive Eve—"For softness she and sweet attractive grace"—but with the usurper of God's creative potential, Satan.

> Similar feelings has Milton's pleasing picture of paradisiacal happiness ever raised in my mind; yet, instead of envying the lovely pair, I have, with conscious dignity, or Satanic pride, turned to hell for sublimer objects. (P. 79 n.3)

Milton's "paradisiacal happiness" deprives woman of soul, reason, and creativity. Like her literary daughters in the nineteenth century (including her biological daughter, Mary Shelley), Wollstonecraft, as both writer and woman, can overcome the anxieties created by Milton's spectre only by identifying with his rebel, by opting not for paradise, but for chaos.

Wollstonecraft's rebellion against the central text of Western patriarchy and her rejection of the fictions of authority that structure its philosophy reveal the dilemma posed by her writing. The more she struggles to rid her language of the ideologies of her bourgeois upbringing, the more they strangle her creativity. Because she defines her rhetorical self to conform to the strictures of male-dominated philosophic discourse, her solution to the problem of feminine dependence must be cast in a language tainted by that dependence. Feminine creativity in *Rights of Woman*, then, is experienced as a problem, a tension between the text as a creative act—the forging of a new rhetoric—and the text as necessarily parasitic—the site of a struggle with masculine authority.

The great achievement of *Vindication of the Rights of Woman* is that as Wollstonecraft strives to "make human conventions conform more closely to human need,"[26] she reveals just how profoundly those conventions—writing in particular—shape and define human needs. Her text not only articulates a revolutionary critique of society, but shows how difficult revolution is.

Notes

1. *The Letters of Horace Walpole*, ed. Mrs. Paget Toynbee (Oxford, 1905), 15:131–32, 337–38; cited in Ralph Wardle, *Mary Wollstonecraft: A Critical Biography* (Lincoln: University of Nebraska Press, 1951), pp. 159, 318.

2. James Fordyce, *Sermons for Young Women* (London, 1792) 1:272; cited in Wardle, *Wollstonecraft*, p. 140.

3. Mary Wollstonecraft, *An Historical and Moral View of the Origin and Progress of the French Revolution* (London, 1796), pp. v–vi; cited in Wardle, *Wollstonecraft*, p. 211.

4. Mary Wollstonecraft, *A Vindication of the Rights of Woman*, ed. Carol H. Poston (New York: Norton, 1978), p. 15. All subsequent references to this edition will be noted parenthetically in the text.

5. William Godwin, *Memoirs of the Author of "The Vindication of the Rights of Woman"* (1798; rpt., New York: Garland, 1974), p. 83. Mary Hays, cited in Poston, *Vindication of the Rights of Woman*, p. 212; Wardle, *Wollstonecraft*, p. 156; Eleanor Flexner, *Mary Wollstonecraft: A Biography* (New York: Coward, McCann and Geoghegan, 1972), p. 164.

6. For a critique of this notion of philosophic rhetoric see Susan Bordo, "The Cultural Overseer and the Tragic Hero: Comedic and Feminist Perspectives on the Hubris of Philosophy," *Soundings* 65 (1982): 181–205; Richard Rorty, *Philosophy and the Mirror of Nature* (Princeton: Princeton University Press, 1979); and John Richetti, *Philosophic Writing: Locke, Berkeley, Hume* (Cambridge: Harvard University Press, 1983), pp. 4–32.

7. Anca Vlaspolos, "Mary Wollstonecraft's Mask of Reason in *Vindication of the Rights of Woman*," *Dalhousie Review* 60 (1980): 462.

8. Virginia Woolf, *The Second Common Reader* (New York: Harcourt, Brace, 1932), p. 176. For a perceptive discussion of the conflict between radical and conservative ideologies in Wollstonecraft's political thought see Zillah Eisenstein, *The Radical Future of Liberal Feminism* (Boston: Northeastern University Press, 1981), pp. 89–112.

9. Vlaspolos, "Wollstonecraft's Mask of Reason," p. 462.

10. Review of Brian Vickers, *Classical Rhetoric in English Poetry, College English* 33 (1972): 615.

11. Mary Poovey, *The Proper Lady and the Woman Writer: Ideology as Style in the Works of Mary Wollstonecraft, Mary Shelley, and Jane Austen* (Chicago: University of Chicago Press, 1984), p.80. See also Bordo, "The Cultural Overseer and the Tragic Hero," pp. 181–85.

12. On the relationship of truth and rhetoric in philosophic writing see Richetti, *Philosophic Writing*, pp. 6–8, and Rorty, *Mirror of Nature*, passim.

13. Hays, cited in Poston, *Vindication of the Rights of Woman*, p. 212.

14. Poovey, *The Proper Lady and the Woman Writer*, p. 78.

15. Miriam Brody, "Mary Wollstonecraft: Sexuality and Women's Rights (1759–1797)," in

Feminist Theorists: Three Centuries of Key Women Thinkers, ed. Dale Spender (New York: Pantheon Books, 1983), pp. 40–59.

16. For a discussion of the masculine and feminine aspects of Wollstonecraft's prose see Poovey, *The Proper Lady and the Woman Writer*, p. 68.

17. Mary Wollstonecraft, *Letters Written during a Short Residence in Sweden, Norway, and Denmark*, ed. Carol H. Poston (Lincoln: University of Nebraska Press, 1976), p. 160.

18. Bordo, "Cultural Overseer and the Tragic Hero," pp. 192–93.

19. Elissa S. Guralnick, "Radical Politics in Mary Wollstonecraft's *Vindication of the Rights of Woman*," *Studies in Burke and His Time* 18 (1977): 159.

20. Ibid., p. 161.

21. Poovey, *The Proper Lady and the Woman Writer*, pp. xiii–xv; Terry Eagleton, *Literary Theory: An Introduction* (Minneapolis: University of Minnesota Press, 1983), pp. 14–15; Hayden White, *Tropics of Discourse: Essays in Cultural History* (Baltimore: Johns Hopkins University Press, 1978), pp. 68–71.

22. Michel Foucault, *The Order of Things: An Archaeology of the Human Sciences* (New York: Vintage Books, 1970); see also Herbert L. Dreyfus and Paul Rabinow, *Michel Foucault: Beyond Structuralism and Hermeneutics*, 2d ed. (Chicago: University of Chicago Press, 1983), pp. 184–204.

23. Wardle, *Wollstonecraft*, p. 163.

24. In this connection see also Dreyfus and Rabinow, *Michel Foucault*, pp. 184–88.

25. Sandra Gilbert and Susan Gubar, *Madwoman in the Attic: The Woman Writer and the Nineteenth-Century Literary Imagination* (New Haven: Yale University Press, 1979), p. 206. I am indebted to Gilbert's and Gubar's discussion of Milton's influence on woman writers; subsequent references to their book will be noted parenthetically in the text. For another discussion of Milton's influence on Wollstonecraft specifically see Poovey, *The Proper Lady and the Woman Writer*, pp. 72–80.

26. Virginia Woolf, *The Second Common Reader*, p. 176.

8

"Ardor of Youth":
The Manner of Hume's *Treatise*

DONALD T. SIEBERT

My Principles are . . . so remote from all the vulgar
Sentiments on this Subject, that were they to take place,
they wou'd produce almost a total Alteration in Philosophy. . . . (1739).

I shall acknowledge . . . a very great Mistake in Conduct, viz my publishing at all the Treatise of human
Nature, a Book, which pretended to innovate in all the
sublimest Parts of Philosophy, & which I compos'd before I was five & twenty. Above all, the positive Air,
which prevails in that Book, & which may be imputed to
the Ardor of Youth, so much displeases me, that I have
not Patience to review it. (1754)

David Hume was of two minds regarding his prodigy, *A Treatise of Human
Nature* (1739–40). At the time of publication he believed that it would
revolutionize philosophy; later he apologized for rushing the work into
print, thinking of it as a youthful indiscretion, and finally disowning it
completely.[1] How much the work's falling *"dead-born from the press,"* as he
put it later, contributed to his change of heart is open to speculation.
Still, one must be chary of Hume's repudiation of the *Treatise*. Is it any
wonder that an author whose "ruling Passion" was the "love of literary
fame," having achieved the desired success with later works, would
dismiss his early failure as a juvenile production when its only notice,
when noticed at all, was misunderstanding or ridicule? The disappointment of the whole experience persisted into old age: Hume demurs in
My Own Life that it did not even "excite a murmur among the zealots."[2]
However disappointment may have altered his later judgment, Hume
was right the first time: *A Treatise of Human Nature* ultimately revolution-

ized philosophy. Its distinction is well-known for having awakened Kant from his dogmatic slumber. Confronted with the *Treatise*, Bertrand Russell speaks of Hume as

> one of the most important among philosophers, because he developed to its logical conclusion the empirical philosophy of Locke and Berkeley, and by making it self-consistent made it incredible. He represents, in a certain sense, a dead end: in his direction, it is impossible to go further. To refute him has been, ever since he wrote, a favorite pastime among metaphysicians. For my part, I find none of their refutations convincing; nevertheless, I cannot but hope that something less sceptical than Hume's system may be discovered.[3]

Even Hume might have been surprised at that reaction, though he would doubtless be pleased, if not with the judgment, certainly with having so distinguished and percipient a judge. In any case, the nineteenth- and twentieth-century impact of the *Treatise* has been far-reaching, and the *Treatise* renounced by Hume is the work on which his reputation as philosopher rests. The philosophical literature of this century on Hume deals almost exclusively with the *Treatise*, paying scant heed to the supposedly more canonical versions in the two *Enquiries*, not to mention Hume's other works.[4] Recently, T. E. Jessop has raised questions about this overemphasis on the *Treatise*, of knowing the Hume of only one book, of treating Hume as primarily an epistemologist rather than what he preferred to style himself, a moral philosopher and man of letters. Jessop's advice to consider Hume's work in its entirety and in the context of eighteenth-century culture—not just as a tissue of "objective propositions to be studied merely by formal and empirical logic"—is helpful.[5] But to take Hume at his word and ignore the *Treatise* is unwise in light of the strong personal inducement Hume had to dissociate himself from his failure, and for other reasons I shall make clear.

A *Treatise of Human Nature* remains the first, the most detailed, and the most emphatic statement of Hume's philosophy. His restatements are essentially that: Hume changes the arrangement of his arguments, he deletes some and stresses others, and he polishes the style, especially refining the tone of discourse. Important new material is in the essays and *Enquiries*, but in terms of Hume's philosophy itself the alteration is less in substance than in spirit.[6] The explanation offered in *My Own Life* is significant: "I had always entertained a notion, that my want of success in publishing the Treatise of Human Nature, had proceeded more from the manner than the matter. . . ." Indeed, all of Hume's reservations about the *Treatise* stem from his regret about the manner, not the matter of that work. A letter (1751) to Gilbert Elliot of Minto reiterates these concerns:

I believe the philosophical Essays [i.e., the first *Enquiry*] contain every
thing of Consequence relating to the Understanding, which you woud
meet with in the Treatise; & I give you my Advice against reading the
latter. By shortening & simplifying the Questions, I really render them
much more complete. *Addo dum minuo.* The philosophical Principles
are the same in both: But I was carry'd away by the Heat of Youth &
Invention to publish too precipitately. So vast an Undertaking, plan'd
before I was one and twenty, & compos'd before twenty five, must
necessarily be very defective. I have repented my Haste a hundred, &
a hundred times. (*HL,* 1:158)

Addo dum minuo clearly endorses the first *Enquiry* over the *Treatise*, and if
"the philosophical Principles are the same in both," what is mainly
defective about the *Treatise* is the manner of presentation, a tone sometimes recklessly personal. It was a defect of which Hume became pain-
fully aware, but he had tried to remedy it even before publication. As he
told Henry Home in 1737, "I was resolved not to be an enthusiast in
philosophy, while I was blaming other enthusiasms"; hence "I am at
present castrating my work, that is, cutting off its nobler parts; that is,
endeavouring it shall give as little offense as possible . . ." (*HL,* 1:25).
The castration he had in mind was mainly of an early draft of the essay
"Of Miracles," a "noble part" which finally appeared in 1748.

Unfortunately the castration, though undoubtedly painful, was more
a witty metaphor than a cure for philosophical enthusiasm, for cutting
out a few offensive sections would hardly render the style of the *Treatise*
more docile. Philosophical enthusiasts, unlike those in religion, as we
learn in the Conclusion to Book I, are "only ridiculous," not dangerous
(I.vi.7).[7] But if "enthusiast" was a sufficiently scurrilous epithet in the
eighteenth century, for Hume it was anathema. It was surely the enthusiastic manner of the *Treatise* that so provoked Hume's later rejection of
his youthful masterpiece, for inadvertently he had become the very type
of what he was blaming, even as he feared. Yet it is not incumbent on us
to blush with Hume at his youthful indiscretion. The *Treatise* is in places
as extravagant and cavalier in its expression as it is bold in its ideas.
Commentators on the *Treatise* have deplored the style as a distraction
from the substance of Hume's thought. T. E. Jessop is quite severe in his
judgment: "Here and there is a burst of rhetoric that is blatantly maudlin,
problems are overanalysed as if Hume were wanting to display his
analytic virtuosity, and there is an obvious relish in flourishing denials.
He can be both tedious and puzzling when an exposition is being
overdone."[8] Admittedly, if objective and efficient exposition is the standard, then such criticism is valid. Yet if we are to know the complete
Hume, the Hume of the eighteenth century, even as Jessop elsewhere
urges us, then it is well to begin by studying the whole *Treatise,* its tone

as well as its ideas. Otherwise we make Hume's castration of the work more complete, and by studying ideas apart from their author's person-ality, we risk making Hume himself into a philosophical eunuch. Instead, our concern in this chapter will be to find Hume's meaning in *manner* as well as in *matter.*

I

A Treatise of Human Nature is a very personal work, perhaps more personal than anything else Hume ever published, including his auto-biography. One of the hallmarks of Hume's style is a detachment, a striving for control, and hence a frequent resort to irony as a means of enforcing that distance, that air of Olympian superiority.[9] The impor-tance of detachment and self-possession is what Humean philosophy teaches. Without question this sense of control colors the *Treatise,* though other elements work at cross-purposes. One style reflects the idealized philosopher, calm and wise, but another style reflects a more uncertain, more involved and emotional, even troubled young man. Hume's guard is not always up, and we can see a philosopher not quite as self-assured and composed as he prefers, one not entirely at peace with the implica-tions of his doctrines. That frightening dead end deplored by Russell may have been glimpsed by Hume.

The mention of a troubled Hume may seem ludicrous to anyone familiar with *My Own Life.* There Hume reviews his life and pronounces serenely, "I have little to regret; it was a success." But the Hume of the *Treatise* is not the elderly man of letters, carefully composing his last words. During the gestation of the *Treatise* occurred something close to Hume's dark night of the soul. If we must look for autobiographical documents to understand Hume's personality, we should turn back from *My Own Life,* written at the close of his career, to another self-revelation composed while the *Treatise* was taking shape—Hume's long confessional letter presumably to Dr. John Arbuthnot, the famous physi-cian, scholar, and wit.[10]

Hume experienced a nervous breakdown at about this time and in the letter describes his illness, with its apparent prognosis and cure. As Ernest Mossner remarks, "Although not written in modern technical terminology, Hume's case-history of his psychosomatic disorder is as clear as could possibly be penned by a highly intelligent person today, and, as such, is diagnosable by modern psychiatrists."[11] A significant resemblance exists between the letter and aspects of the *Treatise,* par-ticularly the concluding section of Book I, and the letter provides insight into Hume's highly wrought-up state of mind during the genesis of the

Treatise. Hume tells his correspondent of how he felt when the possibilities opened by the *Treatise* became fully apparent. It is no serene philosopher who exclaims with pride:

> Upon Examination of these [endless disputes of previous philosophy], I found a certain Boldness of Temper, growing in me, which was not enclin'd to submit to any Authority in these Subjects, but led me to seek out some new Medium, by which Truth might be establisht. After much Study, & Reflection on this, at last, when I was about 18 Years of Age, there seem'd to be open'd up to me a new Scene of Thought, which transported me beyond Measure, & made me, with an Ardor natural to young men, throw up every other Pleasure or Business to apply entirely to it. (*HL*, 1:13)

The mood described here Hume later associates with the *Treatise*—that "Ardor of Youth," that "Heat of Youth & Invention." Then comes a collapse, a transformation from excited activity to lethargy and indifference: ". . . all my Ardor seem'd in a moment to be extinguish'd, & I cou'd no longer raise my Mind to that pitch, which formerly gave me such excessive Pleasure. . . . In this Condition I remain'd for nine Months. . . ." Hume does not indicate the exact reason for the depression or the explanation of how he freed himself from it. The pattern of Hume's movement from ecstatic discovery to bewilderment and anxiety, and then to salvation through common life, is reenacted in the *Treatise*, Book I, and is likewise a pattern informing Hume's philosophy.

When Hume wrote the Conclusion to Book I of the *Treatise*, a few years after the letter to Arbuthnot, he had largely resolved his doubts, and so his account is for the most part retrospective and objective. That is, he is capable of looking back on his malaise and describing it with self-humor and exuberance. Yet we still sense how close he is to that state of anxiety. He shows the frenzied jubilation of a man who has just narrowly escaped disaster and has not quite regained his poise. The first few paragraphs may be what Mr. Jessop calls "rhetoric that is blatantly maudlin," but I prefer to see this passage as playfully theatrical. Hume is relieved to be on firm ground once more, yet he knows how terrifying are the dangers he has passed. He declaims, half amused, half still afraid of his shadow:

> Methinks I am like a man, who having struck on many shoals, and having narrowly escap'd shipwreck in passing a small frith, has yet the temerity to put out to sea in the same leaky weather-beaten vessel, and even carries his ambition so far as to think of compassing the globe under these disadvantageous circumstances. . . . [My difficulty] reduces me almost to despair, and makes me resolve to perish on the

> barren rock, on which I am at present, rather than venture myself upon that boundless ocean, which runs out into immensity. . . .
>
> I am first affrighted and confounded with that forelorn solitude, in which I am plac'd in my philosophy, and fancy myself some strange uncouth monster, who not being able to mingle and unite in society, has been expell'd all human commerce, and left utterly abandon'd and disconsolate. Fain wou'd I run into the crowd for shelter and warmth; but cannot prevail with myself to mix with such deformity. I call upon others to join me, in order to make a company apart; but no one will hearken to me. Every one keeps at a distance, and dreads that storm, which beats upon me from every side. I have expos'd myself to the enmity of all metaphysicians, logicians, mathematicians, and even theologians; and can I wonder at the insults I must suffer? (I.iv.7)

And so on. This amazing departure from the style of the book is hardly a passage which professional philosophers fasten on and celebrate. One might conclude that Hume had lost his wits by this point. But it is of a piece with Hume's philosophy, and it is also more understandable and meaningful when we view it within the framework of Hume's mental breakdown.

Hume is eminently sane here, however recent his glimpse of the abyss, and he is at liberty to have some fun, to tease us as he is teasing himself about what is left for us all after both the vulgar and philosophical supports for a reality outside of ourselves have been undermined. The hand-wringing rhetoric finally builds to a climax several pages later, a climax more serious and intense in tone. The absurd metaphors and hyperboles have disappeared. Hume asks a series of questions which a preacher might use to confound his congregation with a due sense of weakness and mortality:

> Where am I, or what? From what causes do I derive my existence, and to what condition shall I return? Whose favour shall I court, and whose anger must I dread? What beings surround me? and on whom have I any influence, or who have any influence on me? I am confounded with all these questions, and begin to fancy myself in the most deplorable condition imaginable, inviron'd with the deepest darkness, and utterly depriv'd of the use of every member and faculty. (I.iv.7)

These anguished questions could very well have come from the letter to Arbuthnot, for they are appropriate to the state of mind which made Hume write that letter; they are even more desperate and unguarded than anything in the letter. We see how extravagant and personal the *Treatise* remained, despite Hume's desire to tone it down.

Hume apparently justified this excess as the culmination of his drama, which like many eighteenth-century tragedies would have a happy ending. The denouement is almost bathetic, but it is faithful to his own experience. His intention is to shock the reader with the primacy of nature. Windows must be flung open, light and air must be let in to drive away the fumes of philosophical enthusiasm:

> Most fortunately it happens, that since reason is incapable of dispelling these clouds, nature herself suffices to that purpose, and cures me of this philosophical melancholy and delirium, either by relaxing this bent of mind, or by some avocation, and lively impression of my senses, which obliterate all these chimeras. I dine, I play a game of backgammon, I converse, and am merry with my friends; and when after three or four hours' amusement, I wou'd return to these speculations, they appear so cold, and strain'd and ridiculous, that I cannot find in my heart to enter into them any further.

Has any other propounder of a system, ever before or since, so lightly dismissed the thinker's own arguments? If not the self-contradiction of a madman, then it is the sense of humor and perspective, the confidence and self-assurance, which so characterize Hume's mind. He has pulled the reader's leg. Hume has presented his reader with a spectacle of despair, one apparently requiring miraculous deliverance, only to reassure the reader that the remedy is quite simple—and unavoidable.

That may be the significance of Hume's strategy, but his handling of it here is much more whimsical and personal than elsewhere in his works. Hume wishes to illustrate the bankruptcy of Pyrrhonian skepticism and its inevitable cure. Only here, though, does Hume himself act out the part of the Pyrrhonist and then metamorphose before our eyes into a true skeptic—that is, one skeptical of his own doubts. A constant theme with him is that Pyrrhonism is impossible for a human being to maintain. He knew so from firsthand experience, and here confesses his human weakness. Hume's famous injunction in the first *Enquiry* is, "Be a philosopher; but, amidst all your philosophy, be still a man."[12] He is wont to teach that lesson throughout his philosophical discourse; here he relives it.

Note that after the *Treatise* Hume continues to warn against Pyrrhonism, but it is never Hume himself who might be the victim of this malaise. By 1748, in the first *Enquiry*, intent on improving the manner of the *Treatise*, he speaks from a comfortable distance of the errors of Pyrrhonism; he pities the unfortunate Pyrrhonist whose principles, unlike those of other philosophical sectarians, can have nothing to do with human life or conviction. Luckily, nature will rouse him from his dreams and cure him of his life-threatening paradoxes:

. . . were his principles universally and steadily to prevail[,] All discourse, all action would immediately cease; and men remain in total
lethargy, till the necessities of nature, unsatisfied, put an end to their
miserable existence. It is true; so fatal an event is very little to be
dreaded. Nature is always too strong for principle. . . . When [the
Pyrrhonist] awakes from his dream, he will be the first to join in the
laugh against himself, and to confess, that all his objections are mere
amusement, and can have no other tendency than to show the whimsical condition of mankind. . . . (*EHU,* 160)

The description of the problem matches exactly that in the Conclusion of
the *Treatise,* corroborating the interpretation of a Hume willing to laugh
at himself. Yet in this instance Hume describes the problem in the third
person, not the first. Hume views the extreme skeptic objectively; it is
not *his* experience but that of some hypothetical enthusiast. Hume has
assumed a more decorous control of his material, losing thereby the
immediacy of the first-person narration. But Hume was probably only
too ready to separate himself from the philosophical malady. Three
years before the first *Enquiry,* attempting in vain to defend himself in an
anonymous pamphlet, he had done his best to explain away the dark
implications of this last section of the *Treatise,* Book I: The Pyrrhonism
"was never intended to be understood *seriously,* but was meant a *mere*
Philosophical Amusement, or Trial of *Wit* and *Subtilty.* . . . And all those
Principles . . . are positively renounced in a few Pages afterwards, and
called the Effects of *Philosophical Melancholy* and *Delusion.*"[13]

One reason that the manner of the Conclusion was a problem at all is
that the reader is not prepared for it. Although there are exceptions, the
style of Book I is otherwise fairly plain, dignified, and even lackluster, if
one is looking for figures of speech, brilliant aphorisms, or elegant
periods. To be sure, Hume leads the reader through the demonstrations
with a flair, constructing proofs, marshaling evidence, pressing questions with relentless zest. He seems a lecturer, convinced of his ideas
and determined to explain them fully. But he is serious about his lecture,
and so the turnabout at the end, complete with posturing, undercutting,
and ridicule, is out of character. This inconsistency of tone is the essence
of the problem regarding manner. Besides the conflict between reserve
and exuberance, one observes other contrasting manners: modesty and
arrogance, moral high-mindedness and libertinism. These were personal qualities of Hume that he learned later to manage with more
consistency; in his juvenile work they are unmistakable evidence of the
"ardor of Youth."

Hume seems aware of these disparate elements in his text. At one
point he writes explicitly of the proper tone and consistency of philo-

sophical discourse, calling his effort to mind with the very word "treatise": "Shou'd an author compose a treatise, of which one part was serious and profound, another light and humorous, every one wou'd condemn so strange a mixture, and wou'd accuse him of the neglect of all rules of art and criticism. These rules of art are founded on the qualities of human nature; and the quality of human nature, which requires a consistency in every performance, is that which renders the mind incapable of passing in a moment from one passion and disposition to a quite different one" (II.ii.8). It is an apposite commentary on his own manner, although at the time he was probably unaware of how well it applied. Thus we see him trying to maintain a decorum, but sometimes finding it difficult to reject the amusing or slightly risqué examples: "To begin with the advantages of the *body;* we may observe a phaenomenon, which might appear somewhat trivial and ludicrous, if any thing cou'd be trivial, which fortified a conclusion of such importance, or ludicrous, which was employ'd in a philosophical reasoning. 'Tis a general remark, that those we call good *women's men,* who have either signaliz'd themselves by their amorous exploits, or whose make of body promises any extraordinary vigour of that kind, are well received by the fair sex . . ." (III.iii.5). Then follows a short explanation of why even virtuous women would be so attracted to these lusty champions of the bedchamber. Hume apparently feels the illustration is too low for the dignity of philosophy, and his justification merely reveals his uncertainty. By the time he got around to using the passage in the rehabilitated version of the second *Enquiry* (1751), he relegated it to a footnote in the first edition and thereafter purged it entirely.

We see, then, that Hume is caught between the desire to appear dignified, modest, dispassionate, and the satisfaction of youthful qualities chafing against that restrained demeanor. He wants to be modest, but at the same time he is proud of his momentous discoveries. Occasionally the two Humes rub shoulders awkwardly: "I am much afraid, lest the small success I meet with in my enquiries will make this observation bear the air of an apology rather than of boasting" (I.iii.15). What a strange remark: one is modestly afraid that one's humility will mislead a reader to overlook one's boasting! Confidence is stronger than any impression of humility, however, and statements like this are more common: "I dare be positive no one will ever endeavour to refute these reasonings otherwise than by altering my definitions . . ." (II.iii.1). All too often the peremptory dismissal of rival philosophers, besides being haughty, tends to backfire: "Whatever has the air of a paradox, and is contrary to the first and most unprejudic'd notions of mankind, is often greedily embrac'd by philosophers, as shewing the superiority of their science, which cou'd discover opinions so remote from vulgar conception" (I.ii.1). As he admits later in the Conclusion, Hume fits the description as well as anybody. One cannot help remembering Samuel Johnson's criticism of Hume and other innovators: "Truth, Sir, is a cow which will yield such people no more milk, and so they are gone to milk the bull."[14]

Thus, Hume can sound as positive and arbitrary as anyone whom he opposes. In the last paragraph of Book I, he good-naturedly confesses his possibly overbearing manner, and recants. At least he will be his own best example of the dangers of dogmatism, "so natural a propensity" to human beings when they examine *particular points* with great intensity:

> . . . we are apt not only to forget our scepticism, but even our modesty too; and make use of such terms as these, *'tis evident, 'tis certain, 'tis undeniable;* which a due deference to the public ought, perhaps to prevent. I may have fallen into this fault after the example of others; but I here enter a *caveat* against any objections, which may be offer'd on that head; and declare that such expressions were extorted from me by the present view of the object, and imply no dogmatical spirit, nor conceited idea of my own judgment, which are sentiments that I am sensible can become no body, and a sceptic less than any other. (I.iv.7)

Hume has put himself in a tenuous position. He cannot very well write persuasively without appearing to be convinced of what he says, even though the ultimate point of his doctrine is that all such confidence is mistaken. So he gives with one hand and takes away with the other. The way out of the dilemma, learned after the *Treatise,* is to guard against a dogmatic, personal tone from the very first, and then never make a spectacle of oneself by indulging in melodrama and confession.[15]

Only about a year after the first two books of the *Treatise* had appeared, Hume reviewed his efforts with the objectivity of a third person. He puffs his book, revealing pride in his achievement, and yet at the same time we smile at the reviewer's attitude of conservative wonderment at the author's boldness: "I shall conclude the logics of this author with an account of two opinions which seem to be peculiar to himself, as indeed are most of his opinions. . . . The second volume of this work . . . is of more easy comprehension than the first, but contains opinions that are altogether as new and extraordinary. . . . Throughout this whole book there are great pretensions to new discoveries in philosophy."[16] With only a little distance from the *Treatise,* and viewing himself from the third person, Hume could still admire his achievement—the matter—while already showing sensitivity to the tone—the manner—of his great work.

II

Hume would never have offended conservatives by making too much of himself, or by appearing overconfident and then confessing his errors. Such behavior, like James Boswell's dressing as a Corsican chieftain, is more a violation of gentlemanly dignity than a moral transgression. Yet Hume did offend the orthodox. In one sense it was fortunate for him the *Treatise* was unnoticed, even though it was still a sufficient impediment to his career for the next twelve years or so. That his candidacy as a professor was twice rejected was owing to the reputation of the *Treatise* as impious and immoral. A good part of this reputation stems from arguments which *are* heterodox, such as the section arguing the materiality, or more likely the nonexistence, of the soul (I.iv.5). This section cannot be phrased so as to render it orthodox, and Hume's enemies in the Scottish Kirk were adept at scenting out heresy even in piously intended sermons. Hence, we should not conclude that if only Hume had mended his manner, the *Treatise* would have been quoted in the churches.

Yet Hume would not so much have minded appearing impious as he would have objected to appearing reckless and immoral. Hume was a moral man: he was writing ultimately as a moral philosopher: to appear otherwise would be self-defeating. Nonetheless, the Hume of the *Treatise* does occasionally appear worldly, libertine, and cynical—more bent on iconoclasm than moral reassurance. This is another problem of tone and manner, one manifestly corrected in later versions of the identical subject matter. Let us look at this aspect of manner more closely.

When we turn to Hume's moral theories, as found in Books II and III, we must acknowledge that Hume's ethics is essentially worldly and materialistic. When one hangs an ethical system on an opposition between pride and humility (what we think of ourselves) and love and contempt (what we think of others), completely ignoring any spiritual or other-worldly dimensions, then one is prone to appreciate only intelligence and wit, bodily strength and beauty, houses, clothes, food, wine, and other such mental or physical possessions. And when Hume asks us what is useful or in our best interests, he does not even imagine that we will think of our immortal souls. That "men are always more concerned about the present life than the future . . ." (III.ii.5) is not said with regret but approval. This emphasis is not peculiar to the *Treatise*. Even in the improved version of the second *Enquiry*—for Hume the most successful statement of his moral principles—we end up admiring the worldly while condemning those "monkish" virtues that many moral works, including the New Testament, regard as the *only* virtues. Nevertheless, one can be a man of the world without appearing a libertine. That would be an unwanted identity.

Earlier we considered Hume's use of an enthusiastic "I"; in a few places we note the appearance of an iniquitous "I." The problem arises from Hume's using himself as example. In places he appears to understand the motivation of the dissolute man all too well. As Hume illustrates the curbs that must be placed on individuals who might be tempted to cheat on a system of justice, we learn firsthand what the dishonest man is thinking. Why should he alone be honest? We enter the mind of this wicked fellow: "Your example [of injustice] both pushes me forward . . . by imitation, and also affords me a new reason for any breach of equity, by shewing me, that I should be the cully of my integrity, if I alone shou'd impose on myself a severe restraint amidst the licentiousness of others" (III.ii.7). Note that in the improved version of the second *Enquiry*, "I . . . the cully of my integrity" becomes a third person to be branded—"a sensible knave" no less. And anyone who might reason so knavishly is almost beyond hope: "I must confess, that, if a man think, that this reasoning much requires an answer, it will be a little difficult to find any, which will to him appear satisfactory and convincing. If his heart rebel not against such pernicious maxims, if he feel no reluctance to the thoughts of villainy or baseness, he has indeed lost a considerable motive to virtue . . ." (*EPM*, 283). The first version may be better psychologically, the second is more conventionally moral. Or when Hume wishes to make fun of the argument that virtue is a matter of right reasoning, of drawing the proper conclusions, he offers the example of an adulterer in action. And who is this sinner but the first-person Hume? " 'Tis certain, that an action, on many occasions, may give rise to false conclusions in others; and that a person, who thro' a window sees any lewd behavior of mine with my neighbour's wife, may be so simple as to imagine she is certainly my own. . . . [But my intention is not to give rise] to a false judgment in another, but merely to satisfy my lust and passion" (III.i.1). We need not envisage Hume as a satyr to agree that the tone of such examples is indiscreet, if one wishes to pass for a straitlaced and serious moralist.[17]

Hume's purpose is to redefine morality, to discredit too narrow or puritanical a conception of virtue, indeed to oppose the Christian ideal of meekness and humility. To argue so is inevitably to offend the righteous. In the *Treatise*, however, Hume goes about his business with an air of unabashed iconoclasm. Consider the following pronouncements:

. . . Women and children are most subject to pity, as being most guided by that faculty. (II.ii.7)

Let us remember, that pride and hatred invigorate the soul; and love and humility infeeble it. (II.ii.10)

. . . By *pride* I understand that agreeable impression, which arises in the mind, when the view either of our virtue, beauty, riches or power makes us satisfy'd with ourselves: . . . By *humility* I mean the opposite impression. (II.i.7)

I believe no one, who has any practice of the world . . . will assert, that the humility, which good-breeding and decency require of us, goes beyond the outside, or that a thorough sincerity in this particular is esteem'd a real part of our duty. On the contrary . . . a genuine and hearty pride, or self-esteem, if well conceal'd and well founded, is essential to the character of a man of honour. . . . (III.iii.2)

This impulse to prefer almost imperious self-confidence while depreciating meekness makes Hume sound like Nietzsche, though tempered by the calculating gentility of Lord Chesterfield. Only two paragraphs after the last quotation above—after implicitly admiring Alexander the Great's arrogance—Hume openly contrasts *"heroic virtue,* . . . [that] greatness and elevation of mind" which he is celebrating, with the opposite recommendations of Christian "declaimers," whose efforts run counter to "the judgment of the world" (III.iii.2).

And yet Hume was sufficiently in the mainstream of his culture to be a man of feeling, or to have thought of himself as one, to have never seriously questioned the assumptions of sensibility or benevolence. One can see a sentimental Hume in many of the essays, certainly in the second *Enquiry,* and even in the *History of England.*[18] But in his zeal to establish the science of human nature on a surer foundation, Hume at times overstated the case in his *Treatise.* What man of feeling, or for that matter anyone more tolerant than the most supercilious snob, would ever say, "Nothing has a greater tendency to give us an esteem for any person, than his power and riches; or a contempt, than his poverty and meanness . . ." (II.ii.5)? Who but a polemical Hobbist would pepper his discourse with so many aspersions on human nature? "Moralists or politicians" can do nothing to correct "the selfishness and ingratitude of men. . . . All they can pretend to, is, to give a new direction to those natural passions, and teach us that we can better satisfy our appetites in an oblique and artificial manner, than by their headlong and impetuous motion" (III.ii.5).[19] These remarks in passing hardly represent Hume's final judgment on humanity. Hume specifically rejects Hobbism at one point for presenting us with monsters, not humankind, for whom generally "the kind affections, taken together, . . . over-balance all the selfish" (III.ii.2). But there is, once again, a confusion of tone, which the

Conclusion of the third book, *Of Morals*, does little to clear up. The
Conclusion was tacked on to reassure, perhaps inspire, the reader and
ennoble the whole work. But more than a tincture of the worldly,
slightly cynical, waggish young Hume remains:

> Were it proper in such a subject to bribe the reader's assent, or employ
> any thing but solid argument, we are here abundantly supplied with
> topics to engage the affections. All lovers of virtue (and such we all are
> in speculation, however we may degenerate in practice) must certainly
> be pleas'd to see moral distinctions deriv'd from so noble a source [i.e.,
> sympathy], which gives us a just notion both of the *generosity* and
> *capacity* of human nature. (III.iii.6)

Why need bribery (even though with emotion, not money) be mentioned in a peroration to human sympathy, or why must the love of
virtue be so qualified?[20] The sincerity of Hume's moral professions in the
Treatise often does not ring true.

Hume was aware of this problem soon after writing the *Treatise*, indeed
while the last book was still in manuscript. He had submitted that part to
Francis Hutcheson, a philosopher whose moral system was decidedly
benevolent and Shaftesburian. Hutcheson had noticed exactly that tone
we have been considering and had questioned it. Hume replies with
concern: "What affected me most in your Remarks is your observing,
that there wants a certain Warmth in the Cause of Virtue, which, you
think, all good Men wou'd relish, & cou'd not displease amidst abstract
Enquirys." Hume then attempts to justify that tone in a very interesting
passage, which I shall quote in full:

> I must own, this has not happen'd by Chance, but is the Effect of a
> Reasoning either good or bad. There are different ways of examining
> the Mind as well as the Body. One may consider it either as an
> Anatomist or as a Painter; either to discover its most secret Springs &
> Principles or to describe the Grace & Beauty of its Actions. I imagine it
> impossible to conjoin these two Views. When you pull off the Skin, &
> display all the minute Parts, there appears something trivial, even in
> the noblest Attitudes & most vigorous Actions: Nor can you ever
> render the Object graceful or engaging but by cloathing the Parts again
> with Skin & Flesh, & presenting only their bare Outside. An Anatom-
> ist, however, can give very good Advice to a Painter or Statuary: And
> in like manner, I am perswaded, that a Metaphysician may be very
> helpful to a Moralist; tho' I cannot easily conceive these two Charac-
> ters united in the same Work. Any warm Sentiment of Morals, I am
> afraid, wou'd have the Air of Declamation amidst abstract Reasonings,
> & wou'd be esteem'd contrary to good Taste. And tho' I am much
> more ambitious of being esteem'd a Friend to Virtue, than a Writer of

Taste; yet I must always carry the latter in my Eye, otherwise I must despair of ever being servicable to Virtue. I hope these Reasons will satisfy you; tho at the same time, I intend to make a new Tryal, if it be possible to make the Moralist & Metaphysician agree a little better. (*HL*, I, 32–33)

Hume is unsure whether his reasoning is sound and to what extent one can be both objectively philosophical and rhetorical at the same time. He patently admits that his *Treatise* lacks that "Warmth in the Cause of Virtue" which Hutcheson had looked for. The distinction between anatomist and painter is in moral discourse essentially the distinction between iconoclast and preacher. In the last paragraph Hume grants that some passages are imprudent in this respect, promising to alter them, and yet he still argues that "except a Man be in Orders, or be immediatly concern'd in the Instruction of Youth," his character does not depend "upon his philosophical Speculations," and "a little Liberty seems requisite to bring into the public Notice a Book that is calculated for so few Readers" (*HL*, I, 34).

Thus, even as he was writing the *Treatise*, Hume was conscious of its bold manner, of his temerity in publishing it, and above all of the unfavorable inferences which might be drawn regarding his character. This sensitivity influenced him in the final drafting of the Conclusion to Book III, most likely written after the exchange with Hutcheson, for the cross-purposes of that Conclusion, as discussed above, reflect Hume's uncertainty and his desire to palliate or excuse the license of his manner. In the last paragraph he makes up for lost time by praising "the *happiness*, as well as . . . the *dignity* of virtue" but then writes: "But I forbear insisting on this subject. Such reflections require a work a-part, very different from the genius of the present. The anatomist ought never to emulate the painter . . ." (III.iii.6). After distinguishing the two, as in the letter to Hutcheson, justifying the anatomist's preparatory instructions to a painter, Hume concludes: "And thus the most abstract speculations concerning human nature, however cold and unentertaining, become subservient to *practical morality*; and may render this latter science more correct in its precepts, and more persuasive in its exhortations." Exactly how that benefit will accrue is not glossed in the *Treatise*, and the claim sounds hollow and perfunctory. It is one more indication of Hume's uncertain state of mind.

When in the letter to Hutcheson Hume promises "to make a new Tryal, if it be possible to make the Moralist & Metaphysician agree a little better," he could be thinking of revising Book III of the *Treatise*. The evidence does not support that assumption, for the only real adjustment is right here in the Conclusion. Without much doubt, Hume is referring instead to future works, in particular his recasting of the third book of the *Treatise* into that favorite of his, *An Enquiry Concerning the Principles of Morals*. There Hume does attempt an alliance of anatomist and painter—and succeeds pretty well. The egregious differences in manner between the two works (not so much in matter), not to mention the pride Hume took in the second *Enquiry* above all his other works, support the argument of this chapter. Whatever is high-handed, imprudent, or cold in the *Treatise* is either modified in the second *Enquiry* or deleted. The "I" is consistently a man warmly interested in the cause of virtue, though he may broaden its definition. On delicate subjects he is discreet; he reproves vice and cruelty; he argues politely; he sweetens his text with inspiring exempla, painting pictures of virtuous men. He is never the harsh realist of the *Treatise*, infatuated with riches and power, scornful of meanness and poverty. Quite the contrary, the virtuous man, like the remodeled Hume, "does not measure out degrees of esteem according to the rent-rolls of his acquaintance" (*EPM*, 248). And though not ready to praise the humble Jesus and his followers, Hume can admire the noble poverty, the unworldliness of Socrates and Epictetus (*EPM*, 256). The same man who in the *Treatise* had scorned the idle fiction of poets can now pronounce Vergil to be greater than "Augustus, adorned with all the splendour of his noble birth and imperial crown" (*EPM*, 259). In a short dialogue he puts the virtuous man on canvas, with each of his speakers giving "a stroke of the pencil to his figure" (*EPM*, 269–70). Hume's language reveals the extent to which the moral philosopher has become more a painter than an anatomist, and even when he remembers his duty to anatomize as well as to paint, he is reluctant to tear himself from the beauties of morality: "But I forget, that it is not my present business to recommend generosity and benevolence, or to paint, in their true colours, all the genuine charms of the social virtues. These, indeed, sufficiently engage every heart . . . and it is difficult to abstain from some sally of panegyric . . ." (*EPM*, 177)—just as Hume has been demonstrating by his previous effusions of praise.[21]

It is as if the implicit antirationalism of Hume's philosophy had found ideal expression in the second *Enquiry*. The philosopher can exchange the scientist's smock for the artist's, knowing that the moral taste can create an ideal world of beauty which reason can never see. This taste "has a productive faculty, and gilding or staining all natural objects with the colours, borrowed from internal sentiment, raises in a manner a new creation" (*EPM*, 294). This is a conception of some moment. Unlike Pope's "true Expression," which "gilds all objects, but it alters none" (*Essay on Criticism*, II, 11. 315–17), Hume's creative taste is surprisingly more akin to Coleridge's creative imagination–or perhaps to Neoplatonic defenses of poetry over history, the poetry that re-creates *la belle nature*.

In any event, the striking shift in tone and manner apparent in the second *Enquiry* further highlights those defects of manner in the *Treatise* about which Hume became increasingly concerned.

III

Two questions remain to be answered. Is the extravagance of Hume's manner in the *Treatise* finally a defect, whatever Hume may have thought? And is that manner relevant to the meaning of the *Treatise*?

How we answer the first question is in some sense a matter of taste, and hence vain to dispute. Whether we like red better than blue, whether we prefer the heedless vitality of youth to the circumspection of maturity, are matters best deferred to the wisdom of Sir Roger de Coverley: "Much might be said on both sides" (*The Spectator*, no. 122). The Hume of the *Treatise* is something of a firebrand, no Tom Paine to be sure, but still more reckless and dégagé than we are accustomed to thinking of Hume. After the *Treatise*, he cultivated restraint, honed his irony, and when he became emotional, it was in the eminently acceptable guise of sensibility—and a rather safe expression of that—not so much as a man of feeling who might lose control but rather as a *gentleman of feeling* who would always observe the proper limits: "But I forget," says the warm but self-possessed Hume of the second *Enquiry*, "that it is not my present business to recommend generosity and benevolence. . . ." Hume preferred his more mature self; in our post-Romantic world we are inclined to appreciate the more unguarded and energetic young Hume. Having demonstrated his existence, it may be unnecessary for me to recommend him.

Hume may have unwittingly preferred his earlier, more daring self, too. A good while after he had virtually given up writing, he explained in a letter (1767) why his present avocation as an under-secretary of state was suitable for an older man of letters: "Learning requires the Ardor of Youth, the full Vigour of Imagination, a Fund of Vanity, and often an unrelenting application, of all which, men past middle Age are generally incapable" (*HL*, II, 137). The invidious phrase "Ardor of Youth" has here become a lost talent.

The principal advantage of Hume's careless manner in the *Treatise* is that we can get to know him better than from any other of his published works, including his autobiography, and can learn as well the personal origin of his philosophy. The characteristic pattern of the *Treatise* is for Hume to engage in long disquisition, displaying a fair degree of rational objectivity, and then to step back and reflect on the significance of the inquiry, as if to say, "Now let me look up from my arguments; where am

I, and what does all this portend?" Sometimes by taking stock he merely sets himself above rival philosophers, and the pause in exposition mainly serves the cause of vanity, a youthful peccadillo. Yet in the process of getting his bearings Hume becomes increasingly aware of his peculiar position, his liability to enthusiasm and error. Even before the Conclusion to Book I, we notice an increase in personal involvement and even confession:

> . . . We ought to have an implicit faith in our senses. . . . But to be ingenuous, I feel myself *at present* of a quite contrary sentiment. . . . Carelessness and in-attention alone can afford us any remedy. For this reason I rely entirely upon them; and take it for granted, whatever may be the reader's opinion at this present moment, that an hour hence he will be persuaded there is both an external and internal world. . . . (I.iv.2)

The stage is set for the autobiographical Conclusion (I.iv.7), part of which has already been examined. Despite the playfulness, we detect Hume's almost anguished need to justify his philosophy, and even more, to defend philosophy itself. Has any philosopher ever so strongly felt the need to justify the very act of philosophizing? We see Hume torn between austere philosophy and nature—and nature, he has just been arguing, and will prove in Books II–III, is decidedly the stronger and more valid force. Indeed, nature cured him of his incapacitating depression. ". . . Does it follow, that I must strive against the current of nature, which leads me to indolence and pleasure. . . ? No: If I must be a fool as all those who reason or believe any thing *certainly* are, my follies shall at least be natural and agreeable." Then, however, not wishing in his heart to give up philosophy, he rationalizes a solution, the paradox that nature herself disposes one person to philosophy as much as she disposes another person toward indolence. Hume says that he has a natural curiosity to know the principles of ethics, political science, pyschology, aesthetics, epistemology, and logic—no small curiosity! Should he resist that curiosity, he says, "I *feel* I shou'd be a loser in point of pleasure; and this is the origin of my philosophy." But this deterministic explanation does not satisfy him, and he goes on to maintain that even if he were not so inclined to take pleasure in philosophy, human limitation makes us all need a guide. Our choice is between superstition (all religion) and philosophy, and philosophy is the better choice, the "safest and most agreeable" guide, because it is less likely to lead our "natural propensities" astray. Back again we come to nature, ever keeping philosophy in its place and yet the staunchest support of philosophy. It is altogether a strange apologia: for philosophy, an impassioned defense and an exposure of its vain pretensions; and for himself, a confession of weakness, and a credo. Here is pride and self-assurance; here is likewise self-deflating ridicule and insecurity.

But here are balance and wisdom, too, qualities which emerge from Hume's manner. By the end of Book I, Hume has eroded the grounds for belief in anything, including his explanations, and yet he has two more books of philosophy to present. In a sense, Book I has been the performance of Reason, yet Reason has led us to the dead end deplored by Russell. Reason must be made subservient to the Passions for the *Treatise* to proceed. But it has been subservient all along, for belief has been defined as *"a more vivid and intense conception of any idea"* (I.iii.10) which is incapable of rational examination. We are struck with the increasing frequency of Hume's "I feel" as an answer to his dilemmas. But though people cannot justify belief rationally, people do believe. Hume never means to destroy our assurance of an internal and external reality; he never implies that our belief in our own existence and the existence of a world outside is to be doubted. In a sense, Book I is an elaborate destruction of epistemology and metaphysics; by the end, belief even renounces itself. Why do we believe anything? "If we believe, that fire warms, or water refreshes, 'tis only because it costs us too much pains to think otherwise." But we do believe. We are prepared to accept the famous dictum of Book II: "Reason is, and ought only to be the slave of the passions, and can never pretend to any other office than to serve and obey them" (II.iii.3).[22]

Thus, the two questions posed earlier concerning the advantages and relevance of Hume's manner do not admit of separate answers, for style and meaning are never neatly separable. If the *Treatise* is a more radical, more emphatic revelation of the basis of human knowledge and belief than we find in Hume's later versions, then the presence of an involved and active "I" is essential. In the *Treatise* we see Hume in the *process* of discovering his philosophy; in later versions we see him presenting an already systematized theory. The later statements gain in clarity and polish, in propriety and caution. But the later statements suffer from oversimplification and dogmatism, when what has long been expounded comes to be taken for granted. The *struggle for belief* is forgotten.

In this chapter I have pointed to Hume's youthful exuberance and indiscretion, strangely tempered with self-doubt and confession. Later in his works, both disappear. Instead, we get that Olympian calm—some might say coldness—for which Hume is noted. But Hume did not grow out of being both spirited and self-deprecating, and playful more than all. We continue to see these qualities in his letters and in the accounts of his friends. Adam Smith reports that during the last days of his life, Hume could imagine how he might try to buy time from the boatman of the Styx:

"Have a little patience, good Charon; I have been endeavoring to open the eyes of the Public. If I live a few years longer, I may have the satisfaction of seeing the downfall of some of the prevailing systems of superstition." But Charon would then lose all temper and decency. "You loitering rogue, that will not happen these many hundred years. Do you fancy I will grant you a lease for so long a term? Get into the boat this instant, you lazy loitering rogue."[23]

He did not grow out of this puckish humor, but he did conceal it better in his published works, right up to and including the last testimonial, *My Own Life*. Never again would he interrupt his serious inquiry to compare philosophizing to pastimes which cannot always be rationally justified. But in the *Treatise* he had compared a philosopher to a hunter "who over-looks a ten times greater profit in any other subject, and is pleas'd to bring home half a dozen woodcocks or plovers" (II.iii.10). Hunting and philosophizing, like gambling, are amusements to prevent life from becoming too tiresome, Hume says.

Can we take such a philosopher seriously? If his intention is to jolt us out of complacent assurance, to wake us from our dogmatic slumber, then his means are just right. Hume's manner in the *Treatise* catches us off guard, but we are apt to believe a philosopher who so bluntly shows the tenuous grounds of our belief—and his. Having experienced with Hume the salutary doubt, we can go on to philosophize in that careless manner he recommends—open-minded, tolerant, resilient. Careless philosophy, after all, is serious business, too, for the stakes are high. From that same bantering Conclusion to Book I, we hear:

Two thousand years . . . are a small space of time to give any tolerable perfection to the sciences. . . . For my part, my only hope is, that I may contribute a little to the advancement of knowledge. . . . Human Nature is the only science of man; and yet has been hitherto the most neglected. 'Twill be sufficient for me, if I can bring it a little more into fashion; and the hope of this serves to compose my temper from that spleen, and invigorate it from that indolence, which sometimes prevail upon me. . . . The conduct of a man, who studies philosophy in this careless manner, is more truly sceptical than that of one, who feeling in himself an inclination to it, is yet so over-whelm'd with doubts and scruples, as totally to reject it. A true sceptic will be diffident of his philosophical doubts, as well as of his philosophical conviction. . . .

Notes

1. See the two epigraphs at the head of this chapter, taken respectively from *The New Letters of David Hume*, ed. Raymond Klibansky and Ernest C. Mossner (Oxford: Clarendon,

1954), p. 3; and *The Letters of David Hume*, ed. J. Y. T. Greig (Oxford: Clarendon, 1932), 1:187—hereafter abbreviated *NHL* and *HL* respectively.

2. The full story of the *Treatise*'s composition and reception is told in Ernest Campbell Mossner's *Life of David Hume*, 2d ed. (Oxford: Clarendon, 1980), pp. 66–133. Quotations above and hereafter from *My Own Life* are from the text given in Mossner's *The Forgotten Hume: Le Bon David* (New York: Columbia University Press, 1943), pp. 3–10.

3. Bertrand Russell, *A History of Western Philosophy* (New York: Simon and Schuster, 1945), p. 659.

4. See the discussion in Norman Kemp Smith, *The Philosophy of David Hume* (London: Macmillan, 1949), pp. 519–40. Smith remarks, ". . . in recent years more has been written upon Hume, and especially upon the *Treatise*, than at any time in the past" (p. 521). Smith's important study is symptomatic of this paradox, for the scholar who argued for the precedence of Hume's moral philosophy over his epistemology devoted eighty percent of his lengthy book to Hume's epistemology.

5. T. E. Jessop, "The Misunderstood Hume," in *Hume and the Enlightenment*, ed. William B. Todd (Edinburgh: Edinburgh University Press, 1974), pp. 1–13. Jessop recommends: "I take it for granted that he knew better than anyone else where that philosophy is to be found and what it is. The ignoring of that injunction has led to a relative neglect of the later works to which alone he directs us" (pp. 6–7).

6. John B. Stewart says that Hume's "later writings are not radically new understakings; instead, they can best be understood as applications and extrapolations of the principles set forth in the *Treatise*." See *The Moral and Political Philosophy of David Hume* (New York: Columbia University Press, 1963), p. 17; also pp. 18–19, 325–39.

7. Quotations from *A Treatise of Human Nature* are from the text edited by L. A. Selby-Bigge (Oxford: Clarendon, 1888) and are cited only by book, part, and section.

8. Jessop, "The Misunderstood Hume," p. 6. Kemp Smith, *The Philosophy of David Hume*, comments, "The over-forcible expressions into which he was betrayed, while effective in arresting the reader's attention, proved dangerously misleading, as he later came to recognise" (p. 543).

9. John V. Price has explored this aspect of Hume's exposition in *The Ironic Hume* (Austin: University of Texas Press, 1965). In his discussion of Hume the historian, Leo Braudy emphasizes Hume's detachment: "Hume's voice remains cool and remote, and his humor is Olympian irony"—*Narrative Form in History and Fiction* (Princeton: Princeton University Press, 1970), p. 88. Basil Willey makes Hume's "unruffled calm of manner" into a key for understanding Hume and his age; see *The English Moralists* (New York: W. W. Norton, 1964), p. 248. And John B. Stewart, *Moral and Political Philosophy*, remarks: "Hume's writing is never rushed or murky. The most that can be said by way of criticism is that in the *Treatise* the young author, eager in his adventure, occasionally breaks pace and throws the reader, and that in most of the later works . . . the unvaried courtly measure and high polish of his prose seem incongruent with the earnestness of his thought. . . . Nothing that might be taken for wild, thoughtless rapture erupts to disturb the urbane equipoise, the calculated balance of this circumspect, elegant prose" (pp. 261, 263).

10. Hume may never have sent the letter, the writing itself being therapy enough; we cannot be sure that Arbuthnot was Hume's intended consultant, though the evidence provided by Mossner is persuasive. See Mossner's *Life of David Hume*, pp. 83–88, and "Hume's Epistle to Dr. Arbuthnot, 1734: The Biographical Significance," *Huntington Library Quarterly* 7 (1944), 135–52. Another possible recipient was Dr. George Cheyne, author of *The English Malady*, although it makes no difference in this discussion who was Hume's addressee.

11. Mossner, *Life of David Hume*, p. 86.

12. *Enquiries Concerning Human Understanding and Concerning the Principles of Morals*, ed. L. A. Selby-Bigge, 3d ed. revised by P. H. Nidditch (Oxford: Clarendon, 1975), p. 9; hereafter *EHU* or *EPM* for the first and second *Enquiries* respectively.

13. *A Letter from a Gentleman to his friend in Edinburgh*, ed. Ernest C. Mossner and John V. Price (Edinburgh: Edinburgh University Press, 1967), p. 20. Note that Hume was referring to the text of the *Treatise* by memory when he wrote the *Letter*; clearly he is referring to the passage in the *Treatise* discussed above.

14. James Boswell, *Life of Johnson* (London: Oxford University Press, 1953), p. 314.

15. This chapter was written before the appearance of Donald W. Livingston, *Hume's Philosophy of Common Life* (Chicago: University of Chicago Press, 1984). These observations by Livingston are relevant to this discussion: "[In the Conclusion to *Treatise* I, Hume,] in Augustinian fashion, launches into a ten-page philosophic confession in which conflicts in the philosophical passions are laid bare. This remarkable piece of analysis appears to be the first attempt of a philosopher to inquire not merely into the conceptual possibility but also into the *integrity* of his own philosophical activity. . . . The author of the *Treatise* does not merely explain and prove things to the reader, he is also a character in the work. . . . But the price Hume paid is that the author becomes the main character of the dialogue, and this sort of exhibitionism was extremely mortifying to the later and more modest Hume" (pp. 38–41).

16. David Hume, "An Abstract of a Treatise of Human Nature," in Charles W. Hendel's edition of the first *Enquiry* (Indianapolis: Bobbs-Merrill, 1955), pp. 194–98.

17. One may similarly contrast the treatment of female chastity in the *Treatise* (III.ii.12) with that of *EPM*, 207–8, 238ff. In the *Treatise* Hume speaks like a Restoration rake, assuming that all women secretly lust after the sport; in *EPM* he is much more circumspect.

18. See the interesting study of J. C. Hilson, "Hume: The Historian as Man of Feeling," in *Augustan Worlds*, ed. J. C. Hilson et al. (Bristol: Leicester University Press, 1978), pp. 205–22.

19. Many remarks on the selfishness of humanity occur, for example, II.iii.6, III.ii.5, and III.ii.7.

20. Kemp Smith, *The Philosophy of David Hume*, says that "the role which Hume assigns to sympathy in the moral life is no less central than that which he ascribes to belief in the sphere of the understanding" (p. 174). Smith quotes this passage as proof of the importance of sympathy to Hume, yet Smith omits the first sentence, which, like the parenthetical clause, considerably qualifies Hume's faith in the moral disinterestedness of humanity.

21. My view of the differences between the *Treatise* and the second *Enquiry* are supported by Stewart, *Moral and Political Philosophy*, pp. 328–37, although Stewart is concerned mainly with thematic differences. In a long metaphor Stewart does compare the *Treatise* to a suspenseful journey of discovery and the *Enquiry* to a smooth passage conducted by "an experienced captain." A good bit is left unsaid, however, when Stewart concludes, "The *Treatise* is a philosophical work, while the *Enquiry* is a masterpiece of elegant exposition."

22. David Fate Norton has recently cautioned against making too much of this startling dictum. See *David Hume: Common-Sense Moralist, Sceptical Metaphysician* (Princeton: Princeton University Press, 1982).

23. *The Philosophical Works of David Hume*, ed. T. H. Green and T. H. Grose (London: Longmans, Green, & Co., 1874–75), 3:11.

9

The Literary Structure and Strategy of Hume's Essay on the Standard of Taste

ROBERT GINSBERG

Le fil du raisonnement n'y est pas toujours aisé à suivre,
les digressions sont relativement fréquentes et longues,
les idées accessoires se mêlent aux idées fondamentales
dans des proportions et dans des combinaisons difficiles
à tirer au clair. Bref l'ensemble de l'exposé laisse une
impression générale de subtilité plutôt que de solidité.

(The line of reasoning in it is not always easy to follow,
digressions are relatively frequent and lengthy, secondary ideas are mixed with fundamental ideas in proportions and combinations difficult to keep clear. In sum,
the totality of the account leaves a general impression of
subtlety rather than solidity.)
Olivier Brunet, *Philosophie et esthétique chez David Hume*

I

The argument of David Hume's essay "Of the Standard of Taste" is that
despite the natural and justifiable variety of judgments in matters of
taste a reliable standard for arriving at correct judgment exists in the
collective discernment of critics who have five qualities: "Strong sense,
united to delicate sentiment, improved by practice, perfected by comparison, and cleared of all prejudice" (p. 278).[1] The standard is subjective, for it is located in identifiable subjects, but it is not thereby arbitrary, since suitable abilities to detect objective qualities may be
perfected. Hence, matters of taste are subject to objective apprehension
and assessment, given the right preparation of the experiencing subject.
Consequently, we can educate ourselves in taste, or if we cannot over-

come our natural shortcomings we may follow the judgment of those who have the best taste.

Why does Hume require thirty-six paragraphs in nineteen pages to present this argument? The problem of finding a standard amid variety must be clarified, distinctions of subjectivity and objectivity must be drawn, explications of each of the five golden qualities must be given, and moral restrictions must be looked into. In sum, an argument needs arguing. Yet Hume does other things here than logically develop a theory. He is writing an essay, and the essay is a work of literature. Hume makes several kinds of imaginative appeal, including proverb, anecdote, and literary allusion, which draw the reader into experiencing what is at stake. Conjoined to this literary content we may consider Hume's literary practice: word choice and word avoidance, repetition and variation, pairing and paralleling, phrasing and sentence structure, paragraphing and progression, and the dramatic highpoints and sudden reversals of the essay. The reader is made to do the work. Hume activates the reader's thinking by stimulation of feeling and reflection. Hume is an architect of reader experience, and to read this essay is quite an experience. So while we speak of the argument in the essay, we must also see the essay as operative within the reader challenged to make sense of the argument by sensing it being made. Most studies of the essay, including the present one, heavily quote and paraphrase because of the difficulty of stating Hume's position in terms other than Hume's presentation. The context of the writing has to be taken into account if the logic of the argument is to be reconstructed, but more than logic is at stake in this way of philosophizing.

The aim of this essay, which is longer than Hume's, is to expose the reasoning as it is embedded in Hume's literary artistry. The guiding question is: What happens in a reading of the essay? We will assess the reasons and the taste evident in the essay while exercising our reasoning and taste. Let us be both twentieth-century readers and eighteenth-century ones.

II

The title of the essay is not "Of Taste," but "Of the Standard of Taste"—already a complexity, for whatever is said about taste must be held in suspension until we are shown its relevance to standards. Hume speaks of standard in the singular. Quite singular. How then is the standard to be distinguished from many proposed standards?

The opening line is:

> The great variety of Taste [1757: "Tastes"], as well as of opinion [1757: "opinions"], which prevails [1757: "prevail"] in the world, is too obvious not to have fallen under every one's observation. (P. 266)

We are immediately plunged into the problem of pluralism by the initial "great variety." "Taste" is capitalized and draws the attention. But the essay inserts another consideration while we are facing taste: "as well as of opinion." Opinion, we shall see shortly, means intellectual position. The great variety which exists both in taste and intellect is given a modifier, "which prevails in the world," before we get to the predicate of the sentence. The prevalence of such variety in the world is an observation. The variety, we are told, is "too obvious" and then we are told in what way: "not to have fallen under" (a negative following the emphatic) "every one's" (universal quantifier) "observation." In other words, if we change the word order, convert the negative to a positive, and soften the emphatics: *All have observed the obvious prevalence of great variety in taste and ideas.* That is the cold logic. Hume, however, is engaging the reader in mental processes—a psychological task. By the time the sentence gets to "every one's observation," the reader has joined everyone. That the reader shares the observation is made *obvious* by the skillful positioning of that word.

This writing is typical of Hume's strategy. We must not dismiss it by labeling it Hume's sophisticated style, while we pay exclusive attention to the content or "opinions." What Hume is doing is part of the content. The opening sentence is typical because it is not in a clear-cut, simple logical form, a propositional arrangement, although it could be. The point is not made by Hume for the reader; instead, the reader reconstructs the point behind the progression of words. The point is that the point is not simple but multiform. It is gathered gradually and partially as one reads, and one has to reread to get the rest of the point. Something alive underneath the words sticks its head out between the commas. Our effort is needed to work it free. While we speak of authors whom we are obliged to read between the lines, with Hume we have to read between the words. The reader organizes the points within the sentence rather than receiving them one by one. The reading is a process of thinking that overcomes gaps as it unifies. We are doing Hume's work for him—and hence for us.

Returning to the first sentence, we find it makes an observational case about a striking fact in the world. It is an objective claim though it refers to something highly subjective, namely taste and views. One can arrive at correct judgments regarding states of affairs imbued with subjective variety. Hume has won the argument of his essay by the time we have understood its first sentence. Consensus—indeed, universal agreement—is possible in reference to matters of disagreement: that variety exists is true. This ironic opening that insists upon variety comes to an indisputable fact. Obviousness confirms the soundness of observation.

The essay opens on the obvious and seeks its shelter many times in getting to what is not so obvious but nonetheless observationally grounded. One can make sound observations concerning ideas ("opinion") as well as taste. The obvious is at the same time the inescapable quality of an objective state of affairs and the certainty of a subjective experience. The obvious, then, will be a model for overcoming the gap between subjectivity and objectivity.

That Hume has set forth all this in the first sentence is far from obvious. The opening is a disarmer. It seems not to engage in argument, and not to introduce the subject of standards, as it makes a harmless observation. An easiness of cadence and form in the sentence stills the critical faculties of the reader. It is artlessly executed and seductively clear.

We could dwell on the initial sentence for several pages but that would be in doubtful taste, since so many riches lie ahead. To do them justice we shall move on apace and leave details by the wayside. The reader may return to Hume's text at any point to perform a more thorough application.

The second sentence picks up the observational mode ("to remark") as applied again to "difference of taste" [1757: simply "difference"], though this time the frame of reference is a small circle of acquaintances. The initial observation is borne out in this test case. "Prejudices" are innocently mentioned; later their consideration will be integral to the clinching definition of the standard.

The third sentence moves toward the extreme of the largest acquaintance with "distant nations and remote ages" (a recurrent phrase in the essay), where one nonetheless encounters "great inconsistence and contrariety" [1757: "contradiction"]: further evidence of the initial observation. Hume has nicely left room for the reader in the two categories of observers: those of "the most confined knowledge" and those "who can enlarge their view." The reader will not care to belong to the first group and is sympathetically helped into the second group by the saving "But" that opens the third sentence. "But" is the most effective word in David Hume's vocabulary; he is the foremost philosopher of "but."

The fourth sentence begins "We are apt," on the surface an impersonal statement, but beneath the surface it strengthens identification of the reader with the cosmopolitan sort in the previous sentence. *We* are now over on Hume's side. We make a judgment about what is far from our "taste and apprehension": it is barbarous. Apprehension is a more active term than feeling. Throughout, Hume pairs taste with other terms to indicate how taste operates. Sometimes the other member of the pair is parallel to the case of taste, as opinion in the first sentence, at other times the term is concomitant to the functioning of taste. Apprehension seems parallel here; later (¶¶ 22, 28) it will become concomitant. A strong judgment is rendered on what is against our taste, and Hume italicizes "barbarous." Italics are a typographical device in Hume's works that suggests keys to topics and issues. The skeleton of the essay can be exposed by listing its italicized words.[2]

But we are in the middle of a sentence marked by that reversing word *but:* we are judged barbarous by others. Further fuel to the variety of judgment associated with the variety of taste is added by the subsequent sentence's opening *And.* Observation is mentioned here as is the pronouncement of judgment, while the "contest of sentiment" [1757: "sentiments"] remains in force. Sentiment is the grounding for the exercise of taste. So the first paragraph is an elaboration of the first sentence by means of a variety of terms *(variety, difference, inconsistence, contrariety, contest)* and a variety of circumstances open to observation.

Let us move more rapidly through the text, stepping from paragraph to paragraph. The second paragraph asserts that the obvious "variety of taste" is not limited to appearance but goes deeper to reality. Here is a contrast between taste and "matters of opinion and science," for differences in the latter domain might reduce to dispute over terms. When thinkers turn to particulars they find they are in agreement. But though "every voice is united in applauding elegance, propriety, simplicity, spirit in writing," disagreement occurs "when critics come to particulars." Thus, the initial inclusion of opinion with taste becomes a useful distinction of the problem for judging taste, in the second paragraph. At stake are our differing sentiments "with regard to beauty and deformity." This pair is central to the object of taste. Variety remains embedded in the paragraph but also present are kinds of unanimity.

The third paragraph takes an odd direction: morals, which if founded on sentiment would be a field like taste, where general agreement occurs on what is to be praised but considerable difference arises about its particularized identity. "It is obvious," says Hume in a line that carefully parallels one used for taste (¶ 2), that writers "concur in applauding justice, humanity, magnanimity, prudence, veracity." Both morals and taste are founded on sentiment and speak a widely shared language of approbation and blame. Hume makes the telling point that the very habit of language with its terms of praise reinforces a common moral outlook. He makes a tie between literature and morality with his first literary allusion:

Even poets and other authors, whose compositions are chiefly calculated to please the imagination, are yet found, from Homer down to
Fenelon, to inculcate the same moral precepts, and to bestow their
applause and blame on the same virtues and vices. (P. 267)

The literary work is aimed at pleasing the imagination, not at guiding
"conduct and manners," but it employs language whose terms are laden
with value. Hence, the moral judgment within the literary work will
conform to common usage: "the word *virtue*, with its equivalent in every
tongue, implies praise."

Having made the sweeping general reference to Homer and Fénelon
(1651–1715), Hume returns to a probing examination of the comparative
portrayal of the virtues and vices in the shared subject matter of the two
epic artists. Hume has put his finger correctly on the crude morality in
the Homeric world contrasted with the noble refinement of the French
archbishop's recreation of antiquity. The *Télémaque* is intended for the
education of Christian princes.[3] Hume makes good use of what will be
called comparative literature; he traces significant differences in jux-
taposing an ancient and a modern work on the same themes. Hume's
literary allusions are usually offered in pairs.

In making the telling comparison that closes the paragraph, Hume
wins the point made earlier in the paragraph that literature from Homer
down to Fénelon praises the same virtues. Everything is covered in
Hume's claim, from the West's oldest epic to the edge of Hume's century
(the *Télémaque* appeared in 1699). Hume is not calling into question the
literary merits of the works compared, nor is he judging their moral
content. Later we will find Hume deciding on the aesthetic impact of
moral attitudes in works of art. The point of this paragraph is to further
illustrate the variety of views. We now have differences in (1) taste, (2)
ideas, (3) morals, and (4) the literary portrayal of morals. "Obvious" is
used three times in this complex paragraph.

Paragraph 4 steps outside the European tradition to adduce as further
example "the Alcoran." It is a "wild and absurd performance" [1757:
"wild performance"]. The absurd is a type of obviousness, for it is
palpably false or tasteless. Again the very words for the virtues carry
praise, but when one examines the instances that "the pretended
prophet" applies that praise to, we find them to be such "treachery,
inhumanity, cruelty, revenge, bigotry, as are utterly incompatible with
civilized society." What Hume takes as the wildness, and, on second
thought, the absurdity of the Koran (edited 651–52) may be its passionate intensity, for it is a collection of unconnected rapturous utterances
ordered by length, rather than a coherent narrative or systematic teach-

ing as found in the Hebrew and Christian scriptures. Hume had a temperamental as well as philosophical block against religious enthusiasm. But refined writers of English letters in the eighteenth century shared the lack of appreciation for the intensity of religious experience expressed in such works. The Koran is only recently receiving the attention it is due in English. Hume's essay relies on judgments its readers would approve. Hume and his readers may not have read the Koran.

What interests us here is not Hume's taste but the taste within Hume's essay, not the person but the persona—the narrative consciousness we detect in the essay. Thus, any literary allusion is to be grasped in the unfolding of the essay as part of the case it makes and the experience it engenders, rather than as documentation of the preferences and defects of the man, David Hume. To condemn Hume's judgments as orthodox eighteenth-century views, as does George Saintsbury, is to miss the rhetorical value those judgments have for the essay's eighteenth-century reader.[4]

The evil deeds Hume catalogues in the Koran echo three previous occasions when lists were strung out of praiseworthy or blameworthy qualities (¶¶ 2, 3). Thus, compositional devices reappear in the essay to build effects. Our sentiments have been played upon in reaching any point in the text. Hume's treatment of the Koran, following the more civilized examples of Homer and Fénelon, is a case of what earlier he called barbarity. Hume's lack of sympathy for the Moslem classic may be viewed by us as disparity between European taste and that of a distant people. Hume's point, on the surface, is that even this work of another culture exemplifies the variation in judgment of which we have been accumulating instances. Under the surface, however, the reader senses an attack upon religion that might extend to the "admirers and followers" of traditions closer to home, closer to Hume. Between the general preaching and the exemplified practice in scripture falls the shadow of what may be immoral but serves "the true believers." Bigotry, last in Hume's list of condemnations of Islam, reappears at the close of the essay in polemics against other faiths. Smuggled into this essay on taste is a critique of the immorality of religion.

Hume moves toward the conclusions to be drawn from his wide-ranging survey of variety. Paragraph 5 (p. 268) makes the point that the ethical term bears the value commitment of praise within it and hence is a recommendation to action. Hume had made the point with the general word "virtue," now he uses "charity" [1757: "modesty"]. Charity had been last in the list of general praise in ¶ 4, where it was subverted by Islam. The use of the same word in ¶ 5 is a backward stab. And so is the phrase "pretended legislator or prophet" in ¶ 5. The theoretical content of ¶ 5 would make it follow ¶ 3; we feel the awkwardness of the Moslem interjection in ¶ 4.

Hume takes another awkward step to a summary statement in the shortest paragraph of the essay (¶ 6): we need a standard of taste. This is the first use in the essay of the titular phrase—capitalized and italicized so we cannot miss it. By such a standard is meant a rule for reconciling or judging "the various sentiments of men": echo of variety in the opening sentence, reiteration of sentiment. This paragraph belongs after ¶ 2. It does not make anything of ¶¶ 3, 4, and 5 on variety in moral sentiment. While both taste and morality are founded on sentiment, Hume has not argued that morality is a matter of taste. The standard of taste we naturally seek is not proposed as a standard of morality. Hume threatens to throw the reader off the track by the extensive discussion of morality.

Paragraph 7 gets into the argumentative heart of the problem. Hume makes the case against the possibility of arriving at such a standard in one of the best statements ever made of the relativity of taste. Indeed, it is so effective that to seriously consider the alternative will be an uphill struggle as we are tempted to fall back into this initial position. In teaching aesthetics during twenty years I have found my students take this as Hume's strongest point; the rest of the essay for them is downhill. Hume draws a distinction between matters of understanding (or judgment or opinion) and those of sentiment. The former can be tested by objective referent: "real matter of fact." But the latter are self-referential. The sentiment is perforce right because, to use T. S. Eliot's term, no objective correlative exists for it. "No sentiment represents what is really in the object," says Hume. Where then are beauty and deformity, first mentioned in ¶ 2, to be found? "Beauty is no quality in things themselves: It exists merely in the mind which contemplates them." Since beauty is in the mind of the beholder, and no necessary connection exists between what is in the object and what is in the mind, only "a certain conformity or relation between [1757: "betwixt"] the object and the organs or faculties of the mind," then "each mind perceives a different beauty." Our differences as subjectivities entertaining varied sentiments will cause the same objects to be greeted differently. Realizing this natural ground of variation, we should accept our sentiments (*it is good if I like it*) and not seek "to regulate those of others." No rule can be found when each person's sentiments rule. "The proverb has justly determined it to be fruitless to dispute concerning tastes" (p. 269). The proverbial is an instance of the obvious, so that common sense agrees with philosophic reasoning.

The case concerning the "conformity or relation" the object has to the mind is weak. The mind imposes itself on the object, making it conform to its sentiments, but Hume concedes "if that conformity did not really exist, the sentiment could never possibly have being" [1757: "have a being"]. Thus, the sentiment requires something outside itself as the material for its occasion. The beauty resides in the mind within the sentiment, yet the beauty does draw upon a correlative in the object. We are left with the difficulty that each person's sentiment will require different qualities from objects, so that to say such-and-such an object is a ground of beauty is problematic.

Paragraph 8 begins with "But," the first of the nine to do so, one out of every four in the essay. A startling reversal is thus in store for the reader. The proverbial and common-sense position may be opposed by another common-sense position. This is in keeping with the proliferation of differences and variety at every level in the essay. Paragraphs 7 and 8 are matched by the closing line of the former and the opening line of the latter, and by a similar phrase in the opening of each: "a species of philosophy" in ¶ 7 and "a species of common sense" in ¶ 8. Hume's case in ¶ 8 is modeled around a set of literary examples with persuasive power:

> Whoever would assert an equality of genius and elegance between [1757: "betwixt"] OGILBY and MILTON, or BUNYAN and ADDISON, would be thought to defend no less an extravagance, than if he had maintained a mole-hill to be as high as TENERIFFE, or a pond as extensive as the ocean. (P. 269)

Modern readers may ask, "Who the hell is Ogilby?" The very question confirms Hume's point, for the disappearance from literary consciousness of that name, while Milton (1608–74) remains near the summit, indicates the objective difference in their merit. John Ogilby (1600–76) wrote translations in verse, which he also published, of Vergil (1649), Aesop (1651), and Homer (1660, 1665), and he was the author of works on Androcles and other classical themes, before becoming a geographer. His editions were popular in his day, but Ogilby fell victim to a change in taste, led by Dryden's harsh judgment of his verse. Katherine S. Van Eerde reports that in the eighteenth century, "Ogilby's fame became that of one of the worst poets in the English language."[5] Neither Hume nor his readers need have read Ogilby. Why should they? What counts is the obviousness of a shared judgment.

To insist on the equality of an Ogilby to a Milton is to make a mountain out of a molehill. Hume is countering proverb with proverb, giving pleasure to the reader in the spectacle of dispute and in the recognition of common attitudes and commonplaces. Hume's case is not dependent on the specific authors chosen. Thus, if present-day undergraduates were to ask, in addition to the query about Ogilby, "Milton who?" one may substitute other names still well-known, such as Shakespeare.[6]

A problem occurs with Hume's second pair. Joseph Addison's (1672–1719) justly deserved reputation as essayist was strong in the eighteenth century. He contributed to the *Tatler* (1710), the *Spectator* (1711–12), the *Guardian* (1713), and the new *Spectator* (1714), and also wrote the phenomenally successful tragedy, *Cato* (1713). No question can arise of Addison's elegance as prose writer, although the power of his genius might now be downplayed. John Bunyan (1628–88), on the other hand, is the author of pious books springing from spiritual experiences and convictions. *The Pilgrim's Progress* (1678) is a radiant allegory of Christian commitment that has rightly received recent praise. Elegance is not the right term for Bunyan's style, but the moving creative power in his writing is eloquent, and we must attribute genius to him. In retrospect Hume's judgment of the inequality between Addison and Bunyan is wrong, though it was right for the intended readership of Hume's essay, by confirming an eighteenth-century preference for the calm, rational writer over the fervent, impassioned one. The religious controversies of the seventeenth century, which saw Bunyan imprisoned for conscience, may have been willingly eclipsed in consciousness by the urbanity and wit of the Age of Enlightenment. Anything that smacks of religious fervor is frowned upon in Hume's essay. Because Milton unquestionably wins out over Ogilby in the first pairing, we are inclined to accept the triumph of Addison over Bunyan in the second contest.

Teneriffe is the largest of the Canary Islands, topped by an impressive 12,192-foot volcano. In case we miss the geographical identification, Hume tacks on the straightforward terms of pond and ocean.

Hume rebuffs "pretended critics" who are blind to the inequalities. In ¶ 4 he spoke of the "pretended prophet" and in ¶ 5 of "any pretended legislator or prophet." "Pretended" is a strong and repeated term in the essay that means fake rather that proposed. Hume has not put to rest the preceding axiom of relativity, for the gross inequalities that are obvious may "modify and restrain" the thesis, though it may hold good in all but extreme cases.

An alternative is disposed of in ¶ 9. It too opens on a note of the obvious: "it is evident" that a priori rules for composition cannot be established by the understanding. The rules of art are not a relation of eternal ideas but take their foundation, as do "all the practical sciences," from experience. They are observations "concerning what has been universally found to please in all countries and in all ages." The Platonic notion of beauty as an immutable ideal which might be grasped by intellect is rejected in favor of the experiential grounding in the observation of what everywhere pleases.[7] That presumes human nature remains the same from place to place and from era to era. Hence, the sentiment of pleasure, that most subjective of matters, is relatable to identifiable stimuli such that the artist can work out rules to evoke the desired pleasure. If the rules of art are not deducible, they are discoverable, and to observation Hume adds as a mode of their discovery that wonderful eighteenth-century touchstone of creativity—genius. However much we may complain that Hume has boxed himself into eighteenth-century neoclassical preferences in art, he has provided the escape hatch of genius.

We experience as beautiful some works which violate the rules. This is because they possess other beauties strong enough to compensate for the deformity. As example of this pleasing despite the rules Hume picks Ariosto (1474–1533). The Italian author pleases,

> but not by his monstrous and improbable fictions, by his bizarre mixture of the serious and comic styles, by the want of coherence in his stories, or by the continual interruptions of his narration. (P. 270)

A powerful string of condemnations is artfully laid down by Hume before reversing their conclusion. The more he condemns Ariosto, the more effective will be his praise of the author. Saintsbury chides Hume for "orthodox cavils at Ariosto."[8] And Hume's critique is quite wrong-headed. *Orlando Furioso* (1516) is entertaining because of the things Hume lists as its faults. His mistake is in taking Ariosto dead seriously instead of giving in to the playfulness and irony of the mock epic. Hume values Ariosto for the more anticipated qualities in style and the portrayal of amorous passions. If someone in Hume's audience detected the error of Hume's judgment in this case, that would not destroy his argument: indeed, that would strengthen the argument, for if the pleasure came from what Hume blames then we would revise the "particular rules of criticism" to recognize that these cannot be faults. The rules follow from the pleasures. This paragraph lays the ground for an observational or experimental science of aesthetics, although Hume does not develop its implications here.[9] The rules based on models also test the critic as well as correct our judgments. Like laws of science, notes Brunet, the rules are subject to revision.[10]

What does happen here is the deflating puncture of another "But" paragraph (¶ 10). While "all the general rules of art are founded only on experience and on the observation of the common sentiments of human nature," a variety of results occurs rather than a uniformity. The reason for this is delicacy of the "feelings" or "finer emotions of the mind" (to use other terms for sentiment), which are easily upset.

Hume introduces a mechanical model of the mind which plays such a large role in his two *Enquiries* into knowledge and morals. The mind is a machine in operation which runs on "secret springs." The ghost of clockwork haunts Hume's theory of mind. We observers can come to know only so much about its operations; some of its springs must ever remain secret. A hindrance of these throws the clockwork out of order. The proper use of the apparatus imposes prerequisites: "a perfect serenity of mind, a recollection of thought, a due attention to the object" (p. 271). An experimental method exists for matters aesthetic. We test the beauty or deformity by the proper functioning machine which is mind. We try to detect "the relation, which nature has placed between [1757: "betwixt"] the form and the sentiment." Here are the correlatives that naturally occur: a kind of form stimulates a kind of pleasure. Observation permits discovery of such relationships.

Since our apparatus may not be working well, the check to idiosyncrasy is the test of time; we can look for the "durable admiration, which attends those works, that have survived all the caprices of mode and fashion." Hence, identification of the great books is obvious. Consequently, by attending to those works known to be excellent we can develop our taste and subsequently apply it judiciously to works without universal recognition. By cutting our teeth on classics we exercise to the fullest the corresponding powers of the mind. The great works do not form our taste as if we were blank slates to be filled in by impressions received. Instead, they conform to our taste, which has the potentiality to respond appropriately to them. A mighty pedagogical program is implicit in Hume's theory of mind.

As example, ¶ 11 offers an old friend: "the same Homer, who pleased at Athens and Rome two thousand years ago, is still admired at Paris and at London." Brunet may have caught Hume in a profound error here, for a different Homer appears to be admired in changing times and places.[11] Though succeeding generations may equally value the same masterpieces, they can see different things in them. Hume might be exonerated by the nuance in his usage. Instead of identical features of a text, the "same Homer" could mean different features of an identical text, so that Homer is still being admired though for different reasons. While variations in circumstances, "prejudice," and authority cause shifting in literary fortunes, in the long run the works of "real genius" will be appreciated for their true worth. By removing obstructions, "the beauties, which are naturally fitted to excite agreeable sentiments" have their effect. This is the preview of the fourth of Hume's criteria for the ideal critic: freedom from prejudice (¶ 21).

Hume drives home the point in ¶ 12: "it appears then, that, amidst all the variety and caprice [1757: "caprices"] of taste, there are certain general principles of approbation or blame, whose influence a careful eye may trace in all operations of the mind." Variety is not denied; it has been insisted upon. Yet general principles of judgment exist, hence, a standard of taste. These may be found in observation of the mind's operations. "Some particular forms or qualities, from the original structure of the internal fabric, are calculated to please, and others to displease." Hume flirts with the position that beauty resides in the object, though it requires a well-functioning mind to detect it. If we miss the beauty inherent in the object we are at fault for not being in proper tune. Only a sound state of mind can provide "a true standard of taste and sentiment" (p. 272).

A new test is proposed for perfect beauty: the consensus in sentiment among people operating with sound apparatus. Hume is not arguing that the majority rules in matters of taste or that authority must be accorded a small group of taste setters. Decisive is the widespread agreement arising out of the proper functioning of a human faculty. Something democratic is latent in Hume's view. As sharers in human nature we all have the potentiality of becoming good judges of art. Noël Carroll puts the point eloquently: "Put bluntly, what do I care for critics? I'll do it myself."[12] Some of us, Hume suggests, have defects, while others take the trouble to refine their tastes. The measure of taste is not every person, but those persons whose mind functions properly, just as the test of color is the eye of the healthy person, not the jaundiced one. While Protagoras had spoken of man as the measure or criterion (*métron*) of all things, and Aristotle spoke of the good man as the standard and measure (*kanòn kaì métron*) of the good, Hume identifies the good critic as the standard of taste. His essay is more concerned with the good critic than with good art or good taste. He closes the ocular example with the concession that "colour is allowed to be merely a phantasm of the sense." So the color is in the sensed appearance rather than in the object, although to talk of the true color as seen by the healthy eye makes perfect sense. This throws in doubt the position Hume was approaching of taking beauty as a quality in things. Instead, beauty is a quality in the mind sensed as conforming to things.

Paragraph 13 continues with the problem of defects which inhibit "those general principles, on which depends our sentiment of beauty or deformity." Hume reiterates that "some objects, by the structure of the mind," are "naturally calculated to give pleasure," but individuals may miss the pleasure because of shortcomings. The imagination is identified as site of the pleasurable sentiment.

Hume turns in ¶ 14 to an "obvious cause, why many feel not the proper sentiment of beauty." Argument by the obvious has continued as we arrive at the heart of the essay with its five criteria for critics. But

Hume enters this subject negatively, noting the existence of a defect in the *"delicacy* of imagination, which is requisite to convey a sensibility of those finer emotions." Delicacy is italicized as will be the other four criteria in the paragraphs ahead. Hume concedes that delicacy is widely discussed. Many (the essay's sole allusion to other theorists?) would use it as the standard of "every kind of taste or sentiment." "But," says Hume, "as our intention in this essay [1757: "dissertation"] is to mingle some light of the understanding with the feelings of sentiment," he proposes to offer "a more accurate definition of delicacy." Thus, only after one-third of the essay does Hume tell us what he is about. Taste is to be approached not merely by sentiment but by understanding. It is subject to a philosophical definition though it operates by means of feelings. Hume aims to mingle ideas and sentiments—the preceding paragraphs illustrate this. But Hume softens the grave turn toward phil- osophic rigor by calling upon the *Don Quixote* (1605, 1615) of Cervantes (1547–1616). A delicate touch.

III

Sancho Panza (in ¶ 15) tells a story to the Don to prove the former has inherited good taste in wine. Two of his kinsmen are invited to judge a cask of wine. One says it is leathery; the other says it is metallic. When the cask is emptied, on the bottom is found "an old key with a leathern thong." Hume's version of the story suppresses details of Cervantes' story or inserts them to fit the philosopher's purposes.[13] Cervantes makes the tasting activity brief: "the one man tasted it with the tip of the tongue; the other did nothing more than sniff it."[14] Then they make their pronouncements in a sentence whose structure mimics the one above. Sancho is concentrating on the wonderful behavior of his kinsmen. Hume also uses two sentences of parallel structure, but he recasts the parts so that the verdict of the first man is joined with his tasting, and then the verdict of the second is joined with *his* tasting. This allows Hume to interject for the first man a period of "mature reflection" before the judgment. The second uses the "same precautions." That he is a sniffer rather than taster has been left out as unessential. Hume's em- phasis is on how pretentious the exercise in taste by the two men seems to third parties. Cervantes' Sancho says that the owner disclaimed any such impurities, but that the connoisseurs reaffirmed their judgments. Hume's Sancho says, "You cannot imagine how much they were both ridiculed for their judgment." But we can imagine. Both judgments appear unfounded, each takes no support from the other, and they spring from men who pretend to be knowledgeable. We laugh at pretentious claims to the standard of taste. "But who laughed in the end?" continues Hume's version. Hume makes it seem that the cask was emptied at once so that the connoisseurs triumph on the spot over their detractors, but in Cervantes time elapses before the wine is sold and the evidence revealed.

The story clarifies the heart of Hume's essay: though variety occurs in taste yet a grounding exists in qualities for the proper operation of taste; the capability of detecting the qualities may be defective or it may attain an unusual delicacy.

The story has been told by Hume with elegant simplicity in a paragraph allowed to stand alone (¶ 15). Of the great unruly mass of Cervantes' masterpiece a single nugget has been brought forward to shine with intensity, an act of remarkable discrimination. The anonymous reviewer in the *Critical Review* quotes the story of Sancho as an example that Hume not only "knows what a delicate taste is, but that he is himself possessed of it."[15] On the other hand, Hume's French translator, "R. du T.," adds a note of objection: "Although this example marvellously explains the Theory of our author, I fear that many readers will find it too low and too ignoble to enter into a serious dissertation, and that we may reproach Mr. Hume with having sinned against the standard of taste in the very place where he wishes to establish it."[16] These opposite judgments would serve Hume as further illustration of the variety in taste of supposed critics and perhaps as example of national differences in taste.

Hume speaks of the anecdote as "noted"; he may have found it in another source. R. du T. mentions with approbation the rendering of the same story into a fable by La Motte. Antoine Houdar de la Motte (1672–1731) translated Homer, took part in the quarrel of the ancients vs. the moderns, and wrote dramas and poetry. His fable, "Le Gourmet," captures the spirit of the anecdote but without relating it to Cervantes' book.[17] Let us not get lost in the pursuit of sources and influences—the red herring of humanistic scholarship in the twentieth century—for our primary interest is how Hume tells the story and puts it to use in his essay.

He proposes to set forth the moral of the story in the essay's longest paragraph (¶ 16, p. 273). He begins with a certainty: "beauty and deformity . . . are not qualities in objects, but belong entirely to the sentiment." We have heard this before. Beauty is a quality of mind, not of things. It is psychologically sited. But, continues Hume, "there are certain qualities in objects, which are fitted by nature to produce those particular feelings." This too is the familiar formula. Nature brings about that conformity between objective qualities and subjective capabilities which produces the pleasure that is beauty. Why is Hume so insistent that beauty is not inherent in things while being equally insistent that things are the stimuli of beauty? Though things cannot be said to be naturally beautiful, Hume repeatedly says things are naturally related to our capability for experiencing beauty. From a pragmatic point of view these differences make no difference: to regard things as naturally beautiful comes to the same thing as regarding them as stimulators, thanks to nature, of the beauty we can experience. Hume is cautious—skeptical— about commitments to a supposed reality other than what is experienced. His philosophical outlook is subject-oriented rather than object-centered. Instead of analyzing the structure of things, he exposes the operations of mind. But in his aesthetics, things and mind correlate. Hume's repetitiveness need not be attributed to forgetfulness or crude persuasiveness. He repeatedly mines great difficulties and shares the struggle with us. We go deeper into the difficulty each time it surfaces.

Delicacy of taste may now be defined as the fine sense of discrimination which detects the details of the object presented. Delicacy is sensitivity and perceptiveness. Hume proposes an elaborate test of one who pretends to delicacy: see if that person can savor the pleasure of a quality, diminished in degree, that we have found by "the general rules of beauty" derived from established works and observation. Hume tries to put too much together in one sentence and this reflects the overextended device he envisions. He keeps open, as earlier in the essay, the double path of taste as the sense of the palate and as the sentiment of the mind. "To produce these general rules or avowed patterns of composition is like finding the key with the leathern thong." A ground for measuring judgment exists. Only deep into the paragraph does Hume draw the story's lesson proposed at the beginning. An object corresponded to the delicacy of taste of the two wine tasters; hence, they are justified, whereas the mockers present, "those pretended judges," are refuted. The key to settling disputes in the literary realm is development of "general principles" of beauty and identification of outstanding examples.[18] By this evidence we are able to demonstrate to the "bad critic"—a delightful phrase—that what the latter does not take pleasure in should give pleasure since it is an instance of that general principle to which "his own particular taste" conforms. The bad critic is brought to the recognition of a self-contradiction in the critic's operations. The recognition is that "the fault lies in himself" rather than in the aesthetic object; what lacks is not the beauty in the work but the delicacy of the critic to perceive it. In sum, taste is debatable. And a Socratic method exists for fruitfully conducting the debate. Hume's ingenious way of dealing with disputes in taste harmonizes the general rule, or principle, and the particular taste. The particular taste can acknowledge the principle as the latter operates in great examples. We can then see how the principle applies to works of the same kind. We must conclude that we should take pleasure in those works to which the principle applies but which happen to displease us. The logic of taste overrules the idiosyncrasies of our taste.

To dispute about matters of taste is meaningful because resolution is possible by reference to common principles. All still revolves upon one's taste, but appeal is possible beyond the shortcomings of that particularity to general rules to which it conforms. Taste, then, can be tested. If emptying the cask "justified the verdict of SANCHO's kinsmen," then the formation of "general principles" and "excellent models" justifies the good critic and disproves the bad one. Unfortunately, this is an enormous paragraph that strains one's concentration. The concluding sentence, beginning "But," contains ninety-one words, of which four are "principle," and eight are third person pronouns; it is punctuated by two semicolons and one full colon. Hume makes us struggle to drain all that can be gotten out of the wine cask. His elaborate solution sounds great in theory but I doubt it will work smoothly in practice. To understand this paragraph we have to go back over it, just as it is engaged in going back over the anecdote. That story serves as a guiding example from which general principles are formulated. Hume is getting us to engage in the operation which he is asserting as the proof of taste. The proof is in the paragraph—and it is the paragraph.

We are drawn into ¶ 17 (p. 274) by one of those general observations we cannot resist: "It is [1757: " 'Tis"] acknowledged" that the perfection of "every sense or faculty" consists in the exactitude and fineness of its "observation" of "objects." Hume substantiates this generality in two subsequent parallel sentences concerning the eye and palate. Graciously, he leaves open to the imagination of the reader the further parallels with the remaining senses. The groundwork has been laid at the first for every faculty, as well as sense. Hume brings in the case of "the perfection of our mental taste." This too consists in a fine observation of the qualities in a discourse. The fine mental taste is more valuable than a perfect palate, for "it is the source of all the finest and most innocent enjoyments, of which human nature is susceptible." Good taste makes accessible the highest human pleasures. In this "the sentiments of all mankind are agreed." This universal stamp of approval refers to the perfection of human nature. Hume obliges us to concur by use of the parallel between that taste whose organ is the mouth and the taste whose organ is the mind. To detect the differences between these two requires a niceness of observation and reflection. The reader experiences the pleasure of conducting that discrimination, gently assisted by Hume, only to arrive at a congratulatory remark about the value of just such pleasures. The reader's experience in reading contributes to the affirmation.

Delicacy of taste is everywhere prized. The test for it, concludes the paragraph, is "those models and principles, which have been established by the uniform consent [1757: "approbation"] and experience of nations and ages." We have moved a long way from the essay's opening in diversity of opinion and sentiment to a uniform consent extending across boundaries and centuries. The anchor is experience, which concurs in identifying great examples. The rules of art underlying these can be exposed to general recognition. The delicacy of taste of the critic is subject to testing by using these models or comparable works founded on the same principles. This is the wine-cask test of taste.

The second requisite of a good critic appears as the practice of ¶ 18, introduced in its opening "But" sentence. Taste can be perfected by specialization in an art or kind of beauty. The "feeling becomes more exact and nice" (p. 275) in dealing with objects of taste if the critic "acquire experience in those objects." This is a matter of clearer perception, but it also involves distinguishing marks of qualities. The experienced critic enjoys nothing less than a "clear and distinct sentiment." The Cartesian hallmarks of truth which adhere to an intuition are given new life by Hume as qualities of sentiment when a critic turns a delicate and practiced taste upon a range of aesthetic objects. Intuitions are trustworthy as knowledge of the world, in Descartes's scheme of metaphysics and epistemology. Clear and distinct sentiments are trustworthy as indicators of the qualities of aesthetic objects, according to Hume, but this occurs when the faculties of the critic and the qualities of an object conform. Hume has been conducting a Cartesian meditation in search for a principle to serve as solid foundation to the edifice of literary judgment. The critic "discerns that very degree and kind of approbation or displeasure, which each part is naturally fitted to produce." Confusion about the merit of unfamiliar kinds of art can be dispelled. We turn to the judgment of the critic experienced in the field, for by familiarity, "the organ acquires greater perfection in its operations." We are still dealing with the operations of natural capabilities and their highest development for use in judging what is available to experience. Hume concludes paragraph ¶ 18 with the observation that while practice contributes to creation of a work, practice may also contribute to judgment of the art. Practice here is not hands-on making but observational familiarity, what Ralph Cohen calls "funded experience."[19]

Practice is clarified in the following paragraph (¶ 19) where Hume notes the value of repeated exposure to the same work. First impressions and confusions give way to accurate assessment of qualities.

We are practiced readers of this essay by the time we arrive at the articulation of practice as a criterion for proper reading. Hume has obliged us to familiarize ourselves with the issues and the feelings by going over them several times in different forms. Our practical training has included repeated mining of the Sancho Panza story.

Comparisons enter ¶ 20 as the activity that naturally arises "in the practice of contemplating any order of beauty." We return to the haunting problem of variety. Different kinds of beauty are to be assessed in their proper terms. Throughout the analysis of the five requirements for the ideal critic we are shown the grounds for giving praise and blame. The standard of taste is normative, judgmental, critical. It is grounded in natural human capabilities developed to conform to qualities of objects. The beauties of the "coarsest daubing" [1757 adds: "of a sign-post"] would please "the mind of a peasant or Indian" (p. 276). Is the American Indian or the Asian Indian relegated to inferiority by Hume? The essay prints nationalities in capitals (1757: in italics), and "Indian" is set in lowercase roman type. Hume also mentions the "most vulgar ballads" as having plausible aesthetic merit. The critic is in the right position to reject these minor efforts in light of the highest development available in the medium. Hume has provided the reader with the comparative opportunity in the examples themselves. We acknowledge the point about comparisons in the course of making them. And we are led to place our taste above that of peasants, Indians, and the vulgar. A social class distinction oversees the standard of taste. The critic whose judgment is decisive is familiar with the many works "admired in different ages and nations," echo of the cosmopolitanism mentioned in the opening paragraph. The democratic possibilities in the question of taste give way to an elitist conception as those with classical and sophisticated education, like David Hume, will be the final judges.[20] By comparison Hume does not mean the examination of different genres or media which treat, say, the same theme, a concern of modern comparative literature. Instead, comparison is conducted with works of the same category of art. Comparison therefore is an extension of Hume's notion of practice: both are a familiarity with the works. Repeatedly the essay makes us consider such works together, as in the case of Homer and Fénelon.

To allow the critic such great weight in deciding matters of taste is dangerous. The elitist and authoritarian tone at the close of ¶ 20 is softened by the "But" introducing ¶ 21, with its criterion of freedom from prejudice. Here prejudice does not quite mean prejudgment. Instead, it is adherence to one's individual nature and conditions, one's point of view. Yet "the very object" submitted requires adoption of the point of view suitable to it as if one were "a man in general." The work, rather than the critic, lays down the perspective from which it is to be viewed in order to see how it produces "its due effect on the mind." That phrase is close to Aristotle's notion in the *Poetics* of the "proper pleasure" (*oikeía hedoné*) found in each genre.

Hume turns to rhetoric to show the importance of putting aside one's perspective to adopt that of the intended audience, for the orator "addresses himself to a particular audience." In the *Rhetoric* Aristotle insisted that the audience was the principle to be considered by the speaker, even in the presentation of the speaker's character. Hume too notes this relationship of character to audience. The critic in another time or place "must have all these circumstances in his eye" in order to judge the discourse. As in judgment of rhetoric so should one proceed in judgment of other works. Not to do so is to be prejudiced, which means that one's sentiments are perverted. "So far his taste evidently departs from the true standard; and of consequence loses all credit and authority" (p. 277). The crowning of authority at end of ¶ 20 is countered at end of ¶ 21 with divestiture of the crown. The work itself may be addressed to the prejudices of its audience; the unprejudiced critic must be aware of these. In the essay Hume tries to judge works of different cultures and times in their proper perspective, though eighteenth-century conservative British preferences affect his framing of such perspectives. In criticizing Hume's failures to find the proper perspectives for works of other times and climes, we are affirming Hume's criterion and opening our judgments to further correction.

To drive the point home about the dangers of prejudice, Hume opens ¶ 22 with another of those disarming general observations: "It is well known, that. . . ." As prejudice is deleterious in intellectual "operations" so it may be in taste: an echo of the pair in the essay's opening sentence. Why throw in the intellect here? To bring forward the fifth requirement for good taste: good sense. Whereas delicacy, practice, comparisons, and freedom from prejudice enter the essay in the first sentence of their respective paragraphs (¶¶ 14, 18, 20, 21), good sense makes its grand entrance in ¶ 22 in the second sentence: "It belongs to *good sense* to. . . ." Hume has had the good sense to first show the intellectual need, as well as the aesthetic need, for countering prejudice. Good sense, the sentence just quoted continues, will "check its influence in both cases." Thus, reason is prerequisite to the proper "operations" of taste. Good sense helps in understanding the relation of parts in a work, the identification of the whole, the identification of the purpose of the work, and the judgment of success in achieving that purpose. Whereas the first criterion, delicacy, was analyzed in terms of fineness of application, the last of the requirements is discussed in terms of overall grasp of the object.

The ends of the arts are specified: "The object of eloquence is to persuade, of history to instruct, of poetry to please." An Aristotelian distinction of the arts of rhetoric and poetry is employed. Since rhetoric had been the example in the preceding paragraph (¶ 21), Hume brings distinctness to that art by an exercise of good sense in this paragraph. While delicacy, practice, and comparison are naturally related to one another, good sense goes hand in hand with elimination of prejudice, for they both consider the point of view or end posed by the work. As adaptation of means to end Hume mentions that poetical compositions must have plausible reasoning, and that characters in tragedy and epic "must be represented as reasoning, and thinking, and concluding, and acting, suitably [1757: "suitable"] to their character [1757: "characters"] and circumstances" (p. 278). Aristotle in his study of tragedy and epic observes the importance of just such appropriateness. (If Hume is reading Aristotle as a model critic in exposition of the requirements for criticism, he does not inform the reader.) The paragraph concludes as it had opened, with the case for good sense as serving both intellect and "the operations of true taste." Those who have good taste and good sense are usually the same. Opinion and sentiment, discussed at the essay's opening, are more than parallel: intellect and taste converge in individuals who develop their human nature. We have gotten somewhere!

A conclusion is signaled by the "Thus" of ¶ 23 to emphasize the shift from democratic foundations to elitism in taste. Though "the principles of taste be universal," few may be said legitimately to be critics. Natural shortcomings occur in the apparatus that lead to "erroneous" sentiments. General principles are frustrated by defects and disorders. To illustrate these failings, Hume goes over the negatives of the five criteria in five distinct sentences, the first beginning "When" and the rest beginning "Where": a brilliant summary of the criteria which have been spread over nine paragraphs in six pages. To close this paragraph Hume crystallizes the criteria in positive form within one sentence as: "Strong sense, united to delicate sentiment, improved by practice, perfected by comparison, and cleared of all prejudice." There in a nutshell is what we have been looking for.

The definition triumphantly conjoins what have been opposites: sense and sentiment, the one strong, the other delicate.[21] Reason and feeling join hands. The strength of the definition is suggested by its self-characterizing opening word and developed in the intellectually pleasing sequence of connectives: united, improved, perfected, and cleared. A rare achievement: a beautiful definition. While sense was analyzed last, it jumps to the head of the definition to organize it; we are exhilarated by that activity of mind. The definition comes out more than the sum of its parts. It is the soul of the essay.

The clarity and power of the formulation strike the reader as having emerged through the labors of reading. The definition arises from the activity of the essay in which we have been engaged. It affirms what we have been doing. We confirm it, for we have been reading the text by means of those criteria which it insists on. Hume has proven his case by putting our experience to the proof.

The criteria define the ideal critic; "the joint verdict of such . . . is the true standard of taste and beauty" (pp. 278–79). The test of taste is a kind of social activity, for it is supported by relevant peer groups, which may be transcultural and cut across time as well.[22] The community of critics are the scientists of taste.

IV

Yet the triumph wavers. A brief paragraph (¶ 24, p. 279) raises the embarrassing question of how to identify those critics who have good taste. The standard for settling a dispute is the good critic, but who is a good critic is subject to dispute. Thus, we are thrown back "into the same uncertainty" that we have sought to remedy "during the course of this essay" [1757: "dissertation"]: a superb dramatic reversal. The explicit self-reference reinforces our inclination to experience the essay as reflecting upon itself. While the double case of intellect and sentiment initially raised in ¶ 1 is harmonized in ¶¶ 22 and 23, the variety of views also introduced in ¶ 1 raises its confusing head again in ¶ 24.

The objecting "But" of ¶ 24 is countered by the opening "But" of ¶ 25. The question is factual as to who is a good critic, but universal agreement holds that a good critic is desirable. So we can dispute about taste, and these disputable questions, like others "which are submitted to the understanding," must be settled by sound arguments and good evidence. A "true and decisive standard" exists; it is to be found in "real existence and matter of fact." Again the objective grounding for the subjective exercise. The answer to disputed variety is a standard. Hume concludes no democratic equality of taste exists but a few people "will be acknowledged by universal sentiment" to have good taste.

The third successive paragraph opening with "But" (¶ 26) strengthens the case that Hume had knocked the wind out of in ¶ 24. A difference is drawn between intellectual work (science, philosophy, theology) and "the beauties of eloquence and poetry." The theories are subject "to the revolutions of chance and fashion." Hume's point is a telling one for those who recently have theorized about revolutions in scientific theory and in philosophical world views. Hume offers a set of philosophical and literary examples:

ARISTOTLE, and PLATO, and EPICURUS, and DESCARTES, may successively yield to each other: But TERENCE and VIRGIL maintain an universal, undisputed empire over the minds of men. The abstract philosophy of CICERO has lost its credit: The vehemence of his oratory is still the object of our admiration. (P.280)

Hume's judgment in these cases is dubious. If he is suggesting that philosophy advances chronologically by disposing of previous contributions this is unfair, for great philosophical contributions perdure rather than are replaced. The four thinkers initially named cannot be dismissed philosophically as part of a brilliant past. Oddly, Hume has got the chronology wrong: Plato (ca. 427–347 B.C.) preceded Aristotle (384–322 B.C.) and was his teacher. If Hume is suggesting that the contributions of philosophers go out of fashion, he is right. This is not a matter of the chronology of the authors but of their use by others. Yet the work of past thinkers comes back into fashion. This is the case with Plato, Aristotle, and Epicurus (341–270 B.C.) before Hume's time, and we have seen it since to be the case with Descartes (1596–1650). Hume displays poor taste in judging the history of philosophy as well as in understanding philosophical progress. But this he shares with the Enlightenment outlook on the progression of human thought.

Vergil's (70–19 B.C.) preeminence in Latin letters continues to be recognized, but although Terence (ca. 190–159 B.C.) has much merit, he is not as great as Hume makes him out to be. Aristophanes and Molière tower over Terence as inventors of comic theater. But Terence's refined comedy of manners, elegantly styled, appeals to the polite audience of Hume's readership. All the philosophers mentioned by Hume as out of date have greater currency and value than Terence. But Hume is right on the mark concerning the fortunes of Cicero (106–43 B.C.). That writer's oratory continues to be regarded as first-class, while his philosophy receives little attention. Cicero the philosopher may yet come back into fashion.

The arrangement of pairs in this complex example is pleasing and persuasive. Two pairs of philosophers are set off against one pair of literary figures. The final pair is one author considered as both philosopher and orator.

Hume presses the argument in ¶ 27 for the real presence of persons of taste. People follow the judgments of critics, resulting in widespread recognition of great works. Over the long run, prejudices and aberrations are overcome, while the work of "true genius" comes to the fore. A natural power in great beauty makes itself felt, and the appreciation of that beauty spreads. Time is a test of the classics. Hume closes this paragraph with a conclusive "Thus," which reflects upon the distinction between philosophy and poetry in ¶ 26:

Thus [1757: "And thus"], though a civilized nation may easily be mistaken in the choice of their admired philosopher, they never have been found long to err, in their affection for a favorite epic or tragic author.

Hume touches upon a truth concerning national epics and dramas. Such works are permanent cultural treasures that contribute to the shaping of a national identity. Consider Shakespeare for Britain, the *Lusiads* for Portugal, Homer and Sophocles for Greece. Again Hume selects the two poetic forms discussed in Aristotle's *Poetics* and mentioned in ¶ 22. The epic writer was most recently discussed, but instead of a tragic author Hume had also mentioned Terence, so a slight variation occurs in the textual connections. One feels Hume is drawing examples with ease out of his cultured background rather than laboriously constructing examples to fit the needs of logic. That a nation is easily mistaken about its favorite philosopher is debatable, since a philosophic world view may come to permeate the culture. Descartes, implied by Hume to be dated, has been honored as the perennially favored philosopher in French culture. Hume speaks of "a civilized nation": those who do not conform to his principle must be barbaric.

The direction of ¶¶ 25, 26, and 27 counters the shock introduced by ¶ 24 and reestablishes the stability of a standard of taste. New shocks are introduced in ¶ 28, with its ominous opening, "But notwithstanding." Natural variation in the constitution of individuals distorts "the general principles of taste" that "are uniform in human nature." This Francis Bacon called the Idols of the Cave. A blameless variation is also introduced by association with people, says Hume, and this Bacon might have called the Idols of the Market Place. In these cases we cannot settle dispute by reference to a standard. Hume sketches an illustration in ¶ 29 (p. 281) of youthful temperament dictating a taste. "At twenty, OVID may be the favourite author; HORACE at forty; and perhaps TACITUS at fifty." It is a beautiful image, a thumbnail sketch of life in a sentence, resting simply on three Latin authors. One moves from the inventive amorousness of Ovidian poetry to the elegant reflections of Horatian verse and then to the worldly probing of Tacitean history. The story need not end there; the reader is free to imagine further preferences with older age; moreover, Hume has gently left a gap of twenty years between enjoyment of Ovid (43 B.C.–A.D. 18) and Horace (65–8 B.C.), so that one may fill it with one's preference. Part of the beauty of the line is this welcoming of our participation in the living thought.

Hume has made the case for a legitimate species of variety in taste. Though we may differ from one another, and from ourselves in the course of years, yet those differences represent a conformity of our nature with the qualities of the objects.

Paragraph 30 contributes . . . , well, I leave this one for you to consult and to take pleasure in analyzing.

The point about variety of taste due to social customs, mentioned in ¶ 28, is taken up by ¶ 31. Because of shifts in customs we are not "so sensibly touched" by manners not our own. "For this reason," adds Hume "comedy is not easily transferred [1757: "transferred easily"] from one age or nation to another" (p. 282). Apparently in comedy the unfamiliar manners are more difficult to assimilate than in tragedy or other genres. Hume gives these curious examples, arranged in pairs:

> A FRENCHMAN or ENGLISHMAN is not pleased with the ANDRIA of TERENCE, or CLITIA of MACHIAVEL; where the fine lady, upon whom all the play turns, never once appears to the spectators, but is always kept behind the scenes, suitably [1757: "suitable"] to the reserved humour of the ancient GREEKS and modern ITALIANS.

Terence who earlier (¶ 26) received praise as recognized by those in all epochs is here found unsympathetic to the modern French and English playgoers, but the problem may lie in the one play whose social restraint is out of fashion. *The Woman of Andros* (166 B.C.) is Terence's first comedy. Since Terence is a Latin author, Hume would have done better to speak of ancient Latin audiences rather than Greek ones, especially since women appear prominently in the comedies of Aristophanes, notably in *Lysistrata*, though their roles were played by men. Hume asserts a difference of customs in times and cultures, for Italian manners, as represented in Machiavelli (1469–1527), are at odds with those of France and England. Hume has missed Machiavelli's *La Mandragola* (1504), a bawdy, exuberant comedy like the *Clizia* (1506), but in which the hero is a woman who occupies the stage. Machiavelli had translated Terence's *Andria* into Italian, and his *Clizia* follows the conventions of Roman comedy, but his *La Mandragola* is an original creation and masterpiece of Italian theater. Hume fails as critic to inform himself of artistic diversity, adaptation of convention, and cultural innovation, as he looks instead to audience attitudes. But Hume's reader is likely to accept Hume's knowledge in these passages.

A reflection ensues on the quarrel of the ancients and moderns (¶ 32). Hume proposes that we be tolerant of "any innocent peculiarities of manners," else "the poet's [1757: "poets"] *monument more durable than brass,* must fall." The citation, unreferenced, is to Horace (with overtones of Simonides and Pindar), *Odes,* bk. III, no.30, v. 1: "exegi monumentum aere perennius."[23] If the reader recognizes the author, then, given an earlier mention of Horace (¶ 29), the reader may enjoy the pleasure of surmising that Hume has reached forty but is not yet fifty years old.

"Continual revolutions of manners and customs" occur, concedes Hume, but he puts a limit on what is to be neglected for that reason: "Must we throw aside the pictures of our ancestors, because of their ruffs and fardingales?" This is a rare reference in the essay to the visual arts. The limit where we must reject other customs is when morality is affected. One cannot enter into vicious sentiments with pleasure. Hence, their portrayal is an aesthetic defect of the poem.

> The want of humanity and of decency, so conspicuous in the charac-
> ters drawn by several of the ancient poets, even sometimes by HOMER
> and the GREEK tragedians, diminishes considerably the merit of their
> noble performances, and gives modern authors an advantage [1757: "a
> great advantage"] over them. (Pp. 282–83)

Hume is not arguing that moral principles theoretically overrule aesthetic values; instead, the moral veto operates by inhibiting our experience of those aesthetic pleasures. The aesthetic sentiment is blocked by the actions or characters we find morally offensive. While Hume says he is making a contribution to the quarrel of the ancients vs. the moderns, he is using that quarrel to make a contribution to the quarrel of morals vs. art. The dubious moral values portrayed in cultures contemporary with Hume's culture would make their poetic works as unpalatable as those of the ancients. Hume is defending an Enlightenment view of the ennobling value of proper aesthetic enjoyment. Yet one may take aesthetic pleasure in artistic portrayal of values one finds morally reprehensible—I do this daily. This is accomplished by recognition that one's morality is not at stake. One may suspend moral judgment during the aesthetic experience or transfer it to the presuppositions of morality within the world of the artwork. Indeed, one may come to enjoy immorality precisely because it is safely experienceable within the aesthetic frame. Hume has missed the saving grace of aesthetic distancing and the harmless joy in vicarious immorality.

Moral principles are a different case than speculative ones, continues ¶ 33 (p. 283). Speculative principles "are in continual flux and revolution." By imagination we can enter easily into some outmoded theory. But one cannot "pervert the sentiments of his heart" by entering into enjoyment of what violates the "moral standard." Moral commitment to which we are habituated is stronger than either imaginative sympathy or speculative freedom. Hume is wrong. The power of imagination encourages us to suspend moral judgment and indulge in enjoyment.

Speculative errors are reintroduced by ¶ 34 in connection with religious matters. We may rightly overlook such errors in appreciating literary works, even those of the pagans. But the limit is reached when such principles infect the heart with *"bigotry* or *superstition."* For here "the sentiments of morality" are insulted. Hume refers us to the principle mentioned in ¶ 33 to account for the blockage of aesthetic pleasure in such works. That "bigotry" and "superstition" are italicized proclaims their weight in the structure of the essay.

The critique of religion continues in ¶ 35 (p. 284) by focusing on Roman Catholic excess. That religion seeks to reduce "all pagans, mahometans, and heretics" to damnable light. But this sentiment also enters "their tragedies and epic poems," and thereby spoils them. Hume's earlier dictum (¶ 27) that a people cannot be mistaken in their choice of epic or tragedy is at odds here with Catholic practice. The earlier proviso referred to "civilized nations" and asserted their errors were not of long duration. The reader might not hold ¶ 35 up to the assertions of ¶ 27, but an echo of criticism may be sensed. The pairing of epic and tragedy in both paragraphs evokes the echo. The attack upon Mahometans echoes the attack in ¶ 4. Hume specifies defective works:

> This bigotry has disfigured two very fine tragedies of the FRENCH theatre, POLIEUCTE and ATHALIA; where an intemperate zeal for particular modes of worship is set off with all the pomp imaginable, and forms the predominant character of the heroes.

The examples are Corneille's *Polyeucte* (1641) on a religious theme and Racine's religious drama *Athalie* (1691). Hume labels them, correctly, as very fine tragedies, although *Athalie* has a happy ending. Hence, his criticism follows from a fine sense of delicacy. The defect of the works he finds in their "intemperate zeal," a label implying considerable condemnation, which causes the moral sentiment to cancel some of the pleasure. Yet that Corneille (1606–84) selects a religious martyr for his hero, does not mean that the play is religious or that the audience must become engrossed in religious sentiments. Of Racine (1639–99) Hume cites a passage from the *Athalie* (act III, scene 5):

> "What is this," says the sublime [1757: "heroic"] JOAD TO JOSABET, finding her in discourse with MATHAN, the priest of BAAL, "Does the daughter of DAVID speak to this traitor? Are you not afraid, lest the earth should open and pour forth flames to devour you both? Or lest [1757: "Or that"] these holy walls should fall and crush you together? What is his purpose? Why comes that enemy of God hither to poison the air, which we breathe, with his horrid presence?"[24]

It is a powerful speech, plucked out of context, filled with allusions to violence, and reeking with venomous sentiments. Even Mathan notes, "in this violence does Joad make himself known."

Let us examine how Hume alters the text in translating it. He inten-
sifies the distasteful fervor of the original by condensation. Thus, following "you speak to this traitor?" the half-line "Do you suffer that he speak
to you?" is dropped. The opening of the earth is a condensed rendering
of Racine's more elaborate formulation: the opening beneath his steps of
the depths of the abyss. Racine's phrase is wilder than Hume's. Hume
quickens the danger in Racine's causal relation, "while falling on him"
the walls "will crush you," by condensing the line to: the walls may "fall
and crush you together." Hume pumps up the religiosity of the passage
by turning "these walls" into "these holy walls." The closing phrase of
Hume's passage which palpitates with displeasure, "with his horrid
presence," is not found in the original. The violence of Racine's text is
restrained by the rhymed alexandrine verse which lifts everything the
dramatist writes to a level nobler than prose. The versification is a poetic
device of aesthetic distancing. Hume's prose rendering pours out as a
series of direct affronts faced by the reader. He has left out the poetry of
Racine.[25]

Racine is open to the criticism that his late religious dramas have
diminished tragic power because of the predominance of pious sentiment. But if we keep in mind Hume's principle (¶ 22) that the sentiment
and thought of a character must be appropriate to that character, then we
have a way of appreciating such passages as he has quoted. We need to
judge the passage within the play. But Hume wins the case by shocking
the reader with the bald presence of the passage. He continues:

> Such sentiments are received with great applause on the theatre of
> PARIS; but at LONDON the spectators would be full as much pleased to
> hear ACHILLES tell AGAMEMNON, that he was a dog in his forehead,
> and a deer in his heart; or JUPITER threaten JUNO with a sound drub-
> bing, if she will not be quiet.

The defect is admired by the French, given their religion, but something
must be faulty in that religion, for the operation of such principles results
in evidently tasteless incidents. Hume may be getting us to employ the
method of proof in aesthetics: take the principle derivable from examples, here the inappropriateness for the stage of the incidents involving
Achilles and Agamemnon or Jupiter and Juno, and apply it to the
materials at hand—Joad and Mathan. Though the taste of London and
Paris has much in common (¶¶ 11, 31), English taste may legitimately
differ from that of France. The latter is defective insofar as Parisian
audiences applaud Joad's tirade. That fault in taste is attributable to
religious zeal. The classical allusions are to that old standby Homer. The

famous altercation between Achilles and Agamemnon is crucial to the story of the *Iliad* (bk. I, vv. 159, 225), while the harsh warning given by Zeus to the scheming Hera (bk. I, vv. 565–67) is important to the Olympian side of the plot. These are instances of the crude morality Hume remarked in Homer (¶¶ 3, 32). Hume does not make the point that what works well in one literary form (epic) or one art medium may not be acceptable when transferred to another (stage). Nor is he criticizing Homer, whose name is unmentioned here. Was there a London theatrical piece that staged the Homeric materials? Is this a hypothetical example of how English taste would be as defective as French taste? Is Hume illustrating a change in taste from ancient Greece to modern Europe, the case made in the first literary allusion? This present allusion is entangled in its pairings. Neither generous nor tolerant in this case, Hume oversteps the boundaries of good taste by making an occasion in the course of a discussion of aesthetic matters to attack a religion and its adherents.

He is not finished. The attack widens in the final paragraph (¶ 36), where "religious principles" in general are criticized when they infect sentiment with superstition. The poet cannot be excused for portraying such sentiments on the grounds that the society is rife with them. While earlier Hume argued that the critic must be willing to adopt the manners of the time for the sake of appreciating the work, his point in the closing paragraph is that a moral limit curbs such tolerance.

> It must for ever be [1757: "be for ever"] ridiculous in PETRARCH to compare his mistress LAURA, to JESUS CHRIST. Nor is it less ridiculous in that agreeable libertine, BOCCACE, very seriously to give thanks to GOD ALMIGHTY and the ladies, for their assistance in defending him against his enemies.

The literary giants of another Latin and Catholic country are called into question. Yet that Petrarch (1304–74) uses divine figures to express love for his lady in the sonnets (first published 1470) is not ridiculous, for a long tradition of courtly love poetry supports this convention. Hume misreads literary convention for cultural defect. Petrarch's Sonnet III, opening on Good Friday, is a moving and beautiful poem to the beloved, using that convention.[26] Boccaccio's (1313–75) call for the help of God and the ladies in the introduction to the Fourth Day of the *Decameron* (written 1351–53) might be read as part of his libertine waggishness or innocent charm rather than pious seriousness.[27] No matter how silly the invocation may appear it can be no defect for our enjoyment of the narratives.

The essay closes on a minor matter and, in our eyes, an objectionable manner, though Hume will receive the moral approbation of his readers, for he has artfully made the Italian cases sound tasteless. But he has strayed far afield from the standard of taste as intellectual subject. We are in a subclass, religion, of a major hindrance to taste: moral turpitude. The latter was introduced as bearing on the quarrel of the ancients vs. the moderns, and this in turn arose in recognizing the differences between cultures. Such differences may or may not fall outside the exercise of the standard of taste.

The essay has moved off under the influence of its extenuating circumstances. It no longer is about taste but about bigotry. It has drifted into becoming another essay: no calling it back, no capping or binding conclusion. In contrast to the memorable opening sentence that fixed attention, the closing dribbles away. It is intellectually dissatisfying. That careful echoing and linkage that occurred in the early part and that bright gathering of the crucial prerequisites in the essay's center give way to these looser, overextended reflections. The sentiments raised here are not pleasant, nor are the thoughts witty. Hume fuels base feelings touching upon religion and nationality. The phrase "*bigotry* or *superstition*" is a flag waved to excite hostility. The essay concludes with a parade of provocative instances of blasphemy.[28]

The reader is left to conclude. This involves another line of thought about the immoral effect of religion upon civilized life, including letters. One is also left with that line of feeling which is a distaste for religious sentiments. The essay on taste enlists our sentiments against superstition by an artful cultivation of our distaste. Earlier (¶¶ 4, 5) some passages on morality and religion seemed out of place. Hume will not allow the autonomy of the aesthetic. The cultural and humane value of the arts is insisted upon. We are better persons for developing our taste. Religious enthusiasm, on the other hand, makes us worse persons. Good taste will overrule bad religiosity in works of art. Since one who has good taste is likely to be one who has good sense, aesthetic experience will provide that person with insight into moral and cultural defects, including those caused by religion and piety. A good understanding coupled with proper sentiments should lead to correct decisions and decent actions. This is a possible continuation of the essay in the reader's mind, though it cannot be pinned on Hume. Typically, his works begin in crystal and end in mist. We are interested in what he works out within them, in his workout with them, and in the work cut out for us by them.

The dissatisfaction which we may sense at the essay's close is a kind of experiencing that the essay has theorized about. If the essay fails at the end it has succeeded in bringing our taste into its domain. It is about us.

We catch ourselves at the end in the act of experiencing. Our taste remains, as the wine cask of the essay is at last drained.

V

The text has been studied here as self-contained whole to be understood in the exercise of reading it. No reason to believe that Hume's readers read it as we have done, or that anyone else, including Hume, has bothered to read the essay in this fashion. We have explored the potentialities for a reading. One must cultivate a taste for reading Hume. Only some of the work at any point will be digested by an actual reader, and some features will be grasped unreflectively, in passing. Moreover, Hume's essay is easy-flowing and economical, in contrast to the interminable drudgery the present study imposes upon the reader. Hume assists even the casual reader to get the point by his rich examples, his literary devices, and his vocabulary.

Hume has created the vocabulary of his essay. Words used repeatedly and in nuanced ways become polished bearers of meaning in the world of the essay. At our peril we do pry them loose from this text to join Hume's usage elsewhere or the usage of his time. In the essay some words are privileged inhabitants, reliable guides, familiar citizens: *taste, standard, beauty and deformity, sentiment, genius, imagination, human nature, judgment, critic, approbation, rules, variety, obvious, observation, pleasure, uniformity, perfection, civilized, general principles, opinion, feeling, praise and blame, operation, in all countries and all ages, bigotry, absurd, perversion, defect, prejudice,* and, my favorite, *pretended.* Pick any five of these and you have a good chance of explaining Hume's efforts in the essay in their terms. If we map the occurrence of these terms across the thirty-six paragraphs a tapestry results with overlapping threads. Though we may miss the pattern of thought in a few paragraphs we are sure to catch it up elsewhere. Even an ordinary word, like *great* or *true*, when woven throughout the text gives intensity to the whole. The essay sparkles. A critical census of the vocabulary, assisted by word processor, will increase our appreciation of Hume's craft as writer and improve our understanding of his subtlety as thinker.

A study of the variants in the essay must await establishment of the critical edition of the text. Hume carefully weighed his words, and in the rereadings he gave this essay over nearly twenty years he made fine adjustments in style and meaning. His revisions manifest taste at work. A range of differences between the first and final editions has been made evident in passages quoted. To provoke further reflection a selection follows of additional variants, grouped by categories which occasionally overlap.

1. Correction of typographical or spelling errors (6 items)

1757: breath	1777: breathe (¶ 35)

2. Change of styling or spelling of a word (36 items)

1757: excellency	1777: excellence (¶ 20)
1757: forgot	1777: forgotten (¶ 21)
1757: bounds	1777: boundaries (¶ 32)

3. Change of plural or singular use of a word (12 items)

1757: humours and dispositions	1777: humour and disposition (¶ 29)

4. Deletion of a word (16 items)

1757: insist very much	1777: insist (¶ 4)
1757: perfect and universal beauty	1777: perfect beauty (¶ 12)
1757: fix or ascertain	1777: ascertain (¶ 17)
1757: very wide	1777: wide (¶ 18)

5. Substitution of a word (31 items)

1757: suppose	1777: maintain (¶ 3)
1757: use	1777: acceptation (¶ 3)
1757: *be modest*	1777: *be charitable* (¶ 5)
1757: natural	1777: literal (¶ 16)
1757: reference	1777: relation (¶ 19)
1757: vogue	1777: applause (¶ 26)
1757: true poet	1777: real poet (¶ 27)
1757: various	1777: discordant (¶ 28)
1757: And	1777: But (¶ 32)
1757: extremely	1777: very (¶ 35)

6. Insertion of a word (7 items)

1757: as is represented	1777: as it is represented (¶ 26)
1757: admit nothing	1777: admit of nothing (¶ 32)

7. Rewriting of a phrase (13 items)

1757: it must also be allowed	1777: we must also allow (¶ 3)

1757: be approved of   1777: meet with approbation
                                                (¶ 17)

1757: A man who has had opportunities of seeing, and examining, and weighing the several performances
1777: One accustomed to see, and examine, and weigh the several performances (¶ 20)
1757: without entering into that required by the performance
1777: without placing himself in that point of view, which the performance supposes (¶ 21)
1757: pictures of characters, which resemble such as are found
1777: pictures and characters, that resemble objects which are found (¶ 31)

8. Change of punctuation (59 items)

9. Change of typography

Names that in 1757 are italicized are in capitals in 1777.

    Over 180 changes distinguish the final from the first edition, entering by degrees through intermediate editions.

    One may enhance understanding of the essay by other modes of study. (1) One may connect its thought to Hume's other writings in aesthetics and to his philosophical work as a whole.[29] (2) One may relate the essay to other British or Continental discussions of taste in the eighteenth century.[30] Yet Hume's essay refers to none of his other works or to the theorizing of others (except perhaps in ¶ 14). (3) One may analyze and expand ideas found in the essay in rigorous philosophical terms. This has been the recent attraction for Anglophone professional philosophers. Hume, however, has not penned a technical treatise on aesthetics. (4) One may use the text as a sounding board or teaching instrument for ideas of aestheticians and philosophers from different times and places.[31] One runs the risk, though, of losing Hume in the crowd.

    What is Hume's essay? An exercise in literary criticism or a dissertation in aesthetics? It uses instances of the former as it seeks to be the latter, though "aesthetics" had not yet displaced "criticism" as the name for theory. Hume has written the equivalent of a literary inquiry on standards,[32] comparable to his empirical inquiries into the principles of knowledge (1748) and morals (1751) (foreshadowing Kant's three non-empirical critiques). He has jampacked the essay with literary criticism to establish his theoretical case. A glittering array of allusions has kept us busy, provoking our response, eliciting our judgment, engaging us in the debate on matters of taste: Homer, the Greek tragedians, Vergil, Horace, Cicero, Ovid, Terence, Tacitus, the Koran, Petrarch, Boccaccio, Ariosto, Machiavelli, Cervantes, Corneille, Racine, Fénelon, Milton, Bunyan, Addison, and poor Ogilby. In this literary work the examples are persuasively literary, including drama, history, oratory, and scripture. As readers of the essay we are at home in the literary realm as we look at examples cut from the same cloth. The essay and its examples share their ontology. The examples are more than examples.

Hume ranges widely in the exercise of his taste as he brings to our experience models of excellence and instances of defects. He embodies the cosmopolitan education and gift of discernment the ideal critic must have. As eighteenth-century readers we admire Hume's judgments, and this assists recognition of the soundness of his argument. Hume's taste makes a strong case for Hume's theory of taste. But we may also exercise our judgment upon the works Hume judges, as well as upon Hume's judgment and practice. Putting his taste to the test as twentieth-century readers, we have found it often disputable and sometimes defective. We are obliged to offer reasons and evidence for our judgments, which in turn invite correction. While no final answers may exist in matters of taste, reasonable resolutions are available. How agreeable to find a domain in which absolutes do not reign but where the development of talent and the genial flourishing of discussion are encouraged.

The shortcomings of Hume's taste in the essay do not detract from it as literature or argument, since they are eminently understandable in terms of the criteria for the ideal critic laid down in the essay. That the reader, of whatever century, may find fault and correct it, is a confirmation of the possibility and desirability of moving in the direction of the true standard of taste. The weaknesses of the essay are among its strengths.

Yet the essay smacks of unsatisfactoriness whether regarded as a literary whole or a philosophical theory. When we reflect, as we must at the end, on what has been gained by struggling through the text instance by instance and paragraph by paragraph, we are perplexed. The *Critical Review* expresses the disappointment that "our author leaves us in the same uncertainty as he found us."[33] What does it add up to— besides a headache? The theory, in summary, is that ontologically beauty is entirely subjective, because it is a sentiment within an individual mental realm, while methodologically, beauty is largely objective, because it is the apprehension of qualities in an artwork verifiable by the community of experts. An objective referent in rules and models is attested by those most able to detect them. Caution: "objective" refers to the object of experience in the sense of the object in experience—the object as experienced—not the object in itself. Hume's ontology is human nature. Beauty is what one happens to experience, given a particular work of art and one's particularized nature, but beauty is also what one should experience, given a work of demonstrable excellence and assuming no defect or neglect of one's natural faculties. Taste, then, is not arbitrary or beyond dispute, because a standard exists—founded on subjective encounter with objective qualities—which allows arbitration of such disputes.[34] Hume might not have been at ease with twentieth-century insistence on a distinction between subjectivity and objectivity; his preferred distinction in the essay is between individual variety and universal or general standards.

This neat theory has been accused of circularity, in which two things are successively used for the grounding of each other, such as the standard of taste and the consensus concerning great works,[35] the critic and the aesthetically valuable,[36] critics and taste,[37] delicate taste and good art,[38] good art and the critic.[39] Peter Kivy exonerates delicacy, freedom from prejudice, and good sense as "identifiable by marks other than the critic's approval of good art," although delicacy must be redeemed by passages outside the essay.[40] Having saved Hume from circularity, Kivy accuses him of relying upon an infinite regress, for the disputed fact of the worth of an artwork rests on the disputable fact of the soundness of the critic. Noël Carroll saves Hume from Kivy's charge of infinite regress, since a finite number of critics exist, but Carroll makes out Hume's argument to be redundant, since good critics are dispensable if we develop ourselves.[41]

Hume's reasoning is circular. All takes place within the circle of human nature. Experience is circumscribed by the limits of the experiencer. Great works of art stand the test of good critics, but great works of art are also the test of good critics. Delicacy detects fine qualities, but fineness develops delicacy. The aesthetically valuable is that which is aesthetically valued, but we should value what is aesthetically valuable. We appeal to ideal critics to settle disputes on taste, but we dispute who is an ideal critic. Supposedly, demonstrable qualities underlie taste and judgment, yet these qualities might only become evident by deduction from taste and judgment. Rules will apply to artistic excellence, but rules are founded on what pleases. Such logical circularity is experientially enriching as forms of mutual confirmation. Hume does not break out of the circle but works within it. He is not trying to give a logically complete theory but a recognizable account of how we live—and how we may better live.

Though to the professional philosopher enamored of passionless logic and literal language Hume may not seem to have gotten anywhere as philosopher in this piece which is a literary wandering, that wandering is the philosophizing. To such a technical philosopher the philosophical content of the essay is less than the sum of its parts, while to us the essay is more than the sum of its philosophical content. The essay is the activity of thought in process. It has obliged us to think: to reason, remember, reflect, compare, apply, judge, object, and question. The writing pulls us into the act and makes us respond by apprehending, feeling, and imagining. Reading the work is a challenge to intellect and taste that affords pleasure and insight, as well as puzzlement and disappointment. We professional thinkers of the twentieth century should be grateful to Hume for conducting philosophy in ways, which we have neglected, that humanize the reader. Cautious and wandering, committed and inconclusive, confounding and clear, circular and skeptical, this curious conjunction of writing and philosophizing is the most engaging and ingenious essay in the history of aesthetic thinking.

Notes

1. The text cited throughout this chapter is the reprint of the 1777 posthumous edition of Hume's Essays, in *Essays: Moral, Political, and Literary*, ed. T. H. Green and T. H. Grose, vol. 1 (London: Longmans, Green, & Co., 1898). "Of the Standard of Taste" first appeared in 1757, as a last-minute entry in *Four Dissertations* (New York: Garland Publishing, 1970; facsimile of London: A. Millar, 1757). The four dissertations were combined with the essays in 1758, and went through several subsequent editions. Green and Grose do not record variants between the editions for this essay. Some differences between the 1757 original and the 1777 final text will be indicated below.

2. Excluding quotations, foreign phrases, titles of works, and words referred to as words, the italicized words are:

P. 266, ¶ 1: barbarous
P. 268, ¶ 5: maxim
P. 268, ¶ 6: Standard of Taste
P. 272, ¶ 14: delicacy
P. 274, ¶ 18: practice
P. 275, ¶ 20: comparisons
P. 276, ¶ 21: prejudice
P. 277, ¶ 22: good sense
P. 283, ¶ 33: bigotry, superstition.

3. The groundwork for identification of Hume's literary allusions in the essay was laid by John W. Lenz in his edition, *Of the Standard of Taste and Other Essays* (Indianapolis: Bobbs-Merrill Co., "The Library of Liberal Arts," 1965).

4. George Saintsbury, *A History of Criticism and Literary Taste in Europe from the Earliest Texts to the Present Day*, vol. 3 (Edinburgh: William Blackwood & Sons, 1949), pp. 159–62, gives a scathing review of Hume's taste as a critic by culling the literary references from Hume's writings. John Laird, *Hume's Philosophy of Human Nature* (London: Methuen & Co., 1932), pp. 273–81, surveys Hume's critical remarks, noting "the frigidity and portentious correctness of Hume's opinions" (p. 278). A comprehensive review of Hume's literary allusions is given by Olivier Brunet, *Philosophie et esthétique chez David Hume* (Paris: Librairie A.-G. Nizet, 1965), pp. 47–73.

5. Katherine S. Van Eerde, *John Ogilby and the Taste of His Times* (Folkestone, England: Dawson, 1976), p. 150.

6. Lenz does this in the introduction to his textbook edition, *Of the Standard of Taste*, p. xx.

7. Giulio Preti in the introduction to his influential Italian translation, *La Regola del gusto* (Milan: Alessandro Minuziano, 1946), pp. 24–30, emphasizes Hume's replacement of a priori metaphysics by psychological inquiry into the pleasure of taste.

8. Saintsbury, *History of Criticism*, p. 161.

9. Teddy Brunius, *David Hume on Criticism* (Stockholm: Almqvist & Wiksell, "Figura" Series no. 2, 1952), pp. 85–86, reminds us that Hume does not bother to give the rules in this essay.

10. Brunet, *Philosophie et esthétique*, p. 735.

11. Ibid., pp. 130n, 775.

12. Noël Carroll, "Hume's Standard of Taste," *Journal of Aesthetics and Art Criticism* 43:2 (Winter 1984): 192.

13. I do not know if Hume read Cervantes in Spanish. Of the English translations of *Don Quixote* antedating 1757, listed by Robert S. Rudder, *The Literature of Spain in English Translation* (New York: Frederick Ungar Publishing Co., 1975), pp. 137–41, I have consulted those by Thomas Shelton (1620, 1652, 1675), Shelton revised by John Stevens (1700), John Philips (1687), "W. O." (1695), Charles Jarvis (1742), Peter Motteux revised by J. Ozell (1749), Tobias Smollett (1755), and the anonymous abridgement of 1704. Hume is not quoting any of these.

14. Miguel de Cervantes Saavedra, *Don Quijote de la Mancha*, ed. Martín de Riquer (Barcelona: Editorial Juventud, 1958), Pt. II, chap. 13, p. 629:

> ¿No será bueno, señor escudero, que tenga yo un instinto tan grande y tan natural en esto de conocer vinos, que en dándome a oler cualquiera, acierto la patria, el linaje, el sabor, y la dura, y las vueltas que ha de dar, con todas las circunstancias al vino atañederas? Pero no hay de qué maravillarse, si tuve en mi linaje por parte de mi padre los dos más excelentes mojones que en luengos años conoció la Mancha; para prueba de lo cual les sucedió lo que ahora diré. Diéronles a los dos a probar del vino de una cuba, pidiéndoles su parecer del estado, cualidad, bondad o malicia del vino. El uno lo probó con la punta de la lengua; el otro no hizo más de llegarlo a las narices. El primero dijo que aquel vino sabía a hierro; el segundo dijo que más sabía a cordobán. El dueño dijo que la cuba estaba limpia, y que el tal vino no tenía adobo alguno por donde hubiese tomado sabor de hierro ni de cordobán. Con todo eso, los dos famosos mojones se afirmaron en lo que habían dicho. Anduvo el tiempo, vendióse el vino, y al limpiar de la cuba hallaron en ella una llave pequeña, pendiente de una correa de cordobán.

> ("Isn't it something, sir Squire, that I possess such a great natural instinct in this matter of knowing wines that given any one to smell I could guess the country, the class, the flavor, the vintage, and the changes it will undergo, with all the circumstances attending the wine? But there is nothing to marvel about, for I am descended on my father's side from two of the most excellent wine tasters that La Mancha has known in many a year; as a proof of which I will now relate what happened to them. The two were asked to sample the wine from a cask, giving their opinion as to the condition, quality, and goodness or badness of the wine. The one tasted it with the tip of his tongue; the other did no more than bring it to his nose. The first said this wine tastes of iron; the second said it tastes more of leather. The proprietor said the cask was clean and the wine had no additives that would give it the flavor of iron or of leather. But notwithstanding, the two famous wine tasters affirmed what they had said. Time passed, the wine was sold, and in cleaning the cask there was found in it a little key, hanging from a thong of leather." [my translation])

15. *The Critical Review, or Annals of Literature* 3 (March 1757): 214.

16. "Dissertation sur la regle du goût," *OEuvres philosophiques de Mr. D. Hume*, vol. 4 (Amsterdam: J. H. Schneider, 1759), p. 110n.

17. Houdar de La Motte, *OEuvres*, vol. 9 (Paris: Prault, 1754), bk. 4, no. 6, pp. 218–19:

> Arrivent deux Gourmets, Docteurs en l'art de boire,
> Le Marguillier Lucas & le Syndic Gregoire;

> On leur fait goûter. Eh bien, qu'en dites-vous?
>   Votre avis n'est-il pas le nôtre?
> Il sent le fer, dit l'un: le cuir aussi, dit l'autre.
> Bon, dit-on, quelle idée! & d'où viendroient ces goûts?
> Le Bacchique Sénat les croit devenus fous.
> On les raille à l'envi; mais courte fut la joie;
>   L'évenement vint les justifier.
> On trouve, en le vuidant, dans le fonds du Cuvier,
> Une petite clef pendant à sa courroye;
>   Et railla bien qui railla le dernier.

("Then came two gourmets, doctors of the art of drinking, / The Churchwarden Lucas and the Syndic Gregoire; / They were made to taste. 'And now, what say you of it? / Is not your opinion one with ours?' / 'It smacks of iron,' said the one; 'of leather too,' said the other./ 'Great! What an idea,' said the people, 'and from whence come these tastes?' / The Bacchic Senate thought they had gone mad. / People competed in mocking them; but shortlived was the delight; / Events proved them justified. / In emptying the Vat there was found at the bottom, / A little key hanging on its thong; / And who laughs last laughs best." [my translation])

18. "To seek the key with the leathern thong," says Redding S. Sugg, Jr., "Hume's Search for the Key with the Leathern Thong," *Journal of Aesthetics and Art Criticism* 16:1 (September 1957): 97, is "to verify aesthetic judgment by experiment, rather than exclusively by authority, tradition, or the operation of a supposed mental faculty."

19. Ralph Cohen, "David Hume's Experimental Method and the Theory of Taste," *ELH* 25:4 (December 1958): 288.

20. In a lively exposition of Hume's case for the ideal critic, H. Osborne, "Hume's Standard and the Diversity of Aesthetic Taste," *British Journal of Aesthetics* 7:1 (January 1967): 50–56, challenges the parochial eighteenth-century class attitude present in Hume's essay which ill befits twentieth-century mass culture.

21. Cf. Stuart Gerry Brown, "Observations on Hume's Theory of Taste," *English Studies* (Amsterdam) 20:5 (October 1938): 194–95.

22. Cf. Peter Jones, "Hume's Aesthetics Reassessed," *Philosophical Quarterly* 26:102 (January 1976): 59, 62.

23. Horace, *Odes et Épodes*, ed. F. Villeneuve (Paris: Les Belles Lettres, 1959), p. 147.

24. Racine, *Athalie*, in *OEuvres complètes*, ed. Raymond Picard (Paris: Librairie Gallimard, "Bibliothèque de la Pléiade," 1950), p. 931:

> Où suis-je? De Baal ne vois-je pas le prêtre?
> Quoi, fille de David, vous parlez à ce traitre?
> Vous souffrez qu'il vous parle? Et vous ne craignez pas
> Que du fond de l'abîme entr'ouvert sous ses pas
> Il ne sorte à l'instant des feux qui vous embrasent,
> Ou qu'en tombant sur lui ces murs ne vous écrasent?
> Que veut-il? De quel front cet ennemi de Dieu
> Vient-il infecter l'air qu'on respire en ce lieu?

("Where am I? Do I not see the priest of Baal? / What! daughter of David, do you speak to this traitor? / Do you suffer that he speak to you? And do you not fear / That from the bottom of the abyss opening under his steps / Fire will suddenly exit, setting you ablaze, / Or that these walls while falling on him will crush you? / What does he want? With what bearing does this enemy of God / Come to this place to poison the air we breathe?" [my translation])

25. Cf. Renée Bouveresse, ed. and trans. David Hume, *Les Essais esthétiques*, pt. II, *Art et psychologie* (Paris: Librairie philosophique J. Vrin, 1974), p. 103n.

26. Francesco Petrarca, *Le Rime*, ed. Giosuè Carducci and Severino Ferrari (Florence: Sansoni, 1957), no. 3, pp. 5–6.

27. Giovanni Boccaccio, *Decameron*, ed. Vittore Branca (Florence: Felice le Monnier, 1960), p. 459, line 40: "E volendo per questa volta assai aver risposto, dico che dallo aiuto di

Dio e dal vostro, gentilissime donne, nel quale io spero, armato, e di buona pazienza, con esso procederò avanti, dando le spalle e questo vento e lasciandol soffiare: . . ." ("And deeming that I have sufficiently replied at this point, I say, that armed with the help of God and yours, gentlest ladies, upon which I count, and with good patience, I will move ahead, turning my back to such a wind and letting it blow: . . ." [my translation])

28. Brunet, *Philosophie et esthétique*, pp. 759–60, is the rare commentator who notes the essay's inadequate termination.

29. The magisterial effort along these lines is Brunet in 955 pages and 3,176 footnotes.

30. Cf. Lia Formigari, *L'Estetica del gusto nel settecento inglese* (Florence: G. C. Sansoni, 1962), pp. 88–93; Guido Morpurgo Tagliabue, "La nozione del gusto nel XVIII secolo: Davide Hume," *Revista di Estetica* 15:2 (May–August 1970): 161–207. On Hutcheson and Hume see Carolyn W. Korsmeyer, "Hume and the Foundations of Taste," *Journal of Aesthetics and Art Criticism* 35:2 (Winter 1976): 201–15.

31. Such is the appearance of the edition by Bouveresse.

32. Ralph Cohen, "The Rationale of Hume's Literary Inquiries," *Southwestern Journal of Philosophy* 7:2 (Summer 1976): 97–115.

33. *Critical Review*, p. 213.

34. Cohen, "David Hume's Experimental Method and the Theory of Taste," pp. 270–89, sees the five criteria as methods for developing the critic by reference to works.

35. Brown, "Observations," p. 196. Cf. Brunius, *David Hume on Criticism*, pp. 84–85n.

36. James Noxon, "Hume's Opinion of Critics," *Journal of Aesthetics and Art Criticism* 20:2 (Winter 1961): 160.

37. Brunet, *Philosophie et esthétique*, p. 771.

38. Korsmeyer, "Foundations of Taste," pp. 205–6.

39. Peter Kivy, "Hume's Standard of Taste: Breaking the Circle," *British Journal of Aesthetics* 7:1 (January 1967): 60–63. Cf. Jeffrey Wieand, "Hume's Two Standards of Taste," *Philosophical Quarterly* 34:135 (April 1984): 138–39.

40. Kivy, "Breaking the Circle," p. 61.

41. Carroll, "Hume's Standard," pp. 191–92.

Notes on Contributors

STEPHEN F. BARKER received his M.A. and Ph.D. from Harvard University. He works in history of philosophy, philosophy of science, and logic. His books include, *Induction and Hypothesis: A Study of the Logic of Confirmation, Philosophy of Mathematics* (translated into four languages), and *The Elements of Logic.* He has taught at University of Southern California, University of Virginia, and Ohio State University, and has held visiting appointments at Harvard University, University of California at Berkeley, Swarthmore College, and Concordia University. He is Professor of Philosophy, The Johns Hopkins University.

LESTER G. CROCKER studied at New York University and the Sorbonne before receiving his Ph.D. from University of California. His research has been in eighteenth-century history of ideas, and in French and Comparative Literature. His books include, *Two Diderot Studies: Ethics and Esthetics, Diderot: The Embattled Philosopher, An Age of Crisis: Man and World in Eighteenth-Century French Thought, Nature and Culture: Ethical Thought in the French Enlightenment, Jean-Jacques Rousseau: The Quest, Rousseau's "Social Contract": An Interpretive Essay, Jean-Jacques Rousseau: The Prophetic Voice,* and *Diderot's Chaotic Order: Approach to Synthesis.* He has edited works by Rousseau, Diderot, Voltaire, Montaigne, Cervantes, and others. He has taught at Queens College, Goucher College, Case Western Reserve University, and University of Virginia, where he was Kenan Professor of French and Chairman of the Department of French and General Linguistics. Visiting appointments include University of London, University of Paris, and City University of New York. He has served as President of the International Society for Eighteenth-Century Studies, as well as of the American Society for Eighteenth-Century Studies. He is Professor Emeritus of French, University of Virginia.

LAURIE A. FINKE completed her Ph.D. at the University of Pennsylvania. She has published articles on Medieval and Renaissance literature, women playwrights in England, and seventeenth-century tragedy. She has coedited two collections of essays: *From Renaissance to Restoration: Metamorphoses of the Drama* and *Medieval Texts and Contemporary Readers.* She has taught at The University of Oklahoma and is currently Assistant Professor of English, Lewis and Clark College.

ROBERT GINSBERG studied at the University of Chicago and in Paris, Vienna, Rome, Stockholm, and The Hague. He received his Ph.D. from the University of Pennsylvania. His work is in eighteenth-century thought, social and political philosophy, and aesthetics and criticism. He has published studies of Hume, Jefferson, Hobbes, Bacon, Diderot, Voltaire, Rousseau, Descartes, Kant, and Grotius. He edited *A Casebook on the Declaration of Independence* and *The Critique of War,* and authored *Welcome to Philosophy* and *Gustav Vigeland: A Case Study in Art and Culture.* He has taught in France and Turkey. In 1967 he was the first faculty member named to the Delaware County Campus of The Pennsylvania State University, near Philadelphia, where he is Professor of Philosophy.

WULF KOEPKE was born in Lübeck, Germany. He studied at the University of Hamburg, University of Paris, and received his Dr.phil. from the University of Freiburg. He has done research on Herder and many other figures of the period of Goethe. His books include *Erfolglosigkeit: Zum Frühwerk Jean Pauls, Johann Gottfried Herder: Innovator through the Ages,* and *Lion Feuchtwanger.* He is coeditor of the yearbook *Exilforschung.* He has served as President of the South Central American Society for Eighteenth-Century Studies and of the German Studies Association. He has taught at University of Singapore, Goethe-Institut in Munich, University of Illinois in Chicago, and Rice University. He is Professor of German, Texas A & M University.

JOHN A. MCCARTHY studied at the University of Munich and the State University of New York at Buffalo (Ph.D.). His research is on literary and cultural developments in Germany, including the relationship between philosophy and literature, the transition from Baroque to Enlightenment, the essay as artistic form, the theory and practice of reading in the eighteenth century, popular comedy, journalism, and freedom of the press. He has lectured in Germany, Denmark, Belgium, and England. He published *Fantasy and Reality: An Epistemological Approach to Wieland, C. M. Wieland: The Man and His Work, The Poet as Essayist and Journalist, Lektüre und Lesertypologie,* and co-edited *Aufnahme—Weitergabe: Literarische Impulse um Lessing und Goethe* and *Christoph Martin Wieland, 1733–1813.* Since 1972 he has taught at the University of Pennsylvania where he is Associate Professor of German.

ROBERT MARKLEY received his Ph.D. from the University of Pennsylvania. He has published articles on seventeenth- and eighteenth-century drama, fiction, and nonfictional prose. He has coedited two collections of essays: *From Renaissance to Restoration: Metamorphoses of the Drama* and *Kierkegaard and Literature: Irony, Repetition, and Criticism.* He is an editor of the journal *The Eighteenth Century: Theory and Interpretation.* He is Assistant Professor of English, Georgia Institute of Technology.

DONALD T. SIEBERT studied at The University of Oklahoma and University of Virginia (Ph.D.). He has published studies on Hume, Swift, Pope, and Johnson and has edited reprints of eighteenth-century works by William Warburton, Viscount Bolingbroke, and John Hoole. Since 1972 he has taught at University of South Carolina where he is Associate Professor of English.

HARRY M. SOLOMON received his Ph.D. in eighteenth-century English literature from Duke University. He is author of *Sir Richard Blackmore* and is completing a book on Pope's *Essay on Man*. He is Hollifield Professor of English, Auburn University.

Index